An Autobiography
by David

*W*inter's
Tale

Living Through an
Age of Change
in Church and Media

A LION BOOK

Published by
Lion Publishing plc
Sandy Lane West, Oxford, England
www.lion-publishing.co.uk
ISBN 0 7459 5000 0

First edition 2001
10 9 8 7 6 5 4 3 2 1 0

A catalogue record for this book is available
from the British Library

Typeset in 10.25/13.25 Garamond
Printed and bound in Great Britain by
Omnia Books Limited, Glasgow

CONTENTS

INTRODUCTION

When I told Richard Harries, the Bishop of Oxford, that I was writing my autobiography, he related to me a wise saying he had been told: 'Everyone has two books they can write. There's a bad one, about "What I believe", and a good one about "My Life".' I suppose I could say that after a lot of 'bad books', this is going to be the 'good' one. Bishop Richard's saying was consequently highly encouraging for the present project, even if something of a bucket of cold water over earlier literary efforts, almost all of which were about belief, in one way or another.

I think I needed that encouragement because in my heart of hearts I couldn't see why anyone should be interested in the story of my life. Looked at from the inside, as it were, it has seemed quite unremarkable, even dull. As it draws into its evening years, I can record no great adventures or triumphs of enterprise or faith. So I don't think it is false modesty to say that if this story has any claim on the reader's attention it is that the person telling it is about as ordinary and unremarkable as you can get. Pretty well anyone can relate to this saga of one who didn't do much, but to whom, and around whom, some interesting things happened.

Indeed, much of what gives this story whatever significance it has is the consequence of events outside my own life. I was born in the year of the Wall Street Crash and passed my childhood in the years of the thirties' depression. Memories of the barbarity and slaughter of war were still fresh in people's memories: my own father served in the trenches of Flanders and suffered to his dying day from the physical consequences. The second world war followed with sickening inevitability, but with a pleasant side-effect for me, in that my younger brother and I spent most of it living with our grandparents in a remote village in mid-Wales, far from war, bombs and rationing. My student years were passed under the shadow of the Cold War and the ever-present nuclear threat, and my work and married life developed through the feverish fifties and the swinging sixties into the brave new world of electronic technology, instant communication and constant social upheaval. Now, in the new millennium, it is possible to look back and try to make some sort of sense of it all, at least in terms of one person's life and times.

The thirties of my childhood were the last years of the 'old' Britain, with its rigid class structure, deference for authority, suppressed emotions and stern personal honesty. All over the land doors were left unlocked, often wide open, without fear of unwelcome intrusion or burglary. From the aristocracy to the poorest families in the slums, people submitted to authority: wives to husbands, children to fathers, workers to bosses, and everyone to those with rank or title. It was that authority which the General Strike of 1926 briefly questioned, sending shock waves through 'the establishment', but also worrying many working- and middle-class people, who feared that the very fabric of society was about to disintegrate.

It was also the era of the growing influence of the new-fangled 'wireless'. One of the crucial battles during the General Strike was the one to preserve the independence of the infant BBC from control by the government, who felt it was too sympathetic to the miners' cause. As the wireless grew in influence, so the churches tended to lose it, slowly at first, but with what seemed to be an inevitable seepage of commitment. As long ago as 1930 there were only just over 2 million Easter communicants in the Church of England. Anyone who thinks that a decline in churchgoing is a recent phenomenon has disregarded the facts. The media (though nobody called them that at the time) and the Church seemed to be heading in opposite directions, the one becoming more and more relevant and important in people's lives, and the other less and less. I would have been astonished, as a nine-year-old when war broke out, to be told that my working life would see a deep involvement with both, during decades when media and church were to go through times of enormous and sometimes traumatic change.

In fact, my first proposal of a title for this book was *All Change*, because that is what the story of my life feels like. Without so much as a by-your-leave, the world I knew insisted on constantly changing itself and forcing me, along with everyone else, to change with it. As the old Latin tag says, 'Times change, and we change with them'.

The contrast between the Britain of the 1930s and Britain at the start of the third millennium is so vast that it is hard to believe that it has all been contained in one lifetime. It is that contrast, and the changes of lifestyle, beliefs and priorities which brought it about, which are the backdrop to my story.

Like most people, I suppose, I never had a great life plan, or even a clearly shaped career ambition. Bit by bit, like an ill-designed house being constantly extended, it grew into its eventual shape. But I never felt like its architect, not by a long way. I simply, as it were, lived in it. The great events that happened along the way were like noises off in a stage play: the second world war, the Korean war, Suez, space exploration, the Cuban missiles crisis, the end of colonialism, the Falklands conflict, the miners' strike, the poll tax riots and the collapse of the Berlin Wall. Some involved me closely, some were simply 'events' in faraway places or in lives far removed from mine.

Yet the cumulative effect was of a shifting, insecure world, in which one longed to find anchors and harbours. I think I found mine, but that did not mean that tides didn't come and go nor the 'wind of change' blow insistently across the waters. It simply wasn't possible to live through the twentieth century without feeling that something quite momentous was happening to the earth and its inhabitants, even if it was almost impossible to work out what it was.

This book offers no definitive answers. In fact, as I suppose any autobiography inevitably tends to be, it is the rambling, extended story of one life, but a life lived out in a set of circumstances shared by millions of others. I have never kept a diary, so memories of details and events can at times be hazy and possibly inaccurate. Equally, I have never felt that there was some Grand Strategy that would change the world or make all the hurts better. My belief in God, which as the reader will soon discover is the determining factor in my life, does not mean that I believe that there is a deity meticulously dictating the course of events, moving people, nations and happenings like pawns on a chess board. The God of the Bible – the God of the Incarnation, the God of Jesus – is less cosy than that. This is a God who takes risks, who creates opportunities, who graciously permits second attempts (and third and fourth ones, too), whose work is redemption, not domination. In the sense that it all has a purpose, it can be said that history is his story, and even that the story of my life is really part of the story of God. That sounds pretentious, but in fact it is a humbling and sobering thought.

Everything we do, as creatures made in God's image, has consequences. In the end I called this book *Winter's Tale*, because that is simply what it is – the story of my life. But, as the reader will discover, it could just as well have been called, rather more simply, *Consequences*.

THE HOME FRONT

Wood Green was, is, and probably always will be, a rather undistinguished suburb of north London, but it is my birthplace – Pellatt Grove Nursing Home, to be precise. It was 1929, the year of the Wall Street Crash. 'Confinement' was then the respectable name for 'giving birth' and the mother – often referred to as being 'in a delicate condition' – was expected to take to her bed for a week or two to recover from it. My mother was 'confined' in the nursing home and then returned to the care at home of a hearty Irishwoman, whom I later got to know when she attended her after my younger brother's arrival. It was certainly some time before my mother was allowed to put a foot to the ground.

I am sure the nurse (for such she was called) was a splendid and willing help to my mother, but for many years I could hardly bring myself to forgive her for suggesting that the newborn infant – me – who was to be named 'David Brian' should actually be known as 'Brian' – such a splendid name, she argued, and a wonderful Irish hero. So 'Brian' I became, though I never liked it, and was delighted when my first schoolteacher, simply following the school register, called me 'David'.

Thus began the awkward process by which I had two Christian names – the one used by my parents, grandparents and brothers (to this day, by those who are still alive), and the one used by everyone else. I never admitted, outside the home circle, to the name 'Brian', and marvelled at my prescience when that wretched film *Life of Brian*, in the 1980s, associated the name for ever with Nobody Man.

Wood Green seemed to me, growing up in it, a rather pleasant place. It had shops, a park or two, Alexandra Palace, a couple of tube stations, lots of red buses and trolleybuses and tidy streets of terraced and semi-detached houses. I assumed this was more or less what everywhere was like. It wasn't until my late teens that I discovered, to my horror, that other people had quite a different view of it. The awful truth was revealed in a novel I was reading, where a pale and spotty faced youth called up for his National Service was described as 'a typical product of Wood Green'. I had never seen my home town mentioned in a book before, but when I did it came as a shock to my self-esteem. I had apparently spent my early childhood years in a breeding ground of pale and spotty people. Sadly, a look in the mirror tended to confirm the truth of this wild generalization.

Still, in many ways I am glad to be able to remember those distant years before the second world war in an anonymous London suburb. My father had stories of the General Strike of the previous decade, and I would hear my parents talking about the hunger marches from Jarrow. Yet there was a sense of order and tranquillity about those pre-war years in Wood Green which was not an illusion. For whatever reason, people like ourselves, who were neither wealthy nor poor, lived a very settled and secure life, at the personal level. Crime was rare, compared with more recent decades. People left doors unlocked and cycles propped against front gates. My older brother, Geoff, who was by now in his teens, was able to walk the streets, play in the park, saunter home from 'the pictures' with his friends without fear of mugging, or worse. The general level of contentment seemed high. At any rate, there is no doubt that my parents' generation always looked back to those years as something akin to a Golden Age.

In our house, at least, tradition ruled. My father, who had served in the Great War – and been invalided out suffering from the dire effects of gassing, before it reached its conclusion – was patriotic in a way barely conceivable today. 'My country, right or wrong', he would declare. He always stood rigidly to attention for the national anthem – for all the world like a pre-war Alf Garnett, though without the crude language (and also, though the word would have meant nothing to him, the racism).

He was a Christian gentleman. That was how people saw him. He believed in God, family, king and country, probably in that order. As a family we all went to our parish church on Sundays, probably twice (to services) and a third time where the children were concerned, to Sunday school in the afternoon. The services were monumentally tedious, but that is the judgment of a child looking back with hindsight. At the time, they were simply what you did on Sundays, as much a part of life as sunrise and sunset, and as unavoidable. My father loved singing hymns, and the sound of one of his favourites – 'Fight the good fight' or 'Through the night of doubt and sorrow' – would echo forth from the bathroom during his lengthy shaving sessions in the mornings.

My mother was also a committed churchgoer. Brought up in the Primitive Methodists, she must have found the arcane and repetitive liturgy of the Prayer Book a bit of a trial, but if she did, she never showed it. As a young woman she was a pillar of the Fellowship of Marriage, and later, of the Mothers' Union. Social life revolved around their gatherings, together with harvest teas, garden fêtes and similar paraphernalia of parish life in the thirties. The vicar, the Reverend J. Hawtrey-May, was a distant figure who appeared on Sundays and if someone was terminally ill, preached incomprehensible sermons, had a young maid in a black and white uniform who answered the vicarage door, and generously opened his large garden to the parish once a year for a garden party. All of this, it must be stressed, in what I suppose the sociologists would have classified as a lower middle-class parish in a London suburb.

The church itself – St Cuthbert's – is a red-brick Edwardian edifice, standing on what is known locally as Chitts Hill, though who Chitt was, and what this little hillock meant to him, is lost in history. From its rear slopes you can see the Spurs ground, probably a mile and a half away. My father was a dedicated follower of Tottenham Hotspur, though my older brother, with filial perversity, had decided to support Arsenal – the aliens from across the Thames, as they were regarded by dad's generation. Saturday teatimes were lively – indeed, at times, anguished – affairs. Arsenal in the thirties were a power in the land, winning just about everything. Spurs, in contrast, got relegated to the Second Division. Despite that, when I was old enough to make a choice it was for Tottenham. It was, I suppose, the perennial one between the broad and narrow roads.

I was at primary school, St Michael's, when war was declared. Actually, I was at home, because it happened on a Sunday, and I can remember the panic that suddenly struck me. War was all right, even fun, in books and films, but the real thing was likely to be exceedingly unpleasant. Even at nine I could see that.

As if to underline the urgency, my younger brother, Alan, not yet five, and I joined the rest of the children from St Michael's School on a fleet of London buses headed for some unknown place of safety in the country. We became 'evacuees', a strange new word, coined by media or government to describe this motley army of bewildered children and their almost equally bewildered teachers.

It was a bizarre experience, probably less so for the children than the adults. I can remember the tearful farewells outside the school as we left, but it was all rather exciting, heading out of London in a long convoy of double-deckers towards the strange delights of the countryside. Although we didn't know it at the time, we were heading into Essex, straight into the flight path of bombers from Germany and any invading army that might make its way across from the Low Countries.

When we eventually arrived at our destination, it turned out to be a village near Braintree called Shalford. We were all moved out of the buses into a fleet of private cars, and then driven to potential hosts. My brother and I were turned down by the first lady – 'we asked for girls', she said, eyeing us with understandable suspicion. However, the second attempt was more fruitful, and Alan and I spent a happy few months living with Mr and Mrs Edwards and their two children – a boy rather older than we were, and a delightful teenage girl.

The family were genuinely warm and welcoming, active members of the Congregational Chapel nearby at Ambrose Corner, which we soon got to know very well. Indeed, I found the services rather more congenial than the low church Anglican ones on which I had been reared – why, we even had a children's talk, and we sang jolly, rousing hymns, too.

So it was rather a surprise when my parents announced that we were leaving Shalford, not to return to London, but to go to live with my grandparents in Wales. Their reasons were simple and convincing, with hindsight. The so-called 'phoney war', during which nothing much happened as the main combatants took up position, had definitely come to an end with the rout of the Allies in the first experience of what Hitler called blitzkrieg – lightning strikes by swift armoured columns. The remnant of the British Expeditionary Force had been evacuated in small boats from Dunkirk and Winston Churchill had warned the nation to arm itself to the teeth to repel the expected massive invasion of our shores. Essex may have looked peaceful in the summer sunshine, but it lay right in the path of any invader from the continent. Wales, so far away and inaccessible, seemed a far safer haven for us.

So we made the long, if exciting, journey from North London to the tiny village of Darowen in mid-Wales. This involved several trains, mainly because my grandfather had worked all his life for the LMS (London, Midland and Scottish) – which gained us cut-price tickets – but not the Great Western, which would in those days have provided the most direct route to mid-Wales, where we were headed.

Frankly, we didn't mind. This was an unfamiliar but exciting world of vast, clanging locomotives and chattering, swaying carriages, of sandwiches flavoured with the aroma of the engine's smoke, of countryside which flashed by the windows and big stations which appeared like oases in the desert. The carriage windows, covered with adhesive tape to protect passengers from bomb blast, were a reminder of the world at war, but for the rest this was the world of childish imagination and delight.

Darowen was yet another totally new experience. We had thought that Shalford was 'country', but compared with this Welsh hideaway about seven miles from Machynlleth and in the hills above the Dovey valley, it was positively urban. We got off the train at Commins Coch halt (which no longer exists) and, with our grandparents, carried our cases for two miles uphill, without seeing a soul and barely a house, until we arrived at the village. By then we were too tired to take much in, but we dropped our cases and our bodies in the tiny parlour of 'Moelfre View', a two-up, two-down cottage warmed by an open fire. This was now to be our home, at least until my parents decided the danger was past. I don't think many people, least of all children like ourselves, could have believed how long that was to be.

My grandmother was a Welsh-speaking girl who had eventually and thankfully returned to her roots after spending almost all of her adult life in London. She had been born in Trefeglwys, a village perhaps 20 miles east of Darowen, but across a green and mountainous desert without roads. Nevertheless, she was 'local', and fitted perfectly into the rural Welsh scene. My grandfather, by contrast, was a sturdy – indeed, rather bulky – Englishman, born in the Midlands, but he also spent his working life in London, driving horse-drawn carts for the LMS railway.

To his dying day his grasp of Welsh never exceeded a few common words and phrases, but the people of the village took him to their hearts. Soon he picked up the routine: buckets of water from the village pump, paraffin lamps to be lit at nightfall, wet batteries to be exchanged every week for a freshly charged one to power the 'wireless' – and the buckets full of waste from the little toilet over the road to be emptied into a deep hole in the garden. It was a long way from the lights, traffic and conveniences of pre-war Haringey, where they had lived, but he seemed as happy as a sandboy, whistling away as he swept the mats in the village street and greeting passers-by with his execrable attempts at their language.

Sundays followed much the same pattern as they had in London, with morning service in the church, afternoon Sunday school and sometimes, as a kind of bonus, an evening visit to the chapel across the road. Grandpa never missed a Sunday service, though the entire proceedings were in Welsh. After all, he argued, it followed the Prayer Book and hymns were sung – and he had both a prayer book and hymn book of his own. What easier, then, than simply to join in, even if it was in English? On the whole this worked tolerably well with the prayer book (once grandma had checked that he was at the right place in the service) but not so well with the hymns. His technique there was simply to turn up the hymn number on the board in church and sing whatever he found in his own book. This seldom worked at all well, mainly because the Welsh hymn book bore no relation whatever, in identity of hymn, number of verses, tunes or metre, to the battered copy of *Hymns, Ancient and Modern* in grandpa's hands. Undeterred, he would press on, singing an extra verse solo if necessary, and manfully struggling to adjust the words to the tune being squeezed out of the church harmonium. It speaks volumes for the affection in which he was held that no one, to my knowledge, ever raised the slightest objection.

My small brother and I sat spellbound through the services. I can't say that we had become entirely fluent in Tudor English, but I suppose matins in St Cuthbert's offered some points of linguistic contact for us. St Tudur's, Darowen, offered none, until eventually this strange tongue began to become familiar to our ears. Our introduction to the Welsh language followed a crash course, because all the lessons (and I do mean all) in the village school were in Welsh, and there were no concessions to the new arrivals from faraway London. The teacher, Mrs Morris, from Corris – a felicitous rhyming combination that pleased me enormously – was kind and patient, but sums in Welsh were what was on offer, and the sooner we learnt Welsh numerals the better we would cope with them.

The school was very small, perhaps 20 children in two classrooms. The pupils were drawn from a wide area, and walked literally miles to school. The whole idea of coming to school by car would have seemed a bizarre luxury – there was only one car in the village, owned by the blacksmith, and the farmers would conserve their petrol ration for essential trips into town. So in the wildest and wettest weather (and west Wales can at times be both wild and wet), the children would struggle along muddy paths and narrow lanes to attend their lessons.

In my year, just two of us qualified for the grammar school in Machynlleth, about seven miles away. Iori was the other one, a farmer's son from just outside the village. He was the same age but much bigger and stronger than I was, blue-eyed and fair-haired, and I must confess I thought him incredibly handsome. He was also good at sport, able to strike a cricket ball right out of the top meadow. During the summer months we cycled to school together, speeding down the slope of Fron Goch, the hill on the side of which the village stood, and then struggling uphill for the next two or three miles until we joined the main Newtown to Machynlleth road. The mere memory of it makes me feel tired and weak-kneed, but even at 11, I could sense how special and beautiful the surroundings were, and when I finally made it home in the evening there were always grandma's special potato cakes to eat.

In the winter I had digs in town from Monday to Friday. Perhaps 'digs' is too grandiose a title. Actually, for half a crown (12 and a half pence) I shared a bed with three other boys above a shop, had bread and jam and tea for breakfast and could eat any food I purchased from the shop for my evening meal. Baked beans were the staple diet, I have to say.

There were compensations for the rigours of life in town, the chief of which, I'm afraid, was the Powys Cinema, where for sixpence (two and a half pence) one could sample the delights of Hollywood twice a week – the programme changed on Thursdays. The Powys provided a vital new element in my education. I saw *The Great Dictator*, with Charlie Chaplin, and *The Mark of Zorro*, and just about every Abbott and Costello film. There were also, of course, the war films, many of them made with the purpose of stiffening morale and patriotic resolve.

I suppose they also served, in that splendidly isolated part of Britain, as a reminder that there was a war on at all. In other respects, it was hard to believe. There was rationing, of course, but with butter and eggs from the farms, and an uncle who was both a farmer and a butcher, I cannot recall any serious limitations on the household menu. I remember a morning when the calm of the village school was shattered by the most appalling screaming, apparently coming from just over the road somewhere. Not only was the screaming loud, but it didn't stop. Indeed, it went on all through the morning. So at the lunch break we all crossed the road to discover what was going on. One boy darkly suggested that old Mr Owen was murdering his wife. Actually, he was on the right lines, though the victim was not the blameless Mrs Owen but the Owen pig, which was being slaughtered, without reference to the law of the land and certainly well beyond the reach of the rationing system. The trouble was that Mr Owen, while an experienced smallholder, was an absolute tyro at the butchery business, with the result that the poor animal was dying in noisy agony from a slow haemorrhage from its neck. Presumably any visiting policeman would have been told it was attempted suicide. The screams persisted well into the afternoon, until, to general relief, silence fell over the village. Any potential police informer was quickly silenced with a generous pack of fresh pork, to be salted away against the rigours of a Welsh winter.

The most disturbing aspect of the war for my brother and me was the news of air raids on London, which we heard of on the nightly news from the BBC. It was hard to believe that my own parents were living in a front-line target area for German bombs, and I don't ever recall seriously worrying that they might have been victims. I suppose that is a tribute to the sheer normality of the life we were living, as well as to the typical insensitivity of the average younger male of the species.

Just before my older brother was called up for National Service he visited us for a kind of farewell holiday. He spent the rest of the war in the RAF, travelling with a mobile radar unit to various parts of the land and eventually, a few days after D-Day, to the Normandy beachhead and then across France through to Germany. Geoff was very much my elder brother, in every way, and I admired him deeply. All through the war I wrote my strange schoolboy letters to him, full of the kind of nonsense that filled my head but apparently something of a whiff of home for a distant serviceman. On this brief holiday we spent a few days at Aberystwyth, staying in a boarding house not far from the promenade and beach, and even playing on the part of the sands not cordoned off with barbed wire or marched over by young men doing their recruit training. The boarding house managed to earn a place in our family's mythology for the notice propped on the top of the toilet: 'Please don't put nothing hard down the lav-WC.' It caused us great hilarity, but in fact it was a pleasant indulgence to use a flush toilet for a week or so.

At that point, Geoff went off to the RAF, my parents – who had joined us for the week – went back to the blitz, and we returned to our rural fastness. The years at Darowen were in many ways idyllic, and as will become clear they had a deep influence on my later life. But they also gave my young brother and me an understanding of what the 'simple life' really is – to realize that millions of people in Britain at that time were without access to such apparent essentials of life as mains sewage and water, electricity or telephones. With regard to the last named, the nearest phone to Darowen was more than two miles away over the hills in Cemmaes Road. Summoning a doctor, for instance, was a formidable exercise in logistics.

There was a weekly bus – from a stopping point in the valley below the village – to Machynlleth, and for many people that was their only regular contact with the 'wider' world, and Machynlleth was hardly New York. Most of them had at some time or other taken the train to Aberystwyth but it was only National Service that introduced the younger generation to places further afield – and many of that generation had to stay at home throughout the war, in the 'reserved occupation' of farming.

Yet this was far from a narrow, or for that matter uncultured, community. They made their own music, and performed it at Friday night concerts in the school. They wrote and read poetry in Welsh. They recited from the Bible or debated with eloquence and passion. They loved a good sermon and a good hymn. And, of course, they sang – not quite as beautifully as popular mythology claims, but fervently and passionately. The Friday night concerts always ended with *Mae'r hen wlad fy nhadau* ('Land of my fathers') and it inevitably earned several encores. Even at 10 or 11 years old, I could feel the spirit of it all and share in it.

Our eventual return to London, when our parents judged that the worst of the hostilities were over, was something of a disappointment. It was, of course, wonderful and reassuring to be back with our parents. But we both had to start in new schools – for me, this was the local 'county' grammar school, where the headmaster, Dr Jones, was a Welshman and chose to conduct my initial interview in Welsh. But my newly acquired accent amused my new classmates and earned me the name 'Dai', which stuck with me to the day I left that school.

My parents, like everyone else, had been rather over-optimistic about the reduction in hostilities. In fact, the Allied invasion of France sparked two new and terrible aerial threats to the south-east of England, the 'doodlebugs' (pilotless planes loaded with high explosives) and, even more terrifyingly, the V2 rockets, which exploded without warning of any kind, having sped through the upper skies powered by the sort of motors that would soon convey men to the moon.

I had found a new pleasure on my return to London – watching cricket. This led to a memorable encounter with a doodlebug, when the calm of a Saturday afternoon visit to Lord's was interrupted by the drone of one of these awesome missiles. I was sitting on the balcony of the old grandstand, and watched the trail of the missile towards the ground. Suddenly, almost precisely over the mound stand, its engine cut out. We all lay flat on the ground – those of us who could, crawling under the benches. I had a brief glimpse of the players also lying prostrate on the pitch. The plane zoomed noiselessly beyond the grandstand, its progress followed, within a few seconds, by an enormous explosion and a cloud of dust and debris rising into the air. We all clambered up from the ground, there were a few nervous laughs but few spoken words (we were British, after all) and play resumed. The batsman, one of my favourites, Jack Robertson, hit the first ball straight up into the balcony for six, the ball's trajectory seeming to follow that of the doodlebug a few minutes earlier. There was a warm round of applause, a few cries of 'Good shot, sir!' and our summer resumed where Hitler had so rudely interrupted it.

The anonymous suburbs of north London had many attractions for a teenager, of course, but there simply wasn't the deep sense of community that had marked Darowen – and I missed it. Of course, my brother and I had also missed the 'spirit of the blitz', as it became known, and came back only to the sober realities of post-war life: shortages, rations, bomb sites, and one of the coldest winters, in 1947, the country had known that century.

POST-WAR BLUES

I do not think those who were born later can possibly imagine how desperate those post-war years were. As a politically aware teenager – certainly by the time I was in the sixth form – I knew that we were all living under the shadow of something far worse even than the bombing of the war. The two atom bombs dropped on Japan brought a welcome end to the conflict, but introduced into the field of international affairs an ugly new element. The wartime Allies had 'the Bomb', but so now did the Soviet Union. Suddenly one was conscious that there was a new and potentially incandescent element in the conflict between the communist world and the capitalist West, with both parties armed to the teeth with atomic weapons and the means to deliver them. The first test of this new situation was the Russian blockade of Berlin, in the late forties. The second was the long-drawn-out Korean war of the early 1950s. I was fortunate, in one sense, that my period of National Service – 1948 to 1950 – fitted neatly in between them. In both cases I was merely a spectator, except that warfare on the scale implied by nuclear weapons has no 'spectators'. All, like it or not, are participants.

This grim scenario was the background to my early adult life, as it was to millions of others. It wouldn't be true to say that it absorbed my every waking thought. Eighteen-year-olds are not that philosophical. But it certainly shaped my reactions, even if subconsciously. Those post-war years felt unstable and impermanent, as though the world were waiting for the next big event and everything was on hold until it happened. The political leaders made soothing speeches, but the facts were too obvious to avoid. The world was a very dangerous, even unstable, place, and at one level events were as much out of their control as mine.

Taken in conjunction with the genuinely harsh rigours of life in post-war Britain, it made a strange backdrop to late adolescence. Food was rationed, in many cases more severely than it had been during the war. During the bitter winter of 1947 there was an acute fuel shortage – we were reduced to chopping up some 'spare' furniture to put on the fire. And the national economy was seriously out of balance. The fledgling Labour government (of which I was a passionate supporter) set about its long-promised reforms, notably the foundation of the National Health Service, but it could not dispel the general atmosphere of disappointment. If this was what it felt like to be the victors, what must life be like for the vanquished? We now know that the answer was, no worse – and possibly a good deal better.

In 1948 I sat my higher schools exams – the forerunner of 'A Levels' – and having done so was promptly called up for National Service. It could have been deferred until I had completed my anticipated university course, but I felt there was virtue in getting the nasty bit over first (a philosophy I have applied generally in life, which meant as a child that I would eat the crust first and then enjoy the butter and jam bit). So in September of that year I set off, armed with a railway travel warrant and a few listed essentials, to report to the RAF recruiting centre at Padgate in Lancashire.

National Service, like life in the pre-scientific age, was nasty, brutal and short. The redeeming feature was the third one – almost anything is bearable if you know that it won't last long. I realize that many of my contemporaries enjoyed their 18 months or two years in uniform enormously – some to the extent that they voluntarily signed on for short-service commissions and the like. And there was, of course, an enjoyable element to the enforced communal life – male, noisy, crude, but often amusing and sometimes very supportive.

I spent my 18 months in the RAF medical service as a 'nursing attendant', which involved a preliminary nursing course – at RAF Moreton-in-the-Marsh, in Gloucestershire – and then work on the wards in the RAF hospital at Halton, before a rather less hectic posting to RAF Andover, the headquarters of maintenance command. Andover was the nearest to an enjoyable period in my National Service, with just two of us manning the station's sick bay and spending the odd afternoon sitting in an ambulance waiting for someone to crash a plane (it only happened once, and with disappointingly slight injuries to the crew).

But it was at Halton that I had an experience that has lived with me ever since. I was working for several months on the tuberculosis wards, where young men – and a few women – mostly of about my age, were having to come to terms with what was then a terminal illness. At least, there was no cure. The TB bacillus was resistant to every drug that had been tried – as one doctor put it during a lecture, we haven't found anything yet that will kill the TB bacillus without killing the patient as well. So tuberculosis could be 'treated', but not cured. As one young fellow said to me, 'It's strange at 19 to know what you're going to die of.'

The regime was simple and highly organized – sputum samples in the morning before breakfast, a 'good, nourishing diet' with plenty of milk, butter and eggs, linctus to relieve the incessant coughing and fresh air, gales of it, blowing across the beds which we wheeled into corridors with their large windows wide open.

Sometimes the disease would take a rest. With negative sputum tests for a few weeks a patient could be sent home on leave, and sometimes, happily, this remission was long-lasting.

But the TB wards were inevitably ante-rooms of eternity and it was peculiarly disquieting to watch the sudden decline of a patient. The poet Keats, who himself died of 'consumption', captured it precisely in 'Ode to a Nightingale':

Where youth grows pale, and spectre-thin, and dies;
Where but to think is to be full of sorrow
And leaden-eyed despairs...

And yet the whole situation was to change, suddenly and dramatically. One day in 1949 we were summoned to a lecture at which a doctor showed us a new drug which we were to start using the following week. We were taken painstakingly through the routine for its administration and supervision. The next Monday we began doling out the pills and pink liquid. The patients were surprised and interested, of course, but neither they nor we were prepared for the quite sensational results. Within a couple of weeks patients began to provide clear samples. Within a month, most of them were infection-free and damaged lungs were actually beginning to recover. They were putting on weight, feeling stronger, no longer endlessly coughing. In fact, the dreaded TB bacillus had met its match at last. It was the dawn of a new era and a great triumph for medical science, indeed, one of the greatest of modern times. But for those few dozen young men and women it was life out of death – truly, a miraculous healing.

A sad footnote to that story, of course, has been the news of the comeback that TB has been making, even in the West, over recent years – largely feeding on poverty and neglect among the deprived minority in otherwise affluent lands.

National Service was followed, in due course, by university. I had had enough of living rough and decided that I would like to spend the next three years in the comfort of home. So I was pleased to get a place at King's College London, to read English. I'm not sure what I expected to 'get' from it – basically it was 'the next thing' which with a bit of luck would postpone more weighty decisions about future life, employment, career and so on.

King's in those days was a strange place, most of the young men having done National Service and almost all of the young women looking distinctly girlish by comparison – though no one was complaining about that. Reading poetry, plays and novels was hardly back-breaking work, especially for someone like me who loved words in almost any form. And it was stimulating to argue and debate with people who were more intelligent than I was.

Perhaps because of the social and age mix at the college, King's was quite politicized, which suited me down to the ground. I flung myself eagerly into all kinds of political protest and action, some of it under the 'official' Labour umbrella, some of it involving various odd left-wing groups and causes that seemed to proliferate in those heady days of the Cold War. Indeed, if they had responded to the endless messages poured out from a couple of leaking Banda duplicators in a dingy backstreet office in Strutton Ground, the populace would have risen up long ago and shaken off the chains of capitalist oppression. Undeterred by their reluctance, we stuck up posters, handed out leaflets, and harangued innocent students whenever they were foolish enough to pause for a moment.

Eventually I was elected chair of the college Socialist Society. At that stage, the adrenaline that should have fuelled my zeal seemed to begin to dry up. It's hard to pin down where the doubts started, though even then I could identify a number of factors. Negatively, I was rather disillusioned by the direction in which the Labour movement and its supporters appeared to be going. Far from a brotherhood (the chosen language for the chosen people) of like-minded idealists, those post-war years revealed much the same sort of self-seeking, self-promoting ambitions in their leaders as I had long denounced on the other side of politics. Envy, or a kind of crude triumphalism ('We are the masters now!' as one newly elected Labour member memorably shouted as the first post-war parliament convened), hardly seemed suitable fuel for the journey to the New Jerusalem. The closer one got to the so-called idealists of the left wing, the worse it seemed to become.

Positively, I found myself drawn more and more towards the Christian faith in which I had grown up. A new, young vicar in my home church and contact with the members of the flourishing college Christian Union were factors in this. I began to feel – rather than reason – that economic and social reform alone would not solve the enormous problems which confronted the human race. The experience of the National Health Service – very definitely part of that vision of the New World of Justice – brought this home in a vivid way.

Like most people in Britain in that strange post-war period, I believed passionately in the principle of the welfare state, and nothing embodied those principles more splendidly than the National Health Service, with its vision of health care for all, solely according to need, and completely free at the point of delivery. Yet in practice the splendid vision was marred almost from the first moment by the greed and stupidity of people dazzled by the prospect of something for nothing. If it was going free, than people wanted it: free milk, free hearing aids, free spectacles, free medicine. Within a couple of years the noble vision was in peril of being swallowed up by people convinced that in the new era of welfare things really could come 'cost free'. The great architect of the NHS, Nye Bevan, was forced to introduce two elements which were anathema to the Marxist fundamentalists – payment for some items, and what amounted to means testing for others. Only by doing that could the overall future of the Health Service be preserved. It was in fact a victory for common sense, but in our grubby underworld of permanent protest it was seen only as a surrender to the malign forces of capitalism.

What this said to me very forcibly was that society and its structures can't be changed unless people are changed. But how on earth, I asked myself, are people to be changed? Human nature seemed to be innately selfish (in the final analysis) and incapable of paying the price of the general good if it involved personal sacrifice. The wealthy and powerful were blamed by my political comrades for virtually every ill on earth, but I came to see that they were not unique in their selfishness. Given the opportunity, most of us could match them for greed and naked self-interest, not least the poor, exploited workers themselves. 'The heart of man is deceitful above all things, and desperately wicked' – I didn't know the saying of scripture then, but I was beginning to learn its truth.

A visit to our college by a prominent former communist, Rose Osment, crystallized my thinking and led to something of a personal philosophical crisis. She put into words, and from her own experience of half a lifetime in the communist party, exactly what I felt. It was not simply a matter of disillusionment but, as she expressed it, a growing conviction that there must be a better way to change the world. She avoided the simplistic kind of message with which I had been toying – 'changed people will change the world' – but demonstrated from her own experience what a difference it makes to be released from a philosophy of blame into a philosophy of love. For her, the answer had come in a living encounter with Jesus Christ – surprisingly, as she said, because she was not only a communist but a Jew. Yet she found in the teaching of Jesus, and above all in the mystery of his life, death and resurrection, a way of looking at the world and at people which was at once both more sublime and more practical.

What she said resonated powerfully with the way I had been thinking. What was difficult for me to take on board, however, was the thought that the answer to my questions lay in the very faith which I had all but abandoned. I suppose it was difficult to appreciate the radical nature of the teaching of Jesus from the background of my own experience of its presentation in church. I had come to think of it as part of the status quo, an inhibitor of social progress and liberation. Yet now I was faced with the disturbing idea that Christianity, rightly understood, was more revolutionary, asked more truly radical questions, than the sloganized socialism of student protest.

Rose Osment's contribution to my conversion (for that, in a real sense, was what it was) provided the intellectual stimulus. It was another speaker at a Christian Union meeting – and sadly I have no recollection of his name – who earthed it in my experience. 'People get it wrong,' he said. 'They think of Christianity as a creed, a set of dogmas or rules or rituals. In fact, it's much simpler than that. It's what the apostle Paul called "knowing Christ" – it's a Person, a Person we can encounter and who can become the centre and motive force of our lives.' Reading that now, it sounds obvious, but to me as a student in 1952 it was mind-blowing. Christianity is Christ – not what I believe, but in whom I believe. I think it was that evening that I decided this was for me, though I suppose, being a cautious soul in some respects, it took a few days for the full impact of such a conclusion really to sink in.

This 'conversion', or rediscovery of the Christian faith, was to become by far the biggest influence on the whole of the rest of my life. Although I have come, over the years, to reassess the rather narrow view of scripture, for instance, into which the Christian Union initiated me, I have never come to doubt the reality of that encounter with Jesus Christ. Nor have I ever doubted that his gospel is the most radical message available to the modern world, dynamic in its power to change not only individuals but situations and systems and true in a sense that transcends (but does not contradict) ordinary logic.

This journey into faith faced an early test with the illness, and eventual death, of my father. He had a stroke, from which he largely recovered, and insisted on going back to work in order to qualify for his civil service pension. It was not a wise decision, because quite soon he had a second and more severe stroke, from which recovery was not possible. For perhaps three weeks he lay on a bed in the front room at our home in Wood Green, almost completely unconscious, and needing constant nursing attention. It was a genuinely rewarding experience for me, who had not been very close to him for some years, to have the privilege of using my RAF nursing training to do him this final service. A moving moment came when the vicar called to pray with him, as he lay silent and unconscious on his bed. Yet as the words 'Our Father' were spoken, dad began to join in, and in fact spoke the whole prayer strongly, right through to the 'Amen'.

Later, in the vicar's study, I was able to share with him what my new-found confidence in Christ had meant to me during the weeks of my father's illness, and the vicar, Douglas Clark, took me under his wing from then on. It was an experience of 'discipling' that not only established me in the faith, but taught me lessons in pastoral care that I was to value after my own ordination more than 30 years later.

By the time I had graduated, with the predicted and predictable 2:1, I was as convinced and crusading a Christian as I had so recently been a socialist. That was 1953, and London's churches were preparing themselves for a visit the following year by the American evangelist Billy Graham. I say 'preparing themselves', but in truth some were getting ready to pull up the drawbridge at this promised invasion of evangelical razzmatazz, while others – including my own parish in north London – were preparing to pull up their sleeves and give it maximum support. For me, and many others, this involved attending 'counsellor training classes', run by an American called, rather improbably, Lorne Sanny. My mother, who also enrolled to attend, persisted to the end in calling him 'Sanny Lorne', which sounded every bit as reasonable. Hundreds attended these classes, many of them from Baptist churches and backstreet mission halls, as well as from the large and mainly middle-class evangelical Anglican parishes.

I had some misgivings, it must be admitted, about the so-called 'course', which seemed to involve learning a large number of texts from the Bible which were said to be vital to the newly converted Christian, with whom we would be dealing at the end of each mission meeting. On the whole, I found it was best not to look these texts up in context, because when you did some of them didn't seem entirely to bear the weight which Mr Sanny put on them. On the other hand, some of the New Testament ones are marvellous 'proof texts' and the fact that I learnt them – from the King James' Version, of course – by heart has provided me with a constant access to foundational truths. Not only can I still recite Paul's marvellous words to the Ephesian church on faith ('By grace are you saved by faith...') but I can do so with the Bible-belt accent employed by the whole Graham team.

Meanwhile, needing to earn a living and lacking inspiration or guidance for the job I would have liked in journalism, I had enrolled for the post-graduate Certificate in Education at the Institute of Education in Gower Street, in central London. There was at that time a chronic shortage of graduate teachers, and at least it was a way of ensuring paid employment at the end of the course. That, I am sorry to say, was the sum total of my motivation for teaching.

Probably because I approached it totally without enthusiasm, I found the course itself vague, impractical and tedious. The lecturers seemed to inhabit a world far removed from the schools I had attended, where the teachers' first problem was control and the second motivation. My two placement schools drove the message home. They were both in inner London suburbs, and in both the first battle facing the teacher was to maintain any kind of control over the pupils. At the secondary school, my supervising tutor took over one of my classes when mayhem erupted, but was as dismal a failure as I had been at doing anything effective about it, eventually fleeing to the safety of the staffroom. Yet no one at the Institute wanted to talk about 'discipline'. The answer was always the same: to awaken interest, to uncover, as one woman said, that 'sunny corner in the child's brain'. But how could you awaken interest or uncover sunny corners when the blighters wouldn't even give you a hearing?

Like most of the more successful teachers I observed, I simply devised my own, alternative methods. I found I could make a class laugh, which helped, and also that ridicule was quite a potent weapon against the kind of classroom subversives who set out to wreck every lesson. Not only that, but provided you could gain a hearing at the start – easier said than done – a busy class was more likely to co-operate than an idle one. These tactics worked better with the older years, I discovered, and depended on rather more demanding preparation for lessons than I had bargained for. Still, it not only got me through my placement teaching sessions, but by some miracle earned me a distinction in 'practical teaching', which helped to off-set the thoroughly appalling marks I got for my examination, for which I had obstinately refused to read any of the enormously long recommended list of books by academic educationalists and sociologists (many of them, I noticed from my recent past experience, icons of the Left). So I left the Institute with my certificate, and also a first teaching post, at a Church of England secondary school at Ware, in Hertfordshire.

My career as a teacher lasted five years, in two schools – the one in Ware, and then a grammar school in Tottenham, quite near my home in north London. I say 'career', but only in that single dictionary definition of a 'wild course, often downhill'. While those years had many amusing and even satisfying moments, I was not a good teacher. Someone has said that what gets taught is the teacher, which in my case was true in a secondary sense – I learnt quite a lot about myself, most of it fairly painful. I discovered that I was rather immature, which led to a dangerous alternation between overfamiliarity with my students and desperate attempts, usually too late to be effective, to coerce or badger them into co-operative behaviour. I also found out that an endemic laziness about preparation, or perhaps it was overconfidence, could lead to disaster in the classroom.

I think I was able to communicate my enthusiasm for the

subjects I taught, however – at any rate, to those students willing and able to suspend their cynicism about either English literature or religion. With the more able ones, I even achieved at times very good examination results. But I was more aware of the gaping holes I had fallen into, most of them products of my own inept shovel.

All of which meant that it was something of a relief, one spring day in 1959, to get a totally unexpected phone call from someone I had never met and barely knew at all. That one call, and my instant response to it, altered the whole direction of my life.

THE *CRUSADE* YEARS

For several years I had taken time off from marking essays to write occasional articles, and even two serial stories, for one or two Christian periodicals. The best of these, professionally speaking, was undoubtedly *Crusade*, a new arrival on the market in the wake of the 1954 and 1955 Graham Crusades. It was a colour-illustrated glossy monthly, priced (rather expensively, for those days) at one shilling and sixpence (seven and a half pence). Unlike its religious contemporaries, *Crusade* had a sense of humour, with cartoons and line drawings, and it also had 'style' thanks to its splendid art editor, Gordon Stowell. Its theology was firmly in the Billy Graham mould, and its contributors were mostly well-established Christian writers. So it was something of a cachet for an unknown schoolteacher, who simply sent a manuscript on spec, to be invited to write regularly for its pages. It was also, I must admit, a welcome supplement to the miserable pay enjoyed by younger teachers at the time.

In 1959 I was in my second term at Tottenham County School. I was enjoying working with the sixth form – a new experience for me – and I also had a very bright and enthusiastic fifth-year group studying for their school certificate. It was a joy to be with students who actually enjoyed, rather than suffered, Shakespeare, Browning, Thackeray and the rest. I had also volunteered for some Religious Instruction periods (that was its rather directive title at the time), and was amused to see the difference in attitude and expectancy of the same pupils when faced with the two different subjects. In a nutshell, practically none of them took 'RI' seriously, but then, to be fair, neither did most of the teachers. At Ware I had been co-leader of a quite flourishing Christian Union, which was given a degree of credibility by the fact that my colleague helping to run it was the very popular young female PE teacher. No such glamour attached to religion in post-war Tottenham, and I noticed that those students who were practising Christians (and there were a number of them) quite wisely kept their heads down in public.

One evening the phone rang, and when I answered it the caller was none other than the editor of *Crusade*, Tim Dudley-Smith (universally recognized by his initials, 'TDS'). I don't think I had ever met him, or if so only briefly at the magazine's offices, but I assumed his call was about a possible article or story for its pages. However, the invitation was rather more far-reaching than that. Would I be interested in succeeding him as editor? He was a clergyman (who later in his career became an archdeacon and then a bishop), and would be moving on to a new post in the summer. Was I interested?

I don't think I even stopped to ask about pay and conditions, though if I had I might have been surprised to find that at that time religious journalism was even less adequately rewarded than teaching. It was both a way out (of a career in which I felt I was a fish out of water) and a way in to the fulfilment of a childhood ambition – to be a 'proper', professional journalist. I suspect that I said 'yes' on the spot, and the next day I handed in my resignation to the headmaster, Mr Nunn. Incidentally his nickname, the product of perverse metropolitan wit, was 'Josh', as 'Joshua was the son of Nun' (Joshua 1:1).

During the summer months I began to familiarize myself with the workings of a monthly periodical and with the staff, including the very affable Gordon Stowell and the editorial assistant, Joyce Manning, whom I found at the time somewhat intimidating. By the time I took up the reins in July I had begun to find my feet in this unfamiliar field. I was full of bright ideas, most of which, the editorial assistant assured me, they had either tried and they hadn't worked, or were totally impractical. I wasn't sure how to take this, but decided that for the time being her experience and skills were more important, both to me and to the magazine, than my bruised feelings. So, with due caution, we manoeuvred our way through the remaining months of 1959.

A very important year for me was 1960, because I met my future wife, Christine Martin. She was first mentioned to me by the vicar of Christ Church, Ware, John King, whom I suspect felt it was time I 'settled down' with someone suitable. At any rate, his description of her – 'a fair flower of Brethren womanhood' were, I think, the exact words – whetted my interest. Christine's brother John had succeeded me as a teacher at Ware, and I had met him a few times. His father, Bernard, was an elder at one of north London's oldest Brethren 'assemblies', Clapton Hall at Stamford Hill, and I was invited to speak at some occasion there. I accepted, partly at least out of curiosity to see if John King's description of Christine was an accurate one.

It was, I very quickly decided. The problem then was somehow to isolate this delightful young nurse from the rest of her large and rather daunting family. I invented a pretext (I can still blush at the nerve of it – I sought her help with a feature we were doing on Christian nurses) and on the strength of that meeting – a meal, I think, at the Chicken Inn on Leicester Square – invited her to a press showing of *Ben Hur*. That was our first 'date', to be followed by a number of others, mostly, in keeping with the evangelical culture of the time, involving her coming to hear me speak at a meeting somewhere. I think she knew I was 'serious' about our relationship when I took her to hear a well-known evangelical clergyman speak on the case for infant baptism!

In fact, she had already, long before meeting me, made her

acquaintance with Anglican ways. She did her midwifery training in Edinburgh, and regularly went with a friend (who subsequently married a vicar nearly 30 years her senior) to St Thomas's, Costorphine. In any case, her family – pillars of their local 'meeting' – were broad-minded where denominational allegiance was concerned, if (again, in the evangelical culture of the time) alert to the slightest degree of 'unsound doctrine' where 'gospel essentials' were concerned. Apparently I passed that test – *Crusade* and Billy Graham were definitely 'OK' – even if I was, in the phrase chosen by Christine's aunt, 'no oil painting'. This, of course, simply demonstrated how very few oil paintings she had seen, but I was well aware that my new girlfriend was out of my league where looks were concerned. Fortunately, such things were not considered of first importance among committed Christians, and I suppose there was just the slightest touch of glamour associated with being editor of a magazine like *Crusade*.

We were engaged that summer, partly because Christine's mother (who was not to be lightly crossed over such matters) felt that we should have the status of an engaged couple if we were to go together to the Keswick Convention house party organized by the Evangelical Alliance. I got a free place by volunteering to drive the minibus, but I think we shared the cost of Christine's accommodation. The following year, as a married couple, we hosted the same event.

My mother, also a formidable woman in her own way, was pleased, or perhaps relieved, to see me safely married. Frankly, she had not approved of most of my girlfriends, but Christine met all of her basic requirements, it seemed. I had been best man at my brother Geoff's wedding 10 years or so earlier, and now my younger brother, Alan, was to perform a similar service for me. We were married at Clapton Hall in a service conducted by my own vicar, Douglas Clark, with an address by an old friend of Christine's family, Mr Falaise, and the register completed by my father-in-law, Bernard Martin. We had a honeymoon in Ireland –

a few days in Dublin, and then a memorable, if exceedingly wet, week or so in County Wicklow.

1960 also saw Joyce Manning leave *Crusade*, to become editor of a Christian weekly. Strangely, although our working relationship at *Crusade* was somewhat strained, we became good friends after she left. I suspect that our views on editorial direction were never going to coincide. I wanted to make the magazine more 'popular', with more colour features, articles on contemporary issues and plenty of humour. This meant a reduction of what I thought of as the 'didactic' content – teaching articles on Bible study, prayer, evangelism and so on. Worthy but dull material simply wasn't read, though our readers hated to admit it.

Still, all through the sixties the circulation grew, not spectacularly, but steadily, reaching a peak of about 26,000 in 1967. These were audited figures – I had insisted that we joined the Audit Bureau of Circulation – and put us well ahead of any other comparable periodical, though still a long way behind a few religious weeklies like the *Sunday Companion*, *Methodist Recorder* and *Church Times*. We were very clearly identified with the Graham campaigns and with what I suppose one would have called 'mainstream' evangelicalism, though I had begun to cast the editorial net a little more widely. For instance, we reported and commented on the historic Second Vatican Council at some length, and, I hope, fairly and objectively.

One by-product of being editor of *Crusade* was the opportunity to sample what one might call the 'inner wheels' of the evangelical world. I had a great deal of respect for the Graham team, for instance, but was mildly shocked to find that a considerable section of the constituency – what might be called the Calvinistic party – were highly critical of his whole approach. Led by the eloquent and charismatic minister of Westminster Chapel, Dr Martyn Lloyd-Jones, this constituency was fundamentally opposed to 'invitation evangelism', as they called it. From a minor note of dissent in the fifties when, frankly,

Graham took British evangelicalism by storm, this had now grown to a substantial body of opposition. Its focus was a large group of ministers and clergy who met as the Westminster Fellowship, very much under the aegis of Westminster Chapel and its thunderous incumbent.

Personally I did not find this group particularly attractive nor their views very convincing. I had my own reservations about the Billy Graham approach to evangelism, but not on the grounds they argued – that it was the work of God to draw people to faith, not human agents, that grace alone was sufficient, and that urging, persuading and cajoling people to believe was not just tactless or counterproductive, but scripturally wrong. Calvin was much quoted, and also many of the Puritan divines, whose books, published at incredibly low prices by the Banner of Truth Trust, were their guiding lights. But above all it was Martyn Lloyd-Jones himself, 'the Doctor', as he was dubbed by the insiders, who was the chief reference point of truth. Asked what he thought about some issue of moment, a young Baptist minister looked at me doubtfully and replied, 'I don't think the Doctor has said anything about that one.' No light there, then.

The Doctor's preaching was treated with something akin to awe by his disciples, though on the one occasion I heard him preach in Westminster Chapel I found him somewhat thin on theology, while strong on sardonic wit at the expense of 'liberals' and 'neo-evangelicals', who seemed to inhabit his personal Pandora's box. He was eloquent, in the manner of Welsh chapel preaching, and his sermons – massively long by modern standards – were 'deep', in the sense that they gave microscopic attention to single words in the text. He was not a Greek scholar, a fact that was occasionally evident in his handling of specific words and phrases, but he wrote one of the very best devotional books on the Sermon on the Mount. As I say, his views were regarded as little short of holy writ by some of his more besotted acolytes.

I suppose this sounds like a kind of personal vendetta against an evangelical icon of the time. That would be untrue, because I had absolutely no cause either to dislike him or to doubt the effectiveness of his ministry in the lives of many people, including friends of mine. And when I say that I found the Westminster Fellowship ethos unappealing, I must instantly exclude from that judgment a number of its members for whom I had, and have, enormous respect – notably Dr Jim Packer. But the aura of infallibility which hung over the Doctor seemed to be catching and led to a most unattractive doctrinal arrogance on the part of some of his followers. Anyone who didn't share their convictions was at best dubiously Christian and at worst an enemy of the Truth. It made any kind of dialogue difficult, as some of the more irenic evangelical leaders were to discover.

The culmination of all this, I suppose, took place at a rally in the Central Hall, Westminster, in the early sixties, organized by the Evangelical Alliance, who were the owners and publishers at that time of *Crusade*. Dr Lloyd-Jones had been invited to speak, in order that his widely-rumoured misgivings about the place of evangelicals in the 'doctrinally-mixed' denominations could be aired, and his own proposals for evangelical unity considered. The Rector of All Souls', Langham Place, John Stott – probably the most respected figure among Anglican Evangelicals at the time – was to take the chair. As a member of the Evangelical Alliance staff I was sitting on the platform, and so had a ringside seat at what turned out to be the evangelical confrontation of the century.

As far as I could tell – and it was to become a topic of acrimonious dispute over the years – the Doctor kept very conscientiously to the brief he had agreed with the Evangelical Alliance Council, which was to speak about evangelical unity as he saw it. The trouble was that they had not fully realized how he did see it. For him, the evangelical cause was weakened by the 'dilution' of evangelicalism where it was located within the historic denominations. How could these 'brethren' bear witness to the truth when the leaders of their own churches were proclaiming error? And how could denominations which were utterly corrupted by liberalism make suitable settings for men who desired to proclaim the 'whole counsel of God'? He ended with an eloquent invitation to those who were in this situation to abandon these leaking vessels and embark on a new venture, the creation of a union or federation of unequivocally evangelical churches across the nation. I am relying on the memory of a speech delivered nearly 40 years ago, but I am tolerably sure that I have got both the feel and the gist of what he said correctly. He did not advocate the creation of an evangelical 'denomination', but of some association that would be a guarantor of orthodoxy and a touchstone of truth. Again, so far as I can remember, that was what the EA Council had expected he would say, though I doubt they could have guessed the force and passion with which it would be expressed.

When the Doctor had finished, the chairman, John Stott, stood up and decided that it was necessary for him to say something. I imagine he had seen, as I had, many young and older evangelical clergy sitting in the hall, listening with rapt attention to the speech. He may have felt that some of them could have been moved by it to precipitate action, even, perhaps, to resigning from their parishes or renouncing their orders. As one who had already dedicated himself to a strategy of strengthening the evangelical 'presence' in the Church of England, he may have felt that his work was about to be undone by a single and spectacular *coup de théâtre*.

At any rate, he politely but firmly disassociated himself from Martyn Lloyd-Jones' position and repeated, with quiet intensity, his conviction that the Church of England was far from a 'lost cause' and that a gospel ministry could be faithfully and effectively carried on within its structures. The Doctor had probably spoken for the best part of an hour, and John Stott for perhaps five minutes, but the Rector of All Souls had the last word, which may well have been crucial. At any rate, that night probably signalled the end of any hope of a genuine 'common cause' between Anglican evangelicals and their Free Church and independent fellows. Anglicans were now aware, if they had been previously in any doubt, that they were doctrinally suspect, second-class citizens in the evangelical world and fundamentally 'unsound'. The rest were now confirmed in their view that Anglican evangelicals were a bunch of compromisers, 'bowing down in the temple of Rimmon', as one Baptist put it to me (the reference is to 2 Kings 5:18), and wanting both to have their establishment cake and eat it. The divisions, in other words, were reinforced rather than undermined, which was not quite what the Doctor had intended.

In the event, two, or possibly three, Anglican clergy resigned their parishes in response to his plea, and all but one of them eventually came back into the fold. On the other hand, these events undoubtedly provided a massive impetus to those who were working to create a new and more 'open' kind of evangelicalism in the Church of England, a movement which reached its climax a few years later in the Keele Conference of 1967, when with remarkable unanimity Anglican evangelicals pledged themselves to work within the Church of England and 'repented' of past divisive and arrogant attitudes. Again, this cannot be quite what the Doctor had had in mind. Certainly, within the next decade there was a remarkable resurgence of evangelicalism in the Church of England, with evangelical theological colleges bursting with ordinands and evangelical clergy being appointed as bishops up and down the land. It was all quite hard to credit, and perhaps it would never have happened if that strange meeting at Westminster had not crystallized the issue quite so sharply.

Dr Lloyd-Jones' influence on British Christianity was almost entirely confined to the evangelical world. It is safe to say that few Christians outside it, and hardly any of the general public, would have known who he was. On the other hand, Billy Graham was probably the best-known religious figure in the land, much loved of cartoonists and comedians, of course, but also treated with a degree of respect because of the impact he had made and the influence he had achieved in public life. He had been back, since the initial 'Crusade' at Haringey, in north London, for several more campaigns – a week in the rain at Wembley stadium and then a longer mission at Manchester in 1961, based on Maine Road, the home of Manchester City football club. There was seldom an empty seat at any of these events and his simple, direct gospel preaching held these huge audiences apparently spellbound.

In many ways, it was hard to account for this, because he was not particularly eloquent, certainly not profound, seldom even memorable. His preaching style involved the constant, hammer-like repetition of the phrase 'The Bible says...' followed by a succession of texts delivered at breakneck speed and each followed by the relevant biblical reference. 'The Bible says we have all sinned. "All our righteousnesses are as filthy rags" (Isaiah 64:6)... "For all have sinned and come short of the glory of God" (Romans 3:23)... "If we say we have no sin, we deceive ourselves and the truth is not in us" (1 John 1:8)' – and so on (and on and on) until the point was driven home. Only then would the voice, with its rich North Carolina accent, slow down, and Graham would move on to explain the remedy for our sin.

Even in the 1950s, this seemed a risky approach in a country where relatively few people had any knowledge of the Bible, though I suppose at that time there was some vestigial popular respect for its authority. As the years passed, and the religious scene in Britain altered, one began to long that Billy Graham would recognize this problem. It was probably hard for a man who had grown up in America's Bible belt, where even today there is enormous respect for the authority of scripture (even where people seem to have only the haziest ideas of its actual content), to come to terms with the culture of western Europe. Talking to men and women who responded to Graham's invitation to 'get up out of their seats and come to Christ' one was struck time and again by how tenuous was their understanding of what he had said or of what their response might involve. Yet something the evangelist had said had struck a chord somewhere, awakened some longing for meaning or purpose, or possibly forgiveness and a new start, that had been strong enough to get them out of their seats in front of thousands of people to take a faltering step or two towards God.

In my role as editor of *Crusade* I saw a good deal of the Graham team. Indeed, for the London campaigns in the mid-sixties I was chairman of the press and publicity committee. At one level, I got to know Graham himself, though certainly not intimately. I had the feeling that few, beyond his wife Ruth and a very small circle of long-time associates like Grady Wilson and Cliff Barrows, were close enough to him to know the real man behind the public image. However, all that I saw of him confirmed the impression of someone who was driven by a sense of divine purpose, who believed that God had called him to preach the gospel wherever and whenever he was given the opportunity. Certainly I never detected the slightest hint that he was other than a sincere, devout and holy man, almost frighteningly without pride, and scrupulously honest. He was also a person who sought, and could take, constructive criticism, and acted on it. These qualities were to stand him in good stead in the light of later revelations about some of the other 'evangelists' spawned in droves during the sixties and seventies. Graham and his organization retained a clean image, and rightly so, through all the scandals of the succeeding years.

I must confess that I was completely bowled over by the Haringey Crusade in 1954. As someone newly come to a personal commitment to Christ, it was unbelievably exciting to see the crowds, to join in the singing, to listen to Graham's preaching – so utterly unlike anything I had heard before. For one thing, he talked in the language of ordinary people and related the gospel message to the world in which I lived. He read the newspapers and kept up with world events. He had understood and could employ for his own purpose the insecurity and latent terror of that first post-nuclear generation. His was a voice to which one simply couldn't be indifferent – as one critic said, 'Graham speaks in neon lights'. I gladly suspended my critical faculties and wallowed in it. It was all meat, drink and sheer delight for someone who had wondered whether the Christian message, which had recently made such an impact on my own life, would ever again make a similar impact on the life of the whole country. Just for a while, as the papers, radio and television were full of Billy Graham, it seemed that it might.

The euphoria of Haringey was to pass, of course, and in the cold light of history the Graham missions did not make any long-term dent in the growing secularity of modern Britain. They did, on the other hand, make an enormous difference to the Church of England, a difference which was to prove very influential in the next 20 or 30 years, as young men and women converted through the Graham campaigns took their place in the leadership of the Church, many of them in its ordained ministry. For that, Graham can take a great deal of credit, and whatever misgivings I may increasingly have felt about his style of evangelism or his theology, I retain a sense of gratitude that, while he did not succeed in winning the whole nation for Christ, he did bring a huge section of the Anglican Church back to gospel priorities.

My misgivings partly centred around a technique at which I have already hinted. I have said that Graham could 'employ for his own purpose the insecurity and latent terror of that first post-nuclear generation'. One instance of this upset me so deeply that I wrote to him about it, emboldened to do so because he had asked me to let him know, frankly and without restraint, if there were anything in his ministry about which I ever felt unhappy.

The precise motivation for my letter to him was the last night of a very successful campaign aimed at young people in London's Wembley Stadium, 'SPREE 73'. There were tens of thousands of teenagers in the crowd. After the inevitable, and inevitably protracted 'preliminaries', the golden-haired evangelist strode up to the podium. 'Let us pray', he said, in a voice that brooked no disagreement. We prayed. We prayed that on this night of a summit meeting in Beijing, when the very survival of humanity and of the planet was at stake, we would hear and respond to the voice of God. 'I do not know what the President and Chairman Mao are saying to each other,' he assured us, but everything in his manner, and in what we already knew of his associations with the White House, hinted that he did. Graham addressed the meeting that night in a highly charged atmosphere, with the clear implication that we were gathering against a background of impending nuclear holocaust, which might begin with a war between the Soviet Union and China. The evening sky drew dark above the floodlights as his voice drew us into a net of horror and foreboding. Was this to be our Armageddon, our day of Judgment? Was time really that short? Did the world's clock truly stand at five minutes to midnight? I reckoned myself a pretty cool and politically shrewd kind of person, but I could feel the tingling of fear and apprehension. One can only guess what impact this was having on the thousands and thousands of teenagers hanging on the evangelist's every word.

It is hardly surprising that when he finally began to offer us the only hope of deliverance, through putting our faith in the Saviour, seeking forgiveness for our sins and opening our lives to him, an exceptionally large number pushed their way to the front in response to his invitation. I imagine some, possibly many, were making a genuine and lasting commitment to Christ, but I am sure there were also many who later on felt slightly cheated, if not exploited, when they discovered that the summit meeting amounted to little, to be honest, and that things on the world scene continued much as they had always done. The remedy he offered was, of course, nothing less than the gospel truth. But the sickness he diagnosed was not the sickness of this audience's sin. I felt it was a crude act of manipulation, of which an evangelist of his stature should have been ashamed.

As I say, I wrote to him, saying all of this in terms which, rereading my letter now, seem arrogant and presumptuous. I suggested that some of those who responded to his appeal that night might have felt themselves 'just slightly tricked'. I went on: 'I do not believe that the prophetic element in the Bible is to be used to scare people into the kingdom. I also do not believe that Revelation was ever intended to be a guide to future events... I do not believe that it has anything specific to tell us about the future pattern of world politics, nuclear war, Israel, Armageddon or anything else of that kind.' I went on, sounding more and more hectoring: 'Why not, as God has so uniquely gifted you in this way, simply preach the kerygma – the life, saving death, resurrection, ascension and coming again of Jesus, the Son of God? I fear for your ministry if you appear to add to this gospel one interpretation or another of parts of the prophetic scripture.'

I think in Graham's shoes I would have written back to suggest that there would be plenty of time for me to dish out advice like this when I had been instrumental in bringing as many people to Christ as he had. In fact, I received a courteous and genuinely humble answer. 'I am deeply grateful,' he wrote, 'that you have spoken boldly... More and more I think you will find that I am sticking rather closely to the kerygma.' Certainly I never heard Billy Graham use this technique of persuasion again.

All of us who have been engaged in the business of persuasion, at any level, will know what a perilous exercise it can be, and how thin is the dividing line between legitimate and illegitimate pressure. Certainly it is a line I have crossed on many occasions, sometimes (as the prayer says) through ignorance, but also and often 'through my own deliberate fault'. I am not sure that I would have taken a rebuke from an insignificant observer as thoughtfully and graciously as Graham did. For me, that is the mark of a truly great man.

I probably saw much more of the Graham team and of the workings of the 'mission machine' than was really good for me. It was hard to ignore the human frailties of the Graham entourage, nor their total commitment to a 'system' which was little more than a finely honed technique of persuasion. With regard to the human frailties, one could instance the almost childish delight in any endorsement, however minimal, from a person of distinction. Minor royalty (and the major ones, too, come to think of it) were sedulously cultivated. Famous names – Winston Churchill was a favourite – were smuggled into sermons and press conferences. The team were desperate to get famous people to attend the meetings – if not the main rallies, then one of other of the smaller gatherings addressed by Graham or one of the team.

They also fed on the press. The morning papers – all of them – were delivered to the team hotel every day, and studied over breakfast for any references to the Crusade. For all the world like anxious performers after a West End first night, they awaited eagerly the media verdict, glowing if it was good, cast down if it was bad. At first it was almost entirely good, partly because the press could use Graham as a stick with which to beat traditional Christianity. But as time went on, and Graham himself became almost part of the 'establishment', the tune became less melodious to the team's collective ear.

All of this was probably natural enough – most of us want to know how we stand in terms of popular approval. Much of the British press comment was in any case needed for recycling to the States, where it became appeals fodder for the giant Graham corporation, which needed a multi-million dollar budget each year to maintain its 'ministry'.

But the addiction to a proven technique was harder to defend. The truth is that no matter how hard anyone tried – and successive British support committees did try – the team was convinced that the precise format which they had used since Graham was a hick preacher straight from college was the one that worked. 'The Lord has blessed this approach,' they would say. 'Why should we change it?' And so it remained unchanged, no matter in which hemisphere, on which continent, or in which outlandish culture the mission was taking place. If it was in Africa, or Poland, or India, then the words could be translated by an interpreter, but everything else remained the same: the gospel songs by Bev Shea, the multi-voiced choir under Cliff Barrows singing hymns mostly from the Sankey and Moody era, the appeal for financial support (always by a member of the local committee), the prayer by a respected church leader and then, when people could wait no longer, the arrival of Billy Graham on the stage. Soon after getting there he would be announced in ringing tones by Cliff Barrows and bounce up to the podium (always the same one) to call the audience to prayer. There followed Graham's address, often on a topic or theme ('The family', 'War and peace', 'Where are we going?', 'The dangers of delay' and so on) but always lasting at least 40 minutes, usually much more. It ended with the same appeal, couched night after night in almost identical words. Those who were ready to give their lives to Christ were urged to 'get up out of their seats' and come to the front. Detailed instructions were given as to how they should do this from various parts of the often enormous stadium, but they were assured that 'we'll wait for you... you come!... While the choir sings quietly, you come!' So the choir sang – always the same hymn, 'Just as I am, without one plea', to a strangely turgid but oddly insistent tune largely unknown in Britain before Graham days. And they came, so that the most memorable thing about a Billy Graham rally was the sound of their feet, hundreds of them, sometimes thousands. Even on the very first night at Haringey, when no one could have known what was coming, hundreds got up at Graham's bidding and made their way to the front, accompanied by the trained 'counsellors', each dutifully carrying his or her 'pack' of follow-up goodies.

What about those who came forward? What did they make of it all? For some – a few – this was familiar territory, in the sense that they came from the mission hall or chapel environment where such appeals were common enough, though hardly ever evoking anything like the response Graham did, of course. For most of those coming to the meetings it was a totally fresh and new concept that Christianity actually required some active step of personal commitment and that such a step might involve walking to the front of a stadium watched by one's friends. Yet still they did it, often from motives which were a great deal less precisely formulated than Graham's message seemed to require.

Over the years I spent many hours in Crusade counselling rooms. A few of the people I talked with had experienced a genuine and sometimes quite spectacular conversion – a 'new birth' in gospel language. A few others were people who had been drawn to faith, perhaps over a long period of time, and now felt themselves ready to make a decisive response. Billy Graham had given them the ideal opportunity. Most, to be honest, were drawn by a much less coherent feeling that they 'needed something more in their lives', or that they lacked any real purpose or meaning. Among those were some who were acutely conscious that they needed forgiveness and a new start in life. It was asking an awful lot of these 'counsellors' to make much sense of this collage of needs, longings and anxieties. I suspect that most, like myself, found it often beyond them. Whether in the end we did more good than harm is a moot point, though I suspect that any step towards God is a step in the right direction and during the Graham years many people did take their first steps on a path of faith.

Our own parish church, St Cuthbert's, was only a couple of miles away from Haringey Stadium, where the 1954 Crusade was held, and we gave the campaign full and enthusiastic backing. Many of our people were counsellors or sang in the choir, and coaches were laid on several nights a week to take potential converts to the meetings. So I suppose we were a fair test of the overall impact of the Crusade on an ordinary church and its congregation. On paper, the response was tremendous. Every post brought forms from the mission office telling us that such and such a person from our area had 'decided for Christ'.

The church was expected to 'follow up' these contacts and nurture them through the early weeks of discipleship.

With a handful of exceptions, this simply didn't work out. All of the people referred to us – over a hundred in all – were faithfully contacted (except for those who had given false or non-existent addresses). Most expressed surprise that anyone should have called, and some degree of shock that their moment of religious excitement the other night should have anything at all to do with joining a church. Some were embarrassed to admit what they had done, some gave extremely odd explanations of their behaviour ('my friend said, "Well, are you going?" so I got up and went') and a few were quite rude. Out of the hundred or so referrals, once the dust had settled after the mission was over, we had two or three genuine converts – that is, people who had come from no faith to faith in Christ – and probably 20 or so people from our own congregation or its fringes who had taken a huge step forward in terms of the reality of their Christian commitment. I suppose, on balance, that was good. It certainly gave the church a considerable lift, and for the next 10 years or so things continued to go well, with a steady stream of people finding faith through the ordinary life of the parish.

One of the converts was Denis Shepheard, a young man from a council estate on the Tottenham edge of the parish. He had recently been discharged from the Navy with an ankle injury – he'd fractured it falling off a roof in Malta, I believe. I never discovered how or why he went to hear Billy Graham, but he did, with remarkable consequences. I met him at church on his first visit after 'going forward' at a Crusade meeting and we became good friends, a friendship which lasted until his death in the 1990s.

Denis was a true Londoner, much more at home in the pub than in church. Indeed, his relationship with churchgoing had been non-existent until his strange decision to go and hear the American evangelist. But his conversion was rock solid. He wanted to know – how to read the Bible, how to pray, what he should do about beer drinking, how he could tell his mates about what had happened to him. His appetite for the things of the Spirit was insatiable and carried him through all his initial encounters with the weird world of Anglican worship in 1954 – Prayer Book matins and evensong were the staple diet at Chitts Hill. He loved the mid-week Bible study and prayer meeting, which had by now grown almost to rally proportions, and joined one of the home-based 'teams' of young Christians, where his enthusiasm and cockney humour provided a healthy contrast to the usual rather restrained tone of the proceedings.

Quite soon – perhaps within a couple of years – Denis felt a call to the ordained ministry. He wasn't put off by his first encounter with the 'system', when he was told that he would need to pass at least a few 'O level' examinations. At that point, he had absolutely zero in the way of academic qualifications. With simple determination, he set about doing it, at evening classes and with help from various of us in the congregation. A year or so later, he had shown sufficient progress to merit a selection conference for ordinands and was recommended for training. He booked his place at Oak Hill College – just up the road, at Southgate – and we all breathed a sigh of relief.

However, at that point a further, and more serious problem arose. The trouble in his ankle had flared up again and cancer of the bone was diagnosed. He was told that the only possible treatment was amputation of his left leg up to the knee. He came to the mid-week meeting in a mood which I can only describe as godly belligerence. How could God at one moment call him to ministry, and the next collude with the removal of his left leg – and the possibility, or probability, of a recurrence of the cancer elsewhere? To Denis' uncomplicated faith, this simply didn't make sense.

In any case, he explained to the vicar and a group of us after the meeting, didn't the Bible say somewhere that if anyone was ill they should ask the elders of the church to pray for them and anoint them with oil, and 'the Lord will raise him up'? If that was so, he was asking for it, and expecting that God would keep his promise.

The rest of us, from the vicar downwards, found it hard either to match his simple faith or to refute his argument, so it was agreed that the following Wednesday such a ceremony would take place. The vicar, Douglas Clark, and a few other senior members of the congregation, joined in the laying on of hands and anointing. I was included, because I was by now a lay reader and hence, presumably, considered an 'elder of the Church'.

The anointing took place as planned and Denis went home convinced that all would be well. I don't think the faith of the rest of us was quite so confident. But the fact is that when Denis went back to the hospital the following week for a check-up his astonished doctors could find no trace of the cancer. Indeed, it had gone, and never returned. He died in his sixties of a heart attack, having had an astonishingly fruitful ministry as a curate, vicar and national evangelist for the Church Pastoral Aid Society. I think it is the only undoubted miracle of healing which I have witnessed at first hand and it has meant that I have never since felt able to rule out the possibility that God will heal by divine intervention in some cases.

It was quickly balanced, as such euphoric experiences often are, by the death – also from cancer – of another friend, an equally gifted young Christian man, a leading figure in youth work in the Church of England. He, too, was prayed for. Indeed, an all-night prayer meeting was held, at the end of which everyone went home absolutely convinced that God was going to heal him. Within a fortnight he had died.

Those two events taught me a hard but invaluable lesson. Gifts can be sought, but never demanded. Prayer is not a matter of 'getting God to do what we want', which was rather how I had seen it, but of seeking, discovering and then co-operating with the will of God, however difficult that might be. Then, and many times later, I found the Gethsemane experience of Jesus both chastening and enlightening. If the Son of God could wrestle in tears with the will of his Father, while submitting to it, it was not surprising that people like me sometimes found the divine purpose not only unsearchable but impenetrable. Yet faith affirms that the Father's will is the only secure and certain way. And Mark's Gospel adds a further clue, for the prayer of Jesus asking whether the cup of suffering and judgment might be spared him was addressed to *Abba* – the loving, intimate, enfolding name, rather than the usual rather austere and formal *Pater*.

Denis Shepheard's story, and several others like it in our church at Wood Green, suggest that it would be quite wrong to emphasize simply the limitations of the Billy Graham approach in a British setting. The truth is that no one, at any rate not since John and Charles Wesley, had had such an impact on the nation's religious life. His campaigns didn't fill the churches and they didn't, in statistical terms, make much difference to the gradual erosion of church attendance. But they did make God and Jesus and the gospel live topics – even on the correspondence pages of *The Times*. And as I have observed, they shifted the Church of England's ministry away from the prevailing rather defeated liberalism towards a greater confidence in the gospel. That, at least, was a lasting impact, which is still being felt almost 50 years later.

On the personal level, the early years at *Crusade* not only saw my marriage to Christine, but a couple of years later the birth of our elder son, Philip, to be followed by our daughter, Rebecca, late in 1964. The third member of our offspring didn't arrive on the scene until 1969 – Adrian. The arrival of the family signalled a welcome move from a small top-floor flat in Holloway to a three-bedroomed semi in Finchley, still in north London, but moving towards the leafier bits. The house was bought for us by the Evangelical Alliance, and a couple of years later we were able to buy it, in turn, from them. Thus we entered the 'property-owning democracy', which, in view of what was to happen to house prices over the next 20 years, was just as well.

In 1963 I wrote my first book, for Hodder and Stoughton's *Christian Guide* series – *The Christian's Guide to Church Membership*. Now there's a title to stir the blood! However, nothing could dilute the thrill of handling one's first book. In fact, it had to take second place to the thrill of handling one's first child, which took place in the same year, but the sensations are rather similar. The difference, in my case, was that the book was followed, over the long years, by 20 or 30 more, each one, I have to say, conveying the same sense of satisfaction that the first (and very modest) venture did.

However, on the horizon, unlooked for and unexpected, was another change in my life, one that had surprising consequences, and not simply for me.

CLIFF RICHARD AND ALL THAT

In the heart of Finchley is a typical suburban park, with a typical suburban name, Victoria Park. It is just off the Ballards Lane shopping centre and bounded on one side by Etchingham Park Road – again, a typically suburban avenue of houses built around the turn of the century or a couple of decades later in some cases.

On a particular summer evening in 1965 I was leading an open-air service in the park organized by some of the local churches and featuring a pop singer (as they were rather quaintly called in those days) who had abandoned a well-documented life of excess for the only slightly calmer waters of pentecostal Christianity. There was some singing, an interview with the former pop star and a few words from me – all of this conveyed by a portable public address system to the crowd of (mostly already committed) onlookers. You would have had to be pretty committed to hang around, as I recall, because it was a typically English 'summer' evening, when it suddenly gets cold and a stiff breeze blows up. Unobserved by me, a young man exercising his dog in the park did stand to listen for a while, however, and that was to be a significant moment in my life.

The young man was Cliff Richard, a rather more

distinguished and better established performer than the one we had on the platform. From the launch of his career in 1958 with the song 'Move It', which reached number two in the charts, through a string of number-one hits, television shows and, by now, four films, he was by some distance the most successful UK performer on the pop scene. The Beatles had recently burst into the spotlight, of course, and for a while tended to dominate the charts, but at that time a 'pop' career lasting all of seven years was a thing of wonder. 'How long could Cliff last at the top?' the music journalists asked. Yet there he was, at that time actually in the process of making his fifth film, at Pinewood studios, *Finders Keepers*.

He was walking a friend's dog, I learnt later. The friend was Bill Latham, who was a teacher at Cheshunt Secondary School, which Cliff himself had attended a decade earlier, and a reader (lay minister) at St Paul's Church, right next to the park, where Christine and I were also members – indeed, I was also a reader. Cliff had Bill's dog on that evening stroll because he had accepted an invitation to stay at the house in Etchingham Park Road which Bill and his widowed mother shared while he was filming at Pinewood, it being a good deal nearer than the very grand house, Rookswood, which he owned in Hertfordshire.

There was, of course, more to the story than that. Ever since his father's death in 1961, and especially since a respected aunt, and then his older sister, had become involved with the Jehovah's Witnesses, Cliff had been on a slightly tentative religious search. Certainly at one point he was very near to joining the Witnesses himself, frequently attending meetings in their Kingdom Halls on tour in various parts of the country. One member of The Shadows (his backing band), 'Licorice' Locking, was an enthusiastic member, and guitarist Hank Marvin was, like Cliff, almost persuaded. Both of them were regularly reading the Bible (in the Witnesses' own 'New World' translation) and had given up swearing. But, especially in Cliff's case, something held him back. He felt that there were missing parts to the puzzle, as it were.

Cliff's former English teacher, Jay Norris, a woman whose advice he seldom ignored, had suggested that before taking the step of joining the movement he should speak to her young colleague Bill Latham. A Roman Catholic herself, she felt that Bill's approach to religious belief might in the long run be more helpful to him than that of the Jehovah's Witnesses.

An initial contact with Bill had led to a genuine friendship, and also the opportunity for Cliff to meet 'orthodox' Christians of his own age and see for himself how genuine their faith was, and to compare it with that of the Jehovah's Witnesses he had met. He was impressed with them but still not quite persuaded. Like many people who have been exposed to the Witnesses' beliefs, he had enormous difficulties over the doctrine of the Trinity (difficulties he shared with most major Christian theologians in church history) and the divinity of Jesus Christ. Bill got the impression that if those problems could be honestly dealt with, Cliff would be ready to commit himself in a wholehearted way to the Christian faith.

I suspect that something along those lines was the topic of conversation in the little living room in Etchingham Park Road that night after the open-air meeting, as a result of which Bill phoned me and asked if I would be prepared to come round one evening and spend a few hours arguing things through with Cliff. I had no idea what to expect. Like almost everybody else in Britain I had seen Cliff Richard on television, but I had no idea how his mind worked, what his anxieties were or in what way I might be able to help. But if Bill thought it was a good idea, I was more than happy to go along with it. There was, incidentally, one condition attached to all of this. No one was to be told about it. No word was to reach the media that the UK's top pop star was 'flirting with religion'.

I turned up at the appointed time, not at all sure what to expect. Nearly 40 years later, with Cliff Richard recognized by everyone as something of a religious icon, it is quite hard to take on board how he stood at that point in the mid-sixties.

He had burst on the scene in 1958 as 'Britain's Elvis Presley', a rock 'n' roller in the true Elvis style, all swagger and curled top lip and shaking hips. His act, which would seem mild enough now, was deemed irresponsibly erotic by some of the newspapers – and heaven knows what churchmen would have thought about him if they had been close enough to the youth scene to know what was going on. And here I was, going into the Lathams' modest front room in a terraced house in Finchley, not simply to meet him, but to argue the case for Christianity.

In the event, Cliff turned out to be incredibly 'ordinary', totally without pretence or embarrassment and simply eager to get answers to questions that had clearly been troubling him for a long time. He seemed very young – he was actually 24 at the time – but yet with a kind of maturity, probably bred of a tough childhood, an ordinary secondary modern school, a strong family and a rapidly developing instinct for survival in the showbiz jungle. He had a friendly, open face and a pleasant, if oddly mid-Atlantic, accent. Those were my first impressions, but nothing I have learnt of Cliff since, over many years, has altered them materially. Over the years since I have met and worked with many showbiz stars, of varying degrees of fame, but I could count on the fingers of one hand those who match Cliff Richard for genuine modesty and friendliness.

We pitched straight into the argument. I use the word advisedly, because there was never any doubt that on this occasion the Christian gospel was under trial, Cliff was the prosecutor and I – God help me! – was the defence. He listened with quiet intensity to my replies, countering some points, asking me to expand on others, and showing a considerable grasp of the New Testament, albeit according to the Witnesses' version of things. His main lines of enquiry were threefold: the doctrine of the Trinity, the divinity of Christ, and the meaning which was to be attached to his death and resurrection. The agenda was a packed one, and after a couple of hours we decided that at least a second meeting would be needed – and it was arranged on the spot.

How had it all gone? That was what I asked myself as I walked home – we lived in an adjoining road, not far away. I felt emotionally, spiritually and intellectually drained, and wondered how Cliff must have felt. I tried to describe to Christine how the evening had gone, but it was very hard to tell whether the whole exercise had got much beyond a matter of words and definitions. I had begun to read up on the beliefs of Jehovah's Witnesses and had come to see that it was very much a religion of 'right believing' – there was little talk of heart, but much appeal to head, though always from a very rigid doctrinal base. Its belief system was coherent, within its own terms of reference, and tidy in a way the Christian faith could never be. There was little room for any personal response or insight other than obedience to the core beliefs, and little encouragement of what Christians would call 'personal faith'. Witnesses were to be 'footstep followers of Jesus Christ', a noble enough aim in itself, of course, but without any real notion of an indwelling presence or an empowering Spirit it all seemed to me slightly joyless and arid. Strangely enough, it was not until I made a documentary programme with and about the Witnesses for BBC Radio many years later that I began to appreciate the real nature of its appeal to a certain kind of temperament and personality.

As for Cliff himself, I would have to say I was really very impressed. I had assumed that most of his talent was in his larynx and his looks – and indeed these were the copper-bottomed bases of his popularity – but I hadn't reckoned on a very sharp mind as well. Within a few years I was to learn exactly how sharp, as I watched him cope with questions and comments from Oxbridge students or tread with consummate skill through radio and television interviews, some of them distinctly hostile. Cliff is not, in the accepted sense of the word, an 'intellectual', but he is (in the kind of language I would have used in my teaching days) distinctly 'bright', and those who assumed otherwise were generally in for a shock.

Our second meeting went well, partly because Cliff had

been thinking over our earlier discussion and had come along with specific points that he wanted clarified. It became obvious that, in spiritual terms, one was pushing on an opening door. He liked what he had seen of 'orthodox' Christians, he was warming to the vision of Jesus which was at the heart not just of what they believed but of the lives they led, and he could see somewhere along this road the answers to questions and needs that had troubled him for several years.

On this occasion his questions were rather different. Although nobody was going to fob him off with glib answers to difficult questions, it was obvious that he was slowly grasping an even more profound truth – that the Christian 'good news' is not about a set of doctrines or propositions to be argued over and eventually accepted, but an encounter with a person, Jesus Christ. He could see that the real difference between his Christian friends and the Witnesses he had met over recent years was not in their beliefs but in the nature of their faith.

At any rate, that evening he put a quite different kind of question to us. As I recall, there were four or five people present on that occasion and I think we were all slightly surprised at the directness of what he said. 'If I want to be a real Christian, exactly what do I have to do?' I think our answers were along sternly traditional lines, despite our surprise. 'Repent of past sin and unbelief, and put your trust in Jesus Christ for forgiveness and new life.' 'And that's it?' he asked. 'That's it,' we said – though we did make it clear that such a step would be the beginning of a whole journey of faith, to be taken in company with God's people.

As the meeting broke up, Cliff said quietly to Bill Latham, 'I'm on my way in.' Events proved that that was so – private events, which concerned Cliff's own personal commitment to Christ, and public ones, which involved his starting to come regularly to services at the local parish church where a number of people he knew well were already members. Up till then, for all his interest in Christian questions (and even his willingness to go to the boys' Bible study group which Bill helped to run) he had declined to set foot in church.

This was the summer of 1965, and by the autumn Cliff felt quite comfortable in church. It had been decided that his Christian commitment would remain a private matter for as long as possible, which involved the collusion of the boys in Bill's 'Crusader' class and also the youth group at St Paul's Church. I think they were surprised – perhaps 'astonished' would be a better word – to see the pop star sitting in a pew week by week in church, and it must be admitted that some of the girls seemed a bit awestruck, but everyone went along with the plan to keep his presence secret. Indeed, when Cliff agreed to sing a gospel song at a youth service that autumn, accompanying himself on the guitar, most of the older members of the congregation had no idea who he was. At Christmas time he joined a group from the church who led a simple service in the local hospital, and when he played and sang in one ward an elderly patient beckoned him over to her bed to tell him she thought he was 'very good', and really 'ought to take it up'.

Cliff's greatest asset in all of this was his complete naturalness. He was, and is, a naturally friendly person with a kind of inborn sense of courtesy – perhaps the product of a secure and generous family background. At any rate, everyone is treated in exactly the same way and this was an important asset in the transition from the self-conscious world of showbiz to the unglamorous world of a suburban London church and a group of people whose lives were a million miles from Pinewood and Wardour Street.

Christine and I got to know him well at that time. In fact, he would often be round at our home for coffee, or a chat. When this became known in the youth fellowship, we had no shortage of volunteers for babysitting, which was a useful bonus. He also introduced us to some of his friends in the showbiz world. I remember a meal at the home of Brian Bennett, who was the drummer with The Shadows and who, like others of the band, had a lot of questions to ask about Jehovah's Witnesses' beliefs. Indeed, I felt in some danger of becoming a self-styled expert on the subject, which I certainly wasn't. All I could do was to set out, as clearly as I could, what I saw as the orthodox Christian position, and try to justify it from the teaching of the Bible. I discovered, of course, that it was not as easy as I had thought, not because the concept of the Trinity is foreign to the New Testament, but because it had not at that stage been developed into the rather sophisticated doctrines which emerged from the early centuries of the Church.

In a way, the great truth which had set me free a dozen years earlier stood me in good stead in all of this. The key to everything is Jesus. If he is, as I believe he claimed and his first followers passionately believed him to be, the unique Son of God, then his life on earth is simply the most important thing that has happened in human history. That means that knowing him, 'encountering' him (in the jargon of the evangelist), is the vital clue to the truth about everything else, including all of these rather elusive and mystical concepts which have become part of received Christian doctrine. It also means, of course, that to get it wrong about Jesus is really to get it wrong about everything, which in a nutshell is the problem of all the pseudo-Christian sects.

At that time I must admit I adopted a very hard and arrogant approach to Jehovah's Witnesses. One unfortunate couple who happened to ring our doorbell were somewhat taken aback by my verbal assault, which included a scathing denunciation of their New World translation backed up with copious instances in Greek and much waving of textual authorities. I am ashamed to say they retreated under the onslaught with the woman in tears and the man white-faced with shock. Even worse, I think I felt proud of it.

It was several years later, during my time at the BBC, that I came to see the corollary of my oft-quoted belief that Christianity is not primarily about dogma, doctrine or creed but about an encounter with Christ. If that is true, then living by the openness and vulnerability of Jesus is more important even than scrupulous doctrinal 'soundness' in our beliefs about him. Most Witnesses are, in biblical terms, sincere Godfearers, however off the mark they are in many of their beliefs. It should be possible (I eventually conceded) to bear a consistent witness to them of a gentler, more open way to God than the one they had espoused, not only by the words we speak but by our total demeanour towards them.

Nevertheless, it was good to watch Cliff emerge from the shadows of what is, even on its own terms, a narrow and exclusive sect into the broader waters of Christian fellowship and worship. We – that is to say, the small group of people who had accompanied him on his pilgrimage to faith – had been very careful to protect him from premature exposure to the media, including (and perhaps especially) the Christian media. But now Cliff himself expressed a willingness to 'go public' about his new-found faith, though in carefully prepared and monitored ways.

So it was that in the winter of 1965/6 Cliff made a couple of fairly low-key appearances at public meetings. The first was at a rally of the 'Crusader' movement – the association of Bible study groups for young people which he had now known for some time through the large Finchley class led by Bill Latham and others of Cliff's friends. That meeting was in the Central Hall, Westminster, where Bill interviewed him about his beliefs in front of an audience of about 2,000 teenage boys, and he sang a couple of gospel songs.

Soon afterwards, he was back in the same hall, with an even larger crowd – 2700 young people, members of the Church Youth Fellowships Association, including a sizeable contingent from St Paul's, Finchley. A week or so before this meeting, at which I was to be chairman, I met a friend from a church in Essex and asked him if the youngsters from his parish would be there. He said they would, but probably not his own teenage daughter, who was going through an anti-church phase (as he put it) – 'all she thinks about, day and night, is that wretched Cliff Richard'. I told him that the 'wretch' himself would be taking part in the meeting, but I think he reckoned I was having him on. 'Look,' I said at last, 'You tell your daughter to come. She'll really kick herself if she misses it. And bring her up to the front afterwards and I'll introduce her to Cliff Richard.'

I don't know what went on in their household, but sure enough she was there on the night, along with a party from their church. I interviewed Cliff this time, and he spoke of how he had found Christ, and then, once again, he sang a couple of songs, accompanying them on his acoustic guitar. I don't think it would be an exaggeration to say that the audience was dumbstruck. At least, they listened in absolute silence (it really made sense of the cliché about hearing a pin drop), erupting into tumultuous and prolonged applause when he had finished.

True to my word, I introduced my friend's awestruck daughter to Cliff at the end of the meeting, but she seemed to have lost the power of speech.

After these carefully planned experiments, we felt that the time could not be long put off – or the general media kept in the dark – much longer. Odd rumours had reached the papers, though mostly suggestions that Cliff might be planning to leave showbusiness, possibly for a career in teaching. The Gang of Four discussed it, very much under Bill's guidance and with Cliff's full participation, but we were not sure what was the right way to proceed. We didn't want to push Cliff prematurely into a sea of media publicity, but we also felt it couldn't be put off indefinitely. As it happened, events took over.

Maurice Rowlandson, then the Graham Association organizer in the UK and a former colleague of mine at the Evangelical Alliance, had dropped me a note asking if Billy Graham could have Cliff's home address, as he'd like to write to him. Maurice recently sent me a copy of my reply. After giving the address, I wrote, 'We – his closest counsellor and I – both feel that a nice letter from Billy G, perhaps inviting him to Earls Court

– but not, we suggest, asking him to make any public pronouncements for the present – could do a lot of good.' I don't know what happened in the transmission, but the next thing we knew was that Cliff had been invited to give a testimony at one of the Earls Court rallies, and he seemed quite keen to do it. A day was fixed, there was some discussion about exactly what Cliff would say and sing, and there was a careful assessment of precisely how the press and media coverage would be handled. The intention was that no one would be told in advance – largely to prevent Cliff being hounded during the time leading up to the meeting. In the event, somehow *The Mirror* got wind of his appearance and trailed the news in its morning edition. Needless to say, the information sped through the mysterious communication channels of his fans.

In fact, it would not be Cliff's first visit to Earls Court. He had already been to hear Graham on at least two occasions, in parties from the youth fellowship at the church, and had warmed to the content and approach of the evangelist's message. He liked Billy Graham's constant appeal to the Bible, and he also admired his ability to direct attention away from himself to Christ. Here, he once told me, was someone who knew how to use the gift and skills of a performer for a greater cause than self-promotion. Impressed, Cliff sent tickets for Earls Court to some of his fans, urging them to go along, and some responded to Graham's appeal – at least one, to my certain knowledge, with a serious and, as the passing of time has confirmed, lifelong commitment. But it was one thing to sit 'in the stalls', as it were, and quite another to be part of the action – a distinction Cliff was well aware of from his own life and career.

When it came to the chosen night, 16 June 1966, there was a distinct air of expectancy in the arena. The crowds outside fighting to get in were younger than usual, the news having spread that Cliff was going to appear that night. In fact, the main hall's 20,000 seats were full long before the scheduled start. Soon the 'overflow' was also full and several thousand people –

by the sound of it, mostly Cliff fans – were gathered in a huge crowd behind the building, hoping for some chance to get involved in the evening's happenings.

I was sitting on the platform, allegedly to give Cliff some moral support. He is always a bit tense before going on stage, but I have never seen him, before or since, quite as nervous as this. I think he knew that a great deal hung on this evening – possibly the shape of his future career, perhaps even the whole way his life would go from this point. He had always recognized that it is the fans who make the performer, not the other way round, and it could be that he was stretching the loyalty of his devoted following too far by 'going religious' on them. I suspect such thoughts were in his mind; I know they were felt, and had been expressed, by some in his highly experienced management team.

But there was also pressure on him as a new Christian. This environment was strange to him. How would people react to a pop singer standing up and speaking of his faith? He knew already that some on the fringes of the evangelical world had no time for the pop scene at all, regarding its music as demonic and its influence on young people deplorable. How would they feel about his involvement in an evangelistic meeting? Possibly Billy Graham was also taking the risk of losing support among some of the most committed of his backers.

I was aware of the tension, and could see it on Cliff's face and in his whole demeanour. When the time came for his contribution, the huge arena fell silent. He gripped the podium – he said later, 'until my knuckles went white'.

'I've never had the opportunity to speak to an audience as big as this before,' he began, 'but it is a great privilege to be able to tell so many people that I am a Christian. I can only say to people who are not Christians that until you have taken the step of asking Christ into your life, your life isn't really worthwhile. It works – it works for me!' He then introduced his song ('It is no secret what God can do'). 'My voice is small,' he said, 'but the message is a big one' – and then sang, accompanied on this occasion not by his acoustic guitar but by the piano and electric organ combination which was favoured by the Graham team.

When it was over he went backstage briefly with Billy Graham, first to the crowd in the regular overflow hall, and then outside to say a few words to the assembled fans. By now the evening was beginning to take on something of a carnival atmosphere. At least it was obvious that the fans – whatever they thought of his decision to walk the Christian path – were not going to desert him because of it. It was, as the music paper *Disc* put it, 'the point of no return for "Christian Cliff"'. Whatever he did from now on would be judged as the action of a Christian, for better or worse.

Cliff himself described that night at Earls Court as 'definitely the most tremendous moment of my whole life'. It certainly represented a watershed, because until then his private decision had been just that, private. Now his faith was a matter of public record. As he once said to me, 'I know the papers would love to print a picture of me drunk in a night club.' Perhaps at that moment he didn't fully appreciate what a burden it might later become being 'Britain's best-known Christian', but that night in June 1966 probably planted the thought in his mind.

Later in that same year Cliff was confirmed at St Paul's Church, by the Bishop of Willesden. We had a bit of a discussion about the name by which the bishop should address him. After all, his 'baptismal name' was 'Harry' – Harry Webb, to be precise, given to him 26 years earlier in a church somewhere in India. But it was literally years since anyone, even his own mother, had called him 'Harry', so the decision was for 'Cliff'. He was prepared for confirmation by the vicar, Paul Betts, along with a dozen or so others, adults and youngsters.

Of course, he was suddenly in great demand on what one could call the 'Christian circuit'. At least we had known it would happen and had prepared for it. There were thoroughly worthwhile opportunities – with students, perhaps, or a boys' club in the East End. But there were also, inevitably, many invitations designed to pack people in ('bums on seats' is the phrase that comes to mind) for little ultimate purpose than to have a good time, or boost a flagging programme, or give an evangelical entrepreneur an undeserved bit of promotion.

The most cheeky I can recall was a man in the Midlands who invited Cliff to come to speak and sing at some event or other. Cliff, aided and abetted by Bill Latham, who tended to watch his diary like a hawk, declined. But apparently this was a man who wouldn't take 'no' for an answer. Worse, he simply advertised that Cliff was coming, and sold tickets on the strength of it – hundreds of them, needless to say. When the day arrived, Cliff didn't (of course). But even at that point the organizer wouldn't come clean. He told the audience that Cliff was stuck in traffic, but hoped to arrive shortly – and maintained the fiction throughout the evening. We wouldn't have known anything about it had not someone in the audience smelt a rat and phoned me up that very night.

When confronted with the deception, the organizer simply claimed that it was all a misunderstanding – though the fictional traffic jams (which I think may have included a crash on the motorway) would have made it a 'misunderstanding' of monumental proportions. The incident was a warning to Cliff's friends of the lengths to which some people – yes, professing Christians, at that – would go to jump on the Cliff bandwagon.

However, there were also many happy and profitable occasions. I recall going with Cliff to a gathering for undergraduates organized by the Oxford Pastorate at St Aldate's Church, when an enormous crowd of articulate and argumentative young students gave Cliff a rare grilling. He emerged, as he invariably did, still smiling, still articulate – and well able to hold his own with the bright, but as yet not worldly-wise, young intellectuals of Oxford.

There was also a very odd television confrontation, in which some smart producer set up a head-to-head on the subject of Billy Graham's evangelism. In the pro corner was Cliff, supported by me. In the con corner was none other than Paul Jones, lead singer with Manfred Mann, public school educated and highly articulate and, at that stage of life, almost desperately anti-religion. He also had a supporter, but I can't remember who it was. Indeed, I remember little about the recording except that Paul Jones insisted he must have his hair washed before going in front of the cameras – an interesting affectation, I thought. I assume Cliff did a good job on that occasion. In any case, Paul was to change his views completely 15 years later, when he and his girlfriend 'went forward' at a Luis Palau evangelistic meeting at Loftus Road, the QPR football ground. Later Paul made some splendid films for schools on the Bible and was himself a formidable exponent of the Christian case.

The whole 'Cliff business' tended to take life over for me for a few years. There was a film made by Graham's World Wide Films and directed by James Collier, *Two a Penny*, in which Cliff starred. I was 'script consultant', and wrote several scenes – a completely new experience. When the film was eventually released it was predictably panned by the critics, enjoyed by Christians and pretty well ignored by everyone else.

It would be wrong to imply that Cliff spent all his time on some kind of Christian Celebrity Circuit. In fact, on the average Sunday he was in a pew at St Paul's Church, asking for and getting no preferential treatment. He got enormous satisfaction from the midnight eucharist on Christmas Eve not long after his confirmation. Just to put the icing on the cake (for once, an appropriate metaphor) there was even a layer of snow on the Finchley roads as we made our way into church. As it happened, I was preaching at that service, and it did indeed have something a bit special in its atmosphere.

Before leaving the subject of Cliff Richard, I will try to answer the two questions I am most frequently asked about him. The first is relatively simple. 'What's he like in real life?' The only honest answer is, exactly the same as he appears in public life. When you see Cliff on screen or on stage, or when, as we did, you get to know him well over a period of many years, what you see is what you get.

Now that is not to say that Cliff is a human being without flaws. That would be a preposterous idea. The tabloid press might dub him 'St Cliff', but I don't think his friends and family are quite ready to canonize him yet. But his human frailties – or imperfections, if you like – are simply the proof that he is, like the rest of us, a sinner in need of God's grace. To be honest, he is probably a bit too sensitive to criticism and tends to remember its source for a long time. He has a tendency to vanity (not an uncommon failing among much-admired people) and he likes what he would call 'straightforward' and others might describe as simplistic answers to complex questions. He does not, in that rather odd English expression, 'suffer fools gladly', which usually means he can be intensely impatient with other people's failures or incompetence. I have seen him reduced to incoherent fury at a logistical failure in the staging of one of his concerts. In those circumstances, a brief tactical withdrawal is the wisest response, because he gets over it quickly and is not above apologizing all round afterwards.

All of this adds up to no more than saying that Cliff is a pleasant and easy companion with the normal ration of human frailties, considerably offset by his understanding of what Christian discipleship means. One would like to give all the credit for this equable temperament to his religious conversion, but I suspect a happy and secure, if quite impoverished, childhood had at least as much to do with it. A natural ease and innate good manners are probably inculcated very early in anyone's life, or not at all.

The second, and more difficult, question is about Cliff's sexuality. People want to know whether he is gay, or not. Indeed, they seem to feel they have a right to know, and I don't just mean fans or blokes in the pub. I was once asked by a leading church figure in Northern Ireland if I could confirm that Cliff was not homosexual, as he had heard rumours about this, and if there were any possibility of its being true he would have to cancel a meeting he had arranged in Belfast.

The short, honest and most commendable answer to such questions is, 'Mind your own business.' However, for those who pursue this topic so relentlessly, it *is* their business, and they are not easily put off, tending to take any hesitation in answering as confirmation of the rumours. I have often pointed out that a person's sexuality is an intensely private and personal thing, unless they choose to flaunt it in public, and that what they do, as well as what are they are by nature, is a matter entirely between themselves and God.

But I am aware that even to have written what I have just done would serve to confirm suspicions that I am covering up some dark secret about Cliff's personal life. All I can say is, that if there is a 'dark secret' I know nothing of it, and that in a friendship lasting over 30 years Christine and I have never had the slightest reason to question his personal morality.

The question about homosexuality is often linked with one about Cliff's 'failure' to get married. Clearly he hasn't lacked opportunity, so why, people ask, has he never managed to settle down with a wife, or even a long-term girlfriend? Cliff's oft-quoted response is that, first, he is not going to jump into bed with someone to prove he's not gay, and second, he has never met the 'right' person. Both replies are not entirely convincing, it has to be said. Indeed, with the passing of time they have more and more the flavour of clever evasions than truthful answers to the questions. And, of course, there is no earthly reason why Cliff, or anyone else, should feel compelled to explain why he hasn't got married, or even why he lacks any great urge to jump into bed with anybody.

The truth is that Cliff has had a number of 'near-misses' (or perhaps one could say 'near-mrs') in the marriage stakes. Back in the early stages of his career there was the actress Una Stubbs, a long-term friend certainly, and a young dancer, Jackie Irving, who was his steady girlfriend for three years in the early sixties. More recently, in the 1980s, it really looked as if the permanent 'bachelor boy' was about to change his status, when he was quite public about his friendship with tennis star, and later television presenter, Sue Barker. Christine and I had dinner with them one evening, and went home quite convinced that it was time to talk serious hats and so on. They were certainly very close and affectionate, and Sue at that time wholeheartedly shared Cliff's Christian faith. What 'went wrong' we were never told and would not dream of asking, but it is a reasonable guess that yet again he had doubts, as a bachelor in his fifties will always have, and – to quote Cliff back in the sixties – 'doubts are no basis for marriage'. As it happens, just about all his bachelor friends from that earlier era were by now married, many with children, but Cliff resisted all promptings to take the plunge. If ever a song from the dawn of one's career was to haunt anyone it was surely 'Bachelor Boy', back in 1962, for Cliff.

Life for me in the late sixties had become, as might be gathered, both hectic and rather starstruck. Two things might have got seriously neglected in this flood of showbiz glamour – the family, and the day job. Culpably, I guarded the day job fairly well – *Crusade* had its record circulation figures in 1967, audited figures of 27,000 a month. But I know I did tend to take Christine and the children for granted, something I have desperately regretted since. Philip and Becky were at that delightful stage of emerging from being toddlers to 'proper' childhood, and I missed most of it. And I left Christine with the two of them on her own far too often. Her sense of Christian duty, hammered into her from childhood onwards, prevented her complaining in the way I suspect a modern young woman would do – and justifiably. For me, it was all pretty heady stuff – the drug of 'fame' and 'glamour' is, I reckon, a seriously addictive one.

Mind you, it was always lovely to come home to the reassuring order and security of the family, and to a certain extent Christine – and even the children – could also enjoy some of the forbidden fruit. We entertained any number of well-known figures from the world of the media and entertainment, and also were sometimes able to go together to the kind of events that would have made our parents stop in their tracks.

One such was the Eurovision Song Contest finals, when Cliff was 'singing for Britain' – the song was 'Congratulations'. He invited Christine and me to go as his guests. That year the contest was taking place in the Royal Albert Hall, and Cliff was widely tipped to win. This was hardly on the grounds of the musical sophistication or imaginative creativity of 'Congratulations', which to be honest has all the subtlety of a combine harvester at full speed, but it was a brilliant piece of music marketing. That accounts for the fact that, while it failed to win the Eurovision Contest (to Cliff's disgust, it came second), it achieved number one position in the pop charts and, even more significantly, became a 'pop standard' – the sort of tune hammered out by three-piece combos at wedding receptions, birthdays and bar mitzvahs. So it was hardly a failure.

There was one other significant development on the showbiz front. At the end of a Sunday night service at St Paul's I spotted a young woman – with extremely long hair, and an expensive-looking fur coat – sitting alone in a pew. I discovered she was another singer, Cindy Kent, who was the lead singer with The Settlers, a pop-folk group who were regulars on Radio 2 and popular performers on the folk circuit. She explained that she was a kind of 'semi-lapsed' Christian – she'd never stopped believing, but had lost contact with church and didn't feel she belonged anywhere. She, and the rest of the band, came from the Birmingham area, but now shared a flat in West Hampstead, which is not very far from Finchley. She'd heard that this was the church Cliff went to, and thought if he was welcomed here, she might be as well. And indeed St Paul's became her 'spiritual home' until she got married some years later and moved a few miles north to Whetstone.

The Settlers were doing a concert in the Purcell Room at the Festival Hall and Cindy arranged for Christine and me, Cliff and Bill to have tickets. None of us quite knew what to expect, but frankly the show was brilliant. This was what 'ensemble performing' was all about. The three voices – Geoff, the bass player, did not usually sing, mercifully – matched perfectly, the items were cleverly varied between pop, 'soft' gospel and folk, and the chemistry on stage was superb. We were all won over on the spot, and an idea was planted that night that was to come to fruition in due course: a series of gospel concerts, starring Cliff, backed and supported by The Settlers. He had wanted to do something professionally that would enable him to witness to his faith through his stage work, and here was the chance.

The boys in The Settlers – Mike, John and Geoff – were not fully signed-up practising Christians, though that was certainly Mike's background, and the others were 'sympathetic'. In fact, they had always done a lot of gospel material in their shows. Now they had the chance to showcase their act on stage with one of the biggest stars of the music scene. But there was also a gain for Cliff – a ready-made gospel band to back him, and to provide support for a full-length programme.

Cliff's management took some persuading. After all, a major part of their role was to save Cliff from hangers-on and bandwagon boarders. But Cliff's enthusiasm, and the limited nature of the project (it would not affect Cliff's normal recording, television or stage programme at all) won them over. A series of gospel concerts was planned, on a theme of which I was the proud creator: 'Help, Hope and Hallelujah!'

The idea was to present the Christian message in the setting of an evening of memorable contemporary music. So 'Help' was the human dilemma, 'Hope' was the story of Jesus and 'Hallelujah!' was our response to it. We all worked together on the content, with Cliff and The Settlers revealing an encyclopedic knowledge of the modern music scene. They seemed able to find a song somewhere to say, well, exactly what you wanted it to say. My role was that of theological watchdog.

Together we assembled a programme which would last a couple of hours, with The Settlers 'warming up' each section of the proceedings (something they were all too used to doing for 'bigger' bands) and Cliff bursting on to stage at appropriate moments to keep the fans happy.

The show was launched at the Royal Albert Hall, which was sold out for the occasion. We also took it to Newcastle, and then to the Hague, in the Netherlands. The most striking thing there was the enormous enthusiasm of the audience and their total rejection of any attempt to translate the proceedings into Dutch. 'No', they shouted with one voice, 'English, please!'

But the highlight for Cliff and The Settlers was undoubtedly Yugoslavia, as it then was, at a concert set up by a group of Christians in Zagreb. Like the previous concerts, it was a sell-out. I wasn't present – I had a magazine and a family, as it were – but the performers returned on something of a high. I don't think they had ever experienced anything like it before. The concert went out live on national television (in what was then a communist state, though of the more relaxed variety), and there was remarkably positive coverage in the newspapers. But it was the audience that left the deepest impression. Not only did they clearly appreciate the music, but there was also an enthusiastic and positive response to the message – a response confirmed later by one of the organizers, a Christian doctor who had prayed for something like this for years.

Possibly as a result of all this, we were approached by Tyne Tees Television, the ITV company based in Newcastle, about the possibility of a ground-breaking television series featuring Cliff and The Settlers. The producer, Max Deas, met with me to brainstorm ideas for it, and we came up with an ambitious (possibly, in hindsight, overambitious) project – retelling some of the parables of Jesus in modern settings, with story and songs. We even devised a name for the series, *Life with Johnny*, after the character who would be central to the narrative each time. Johnny, needless to say, would be played by Cliff.

Amazingly, all the complicated negotiations between Tyne Tees, Cliff's management, The Settlers and their manager, and even their record companies, were fairly speedily resolved, and dates were pencilled in for the recording days in Newcastle. Before then, about 30 original songs (lyrics by me, music by Cliff and The Settlers) and a script for the seven programmes had to be written. And all the while, *Crusade* had to come out each month, and it would also have been nice to spend some time with Christine, Philip and Becky, at a crucial stage in the children's development.

Mind you, they loved the showbiz ambience that occasionally flooded our Finchley semi. Becky, at four years, could do a pretty good imitation of Cindy in full flow, and Philip's ear for music and love of the bass guitar, which have remained with him to this day, probably had their first promptings at the feet of Geoff, The Settlers' red-haired and slightly eccentric bass player. Actually, we have come to recognize bass players as a genre, and eccentric is probably what most of them are: almost aloof, affecting a cool detachment from the excesses of the front row performers – all qualities that would have appealed to our son.

We didn't know it at the time, but Philip and Becky were to be joined, at about the same time as 'Life with Johnny' was due to be broadcast, by a brother, Adrian. To say life was full at the time would be an understatement, and to be honest, looking back, the biggest marvel is that Christine didn't lock me up in a darkened room for a couple of weeks to get over it.

However, she didn't, and even came up to Newcastle a couple of times during the recordings. Our home also provided, we liked to feel, a haven of normality for a number of people whose lives were far from 'normal', including Cliff himself, from time to time, Cindy, who had become, and remains, a close friend, and one or two other refugees from the excesses of the world of showbiz and the media. It was out of this experience that the idea of the Arts Centre Group emerged, but that must take its proper place in the sequence of events.

Life with Johnny was eventually finished, and I think everyone at Tyne Tees was very satisfied with it. We were treated to a showing of all the finished episodes and while the professionals were able to find, as they always can, this and that with which they were not entirely satisfied, the general feeling was that these were quite ground-breaking as programmes for the Sunday evening religious 'slot' which then existed on national television. Tyne Tees had been encouraged by the Independent Television Authority to go ahead with the project and had kept in touch with the networking committee of ITV all through. So it came as something of a shock when the 'Big Five' companies refused to take the series. None of them said that the programmes weren't good enough for networking, but Max Deas felt that television politics were seriously at work. The big companies were unwilling to give one of their smaller 'partners' the chance to perform on the big stage with a big star. And, of course, the series was expensive, which meant that the proportionate cost to the larger companies would be high.

So *Life with Johnny*, which the next year's ITA report described as one of the most imaginative attempts yet made on television to present the Christian message in a contemporary setting, was to be seen only in the areas covered by the six smaller companies. Tyne Tees faced something of a financial crisis over their involvement in the project, which was only partly assuaged by the kind words of critics and viewers. For me it was a sharp introduction to the world of broadcasting politics, which I would learn a great deal more about in due course.

In fact, I was already becoming quite involved in radio and television, beyond the *Life with Johnny* project. We had met Ronald Allison on a visit to Duke Street Baptist Church, Richmond. He was a BBC news reporter, who had also had a stint as a network newsreader and was at that time on 'attachment', as the BBC calls it, to religious broadcasting. Ron was that comparative rarity, especially in those days – a practising Christian who worked at the sharp end of the media. Later he was to become the BBC's Court Correspondent, then press secretary to the royal family and subsequently a senior ITV executive, so he was a person of some weight in the media world.

At any rate, he turned out to be quite a fan of *Crusade*, and suggested I might like to try my hand at some radio talks. This led to one or two broadcasts on a Saturday morning religious 'perspective' slot, and subsequently to my first *Thought for the Day* on Radio 4 – though at that point it was called *Ten to Eight*, a secular substitute for its original title, *Lift Up Your Hearts*. It was recorded, in those days, and I can clearly recall my first effort, on the theme of 'mediators'. (We were in the middle of yet another national strike of one kind or another, a familiar feature of life in the late sixties.) It evoked a satisfyingly positive response from listeners, and for a while I became a regular on the slot – an opportunity denied me, of course, while I was on the staff of the BBC in the seventies and eighties, but one to which I have since returned with a modest degree of satisfaction.

I suppose no one has spanned a longer period as a contributor to *Thought for the Day* – 1968 to the present is a long while, and has seen many changes in the programme's format, content, style and intention. Since the 1970s it has always been live, though shrinking in length from its original five minutes to four and now three. But there it is, the eternal survivor, 'through glory and dishonour', as the apostle Paul wrote, 'through bad report and good report, dying, and yet we live on'. Later, in the seventies, I was for a time producer of *Thought for the Day*, which is not, it has to be said, the easiest job in the Corporation by a long way. What I learnt was the extreme touchiness of politicians if they think the Church is criticizing them. In the Harold Wilson years, his press office regularly phoned with a complaint about something said on *Thought for the Day*, and in the eighties the Thatcher regime, with Norman Tebbit as chief prosecutor, constantly had the programme in the dock. I felt this simply proved that we were doing our job reasonably fairly. Prophets have never been very popular (except the false sort, of course, who cry 'Peace, peace!' where this is no peace).

Working with Ron Allison on these talk programmes introduced me to the world of radio, which I found rather more congenial (less fussy, less complicated, less pretentious) than the world of television. I was at this time also popping up to Birmingham every Wednesday morning to record a late-night programme for ATV. Actually, we always did two programmes in the one studio session, one for early in the week, one for later. *Who Knows?* – as it was cunningly entitled – was a panel show which I chaired, which set out to give answers to viewers' ethical, moral and religious questions. I suspect that most of the questions were actually dreamt up by the producer or his PA, but his lips were sealed on that subject.

Being a late-night offering for regional television, albeit one of the largest companies, it had to be done on the cheap, so it was recorded 'as live'. This meant, in effect, no editing, except in direst emergencies, so that I had to try to round off the discussion (which could get quite heated) at precisely 14 minutes. My natural courtesy and restraint were put to the severest of tests by this, so that ever since I have become quite a tiresome interrupter of other people's conversations. Recognizing the indrawn breath that provides the briefest of pauses for an intervention is an essential knack for the broadcasting presenter, though one that few listeners and viewers, in my experience, really appreciate. But then they do not live by the clock in the way that live broadcasting does – an obsession which one inevitably carries into the rest of life. Many a church choir has been baffled when I have insisted that the procession moves off into church at exactly 11 o'clock, even if Margaret has not quite got her cassock on yet.

I shared the 'green room' at ATV very often with the presenter of the weekly astrology programme. She was, if memory serves me right, editor of an astrological journal of some kind. On one occasion, after we had both finished our recordings, we were sitting quietly drinking coffee when the PA from her programme burst into the room in something approaching panic. 'You must have picked up the wrong script,' she said, 'you've recorded next week's programme.' My companion wasn't going to be deflected from her coffee, nor delayed from taking the taxi she was instantly expecting. 'No sweat,' she replied. 'Makes no difference.' So much for poring over time charts and analysing the intricate movements of the planets.

I was at this time technically (and effectively) self-employed. I had a contract to edit *Crusade*, which probably took three days a week and paid peanuts – but regular and reliable peanuts. I also had a contract with ATV, but in the nature of things these were fragile affairs. Christine ruefully recalled my insistence on commuting from Cornwall to Birmingham in the middle of our holiday with the children because I dared not let anyone else present 'my' programme. In my case, this was due to insecurity – a common weakness in freelance broadcasters.

At the same time, I remember sitting in Cliff's dressing room at the Palladium when he was appearing with The Shadows in *Cinderella*. As we sat talking, with the door open so that he could hear his cue, a young man passed and waved. 'That's my stand-in,' said Cliff. 'He'll never get on stage.' Neither did he, of course. I do not think this determination represented anxiety on Cliff's part, so much as the need of the performer for his stage. Take away the oxygen of performance, and many a star would asphyxiate.

So I pursued the hectic life of an editor-writer-broadcaster, trying, not too successfully, to fit it into the more permanent life of home and family. I have asked myself since whether it was born of a desperate desire for fame, even in the fairly restricted world in which I worked, or a need to prove that I could do it. I can see that for a man approaching 40 I was rather immature, but my age might have had a further significance. People tend to see 40 as the last point in life at which one can hope to achieve new

CLIFF RICHARD AND ALL THAT

things. Possibly, even subconsciously, I was driven by a feeling that if I didn't do it now I never would. Looking back, I can see how utterly daft the whole assumption is, but at the time it all seemed quite 'normal'. After all, this was the end of the sixties – 'go with the flow', and all that. So, in a curiously helpless sort of way, I went.

In 1969 our youngest, Adrian, was born. Fortunately, the older two, and especially his 'big' sister, who was now five, accepted the newcomer with open arms – literally, in Becky's case. However, he was not a good sleeper. Not until he was five did he sleep through the night regularly, which meant many bedroom and landing patrols in the middle of the night or – more often – a little stranger in our bed. As he was often joined by one or other of his siblings, sleep became a rare and treasured commodity. Our solution was to buy a larger bed. We were well aware that child development experts would have frowned, but both Christine and I have always inclined to the 'if you can't beat them join them' school of thought.

In any case, a further big change was coming in my working life. Once again it had its origins in a totally unexpected phone call, and once again it was to point me in another direction altogether.

The BBC Years

In the course of my occasional contributions to BBC radio, I had met the head of religious programmes, John Lang, on one or two occasions. He was a clergyman, of course, but also a typical BBC executive of the time: urbane, ex-army, public school, Cambridge, with a church pedigree calculated to make a deanery or a bishopric a certainty in later life. Starting with a curacy at Portsea (breeding ground of the episcopate), he then had three years on the staff of Southwark Cathedral followed by four as chaplain to his old college at Cambridge. It was really not at all surprising that he later became a chaplain to the Queen and Dean of Lichfield.

None of this is meant to imply that John was not one of the nicest of men, because he was – and very gifted as a musician and writer. He was then a bachelor – a situation soon to be remedied – who lived in a splendidly furnished apartment in Blackheath. But however much I later came to like and admire him, it has to be said that in 1970 he and I inhabited totally different worlds. So I was surprised, to put it mildly, to have a phone call from him one afternoon. I was even more surprised by its invitation, which was to go and see him to discuss whether I might join the religious broadcasting department on a part-time contract as a producer.

The interview clearly went quite well, because very soon a

contract followed, including permission (rarely given) for me to complete my contractual obligations to ATV, which committed me to working half-time as a producer and the BBC to pay me what seemed at the time a princely salary. So it was that in 1970, exactly 40 years old, I started a completely new career as a radio producer. This either meant I was just in time, or that the 'too old at 40' tag was no longer valid. Not without trepidation, I reported for duty to John Lang's office in the Langham, Portland Place.

The old Langham Hotel actually stood at the north end of Upper Regent Street in the West End of London, dead opposite the famous All Souls' Church, Langham Place. I say 'stood' because, although there is still a Langham Hotel on the site, and its outward form bears an uncanny resemblance to the Edwardian pile of yesteryear, inside it is a typically modern 'luxury' establishment, international (in the sense that once you enter its doors you could be anywhere in the world not too far from a major airport) and bland (in the sense that there is nothing here to upset sensitive American business travellers or put them off their hash browns).

But already I digress. In 1970, when I first made acquaintance with the original building, it was owned, as it had been for several decades, by the BBC, whose headquarters in Broadcasting House also stood just across the road, a huge eight-storey white stone creation, rounded at the front like the head of a whale, but more often likened to a thirties-style liner about to be launched down Regent Street. Inside the Langham, perfectly matching the pre-war fittings and Edwardian decor, was located the religious broadcasting department, or at any rate that part of it which was based in London. It occupied the 'entresol', which aptly hung between two floors at the west end of the building, like a secret enclave from the rest of its activities. I got to know the entresol well, first as an occasional contributor to programmes, now in my role as part-time producer, and finally in 1971, as a fully fledged and full-time member of the team.

In those far-off days, broadcasting – at any rate, radio broadcasting – was a truly civilized occupation. Radio producers were seldom expected to break sweat. Programmes were devised, chewed over, planned, discussed over a couple of bottles of claret, scheduled and finally recorded in well-appointed studios staffed by a small army of highly qualified technicians (all of whom seemed to have good honours degrees from the best universities).

The BBC was only just out of the era of the home service and the light programme. A project called 'Broadcasting for the Seventies' had produced a revolutionary scheme which would see no less than four radio networks (1, 2, 3 and 4, needless to say) and also the gradual introduction, over a few years, of as many as 40 BBC local radio stations. All of this had proved quite hard for some of the more traditionally minded producers and managers to cope with, but it was driven through, largely as proof that BBC radio was ready to enter the new competitive era of broadcasting brought about by the advent of commercial radio. Its effect on religious broadcasting was fairly marginal – news of these things took quite a long while to negotiate the pedestrian crossing between Broadcasting House and the Langham, and even then was greeted by many with deep suspicion.

Most of the religious broadcasting producers at that time were ordained. In fact, apart from the statutory woman, there was only one layperson on the production staff in London, Ronald Allison, on attachment from News. There was one former Methodist, the redoubtable Roy Trevivian, now an Anglican priest, and one Roman Catholic, Father Pat McEnroe, filling the rather strange role of 'Roman Catholic Assistant to the Head of Religious Broadcasting' – a post of historical, but little practical, significance, designed to assuage Catholic suspicions that BBC religion was simply the Church of England at the microphone (which at that time it largely was).

I became the second layperson and very much the junior

member of the team, given for starters the production of *Prayer for the Day*, a pre-recorded devotional talk, embracing a Bible reading and a prayer, which in those enlightened days went out just before the *Today* programme.

My first recording was very nearly my last. Having tuned in to hear my maiden broadcast as a BBC producer, I suffered the mortification of a serious technical error: the last paragraph was broadcast twice. As it was not all that memorable the first time, some listeners may not have noticed that they were hearing it again, but I certainly did, my blood running cold at the shame of it. Apparently a retake of the talk (it was too long on the first take) had been ineptly edited so that the tail end of the first, longer version overlapped the new one. Doubtless the studio manager, whose degree was probably in medieval art, felt such chores as cutting and editing tape a trifle vulgar.

I can still remember the embarrassment of being summoned to the boss's office to explain what had happened – it was not really my fault, but I had signed the wretched form confirming that it was 'ready for transmission'. It was the sort of event that breeds future caution.

It was also a sharp reminder of the perils of broadcasting. At *Crusade* a few thousand people, almost all of them sympathetic, were likely to become aware of your embarrassing mistakes. On radio or television, that figure instantly becomes hundreds of thousands or even millions, many of them only too ready to pick holes in your performance. I also rapidly learnt that religion has enemies as well as supporters, many of them articulate and influential people, who feel that 'superstition' and what they see as bigotry have no place in a civilized modern society.

At *Crusade* there was criticism, outrage and disgust, often expressed in extreme language – heresy was always lurking and such correspondents saw it as their duty to root it out and expose it. But at least most people felt the 'cause' was worth fighting for, even if the editor had culpably developed liberal tendencies. At the BBC one became aware increasingly over the years of an opposition to the whole idea of a religious dimension of life which expressed itself in a root and branch rejection of any programme which took religious (and especially Christian) belief seriously.

Of course at first I was too busy trying to make my little programmes to the right length and without editorial glitches to worry much about such issues. In any case, there was enough of the Reithian afterglow still hanging about the BBC for its top people to refrain from any overt moves to restrict religious output. Indeed, it was quite the contrary. With a number of gifted producers in religious broadcasting, inroads were being made into mainstream schedules, both on television and radio, and there were opportunities to offer documentary and feature ideas which had a reasonable chance of being accepted for production. Peter Armstrong – another layman – was one such producer, then something of a tyro, but soon to become a distinguished television producer, especially of major feature series. One of these, on Jesus, and featuring the then largely unknown radical theologian Don Cupitt, caused something of a furore. I do not think Peter had any idea when he started out on the project either how far Cupitt had already shifted from the scholarly mainstream nor, as he once told me, how quickly that shift would accelerate during the course of filming. It was heady stuff, by any standards (though, it has to be said, positively conservative compared to the views Cupitt and his Sea of Faith colleagues were to adopt over the next 25 years). Questioning the nature of the divinity of Jesus or the historicity of miracles, as he did then, was one thing, but arguing that God – in the sense of an objectively existing being – does not exist at all, as he does now, seems a trifle farfetched, even for a Cambridge clergyman and academic. Perhaps that is the difference between 1972 and 2001.

However, it was series like this which gave religious broadcasting a new and higher profile. At a rather less atmospheric level, so did *Songs of Praise*, brilliantly revamped by Ray Short to include brief interviews and to move beyond being simply a programme of community hymn singing. In the process, its audience leapt, reaching at one stage 8 million, which put it above *Match of the Day* and several other high-flying BBC programmes. It also provided a rare, possibly unique, broadcasting platform for the views and experiences of 'ordinary' people, in this case, ordinary Christians. Their straightforward witness to the reality of faith in the day-to-day pressures and even tragedies of life was often deeply moving and memorable.

For myself, having done a brief apprenticeship on *Prayer for the Day*, I was to be tried out on our latest innovation, the *Sunday* programme on Radio 4. The department had wanted to broadcast a regular weekly programme of religious news and opinion and had finally been granted a Sunday morning slot, but only on FM. The placing was fine – 8.15, after the main news and Sunday papers – but at that time relatively few people had FM (or VHF, as it was then known), and those who did seldom tuned to it, preferring the familiar long wave frequency. On FM we were in competition, if that is the word, with network radio's only Asian programme, half an hour of film music from the Indian subcontinent, linked in Hindi.

Colin Semper, later to become Provost of Coventry and subsequently a canon of Westminster Abbey, was the first producer, and I joined him as his assistant. Colin was a born innovator, but would be the first to admit that he rapidly lost interest once the project was established. So it was fun getting *Sunday* on the air, a cheeky, iconoclastic look at goings-on in the religious world, presented by Paul Barnes – chosen for the job because he had no religious qualifications at all, but took a lively interest in anything, including the world of religious belief, and was a quirky, distinctive kind of broadcaster with a sharp turn of phrase. But within a few months Colin was beginning to tire of the chore of assembling the programme each week and then getting into the studio at the crack of dawn for the live broadcast. So, unbeknown to me, I was being tried out as, first, his sorcerer's apprentice and then, possibly, his successor.

Sunday was a great deal more to my taste than *Prayer for the Day*. It resonated with my journalistic experience (which was, I later discovered, the main reason I had been brought into the BBC). And I liked its style – irreverent, without being destructive. This was the sort of job I felt I could do, and even perhaps do well. But again I almost fell down at the first hurdle.

It is one of those occasions you remember with crystal clarity all your life. Colin Semper had asked me, fairly casually, whether I would like to produce that week's programme. It was not an invitation I was likely to turn down even though I had never in my life produced a 'live' radio magazine programme. *Sunday* went out at 8.15 on a Sunday morning, but it was prepared and set up during the week. Various freelance reporters would offer ideas for interviews and features, the BBC's religious news reporter (as the post was then styled), Douglas Brown, would draft a four-minute bulletin of the week's religious news, and most of the actual broadcast material was prepared on Saturday evening in a studio in the basement of Broadcasting House. By the time that preparation session ended – about 11 o'clock – the programme's bits and pieces were pretty well settled and the presenter, Paul Barnes, would have at least drafted his script. Sometimes there was a 'live' item, possibly an interview or even a studio guest, but the main shape of the programme would be settled and timed, so that we had a degree of confidence that it would all fit in when we went on air in the morning.

On Sunday morning the producer, his PA and a couple of studio engineers would be in by 7.30 to have a final run through with the presenter, and then from 7.50 onwards listen to Radio 4 to pick up anything we needed to note in the programme. Sometimes there was something on the news, for instance, that related to an item in *Sunday*, and Paul could reflect that in his links. By the time the 8 o'clock news was on we were all sitting in our places, hoping that everything was ready.

Up to that point everything on this debut morning of mine

had gone very smoothly. I thought the programme was quite strong and I was reasonably confident – having sat in on several programmes already – that it was fine for length and editorial content. I must admit my stomach was doing a few turns as the announcer cued the programme. 'Now it's a quarter past eight, and time for *Sunday*. Here's Paul Barnes.'

Except there wasn't. Paul was speaking – through the soundproof glass I could see that his lips were moving – but nothing was being transmitted. What was the problem? Faulty microphone, lead become detached, failure on our own feedback to the studio? The engineers (their traditional BBC title was 'studio manager') flung themselves into action, one dashing into the studio to fiddle with the mike, the other checking leads and connections in the cubicle. Suddenly, after what seemed an eternity but was probably no more than 30 seconds or so, sound was restored. Paul, who was at his best in a crisis, apologized for the inexplicable delay and welcomed the listeners, a few seconds late, to the *Sunday* programme. It would, he promised them, be worth waiting for. His first link neatly completed, we were into the first taped item.

That was the signal for the studio managers to start a private war. They seemed more concerned with whose fault it was – 'I asked you to check the mike leads'; 'It's your job to see that sort of thing doesn't happen', and so on – than keeping the rest of the programme on the road. I swung round in my chair at the 'desk' and urged them to abandon this pointless discussion (though I think my actual words were a little more crude than that) and to concentrate on the rest of the programme. 'Anyone can make a mistake,' I said. 'Don't let it wreck the whole programme.' They grunted what I took for an apology, and were concentrating fully by the time the first item ended and we were back with Paul's second link. And from then on the programme went exactly as planned, coming out just in time for the pips (the time signal) for 9 o'clock. I thanked the team, breathed a massive sigh of relief – and at that moment noticed that John Lang himself was standing partly hidden by a screen at the back of the studio. Before I could say anything, he had tactfully slipped away.

I learnt on Monday that he had been there all through the programme, which would have induced a minor heart attack if I had known it when we were off-air at the start. Anyway, he professed himself mightily impressed with the way I had handled it. 'No one would have thought it was your first live programme,' he said. He also liked the whole 'mix' and felt I had demonstrated that in due course it was a programme I could take over from Colin Semper. At that point, I think, I realized that sometimes bad things can have good consequences. Nothing could have furthered my cause more dramatically than the disastrous opening minute of my very first piece of magazine programme production.

As though at a hidden signal, Colin Semper 'moved on', some new project having taken his fancy, and I found myself producing *Sunday* every week, holidays excepted. I also, I suppose as a consequence, found myself offered a full-time contract, which meant that my 12 years or so as editor of *Crusade* would necessarily have to come to an end.

Looking back, they had been good years, years in which I had learnt something about magazine journalism and even more about the strange world of organized religion. About journalism, I had come to one firm conclusion: people are easily bored and easily distracted. Consequently, the test of a piece of writing was not so much 'What does it say?' as 'Will anyone actually read it?' I came to appreciate that exactly the same criterion could be applied to preaching (a good sermon is one people listen to, a bad sermon is one they don't) and to broadcasting. Getting and holding attention is the name of the game. Only then can you start to worry about whether what you are writing, saying or broadcasting is worthwhile.

I think that from the mid-sixties onwards, *Crusade* had more often passed that test than failed it, though reading its pages now, 30 years later, it seems terribly pompous and verbose.

Broadcasting demanded a much more immediate style – there was no time for a second innings. The item either captured attention, or it didn't. I quickly learnt how transient is the broadcast word, and how easily misunderstood. Indeed, week by week I spent hours in the office fruitlessly trying to assure listeners that so and so had not said what they claimed to have clearly heard him say.

Broadcasting also taught me to write for speech and not for reading. That is quite a change for someone who had worked in print most of his life. But once one had got into the habit of reading it aloud, of avoiding subordinate clauses and eliding all those pedantic auxiliaries which plague the English language, the transformation was quite dramatic. The difficulty thereafter is trying to get back into literary mode, something I have never really succeeded in doing. On the other hand, the inborn pedantry of the English teacher would still obtrude. I find it hard to use the helpful and immediate phrase 'lots of', or 'like' as a simpler version of 'such as'. And I am positively unbearable about 'different to' and 'hopefully' (used with the meaning, 'one hopes'). But I think in my heart of hearts I know that language is a living thing, and living things adapt or die.

Among the duties of staff producers in religious broadcasting in those days was conducting the daily service on Radio 4. One could be excused on conscientious grounds, but no other excuse was allowed. We were put on a daily rota drawn up by Hubert Hoskins, a producer of the truly older school. He also set out which pages of the book *New Every Morning* should be used on that day, and chose the Bible reading and the hymns. Barry Rose, then director of music at Guildford Cathedral, but also 'music advisor to the head of religious broadcasting', would choose the introit, rehearse the BBC singers and conduct them during the broadcast, which was live every morning from All Souls' Church, Langham Place. The church was connected to Broadcasting House by a land-line, and there was even a small broadcast studio. I realize that all of this will sound antediluvian to the present staff of religious programmes, but at least there is still a daily service, as there has been for well over 70 years.

It originally came into being through the sheer persistence of a Miss Cordeux, of Bushey in Hertfordshire. In April 1926, when the BBC was only four years old, she wrote a letter to the *Radio Times* proposing a brief daily service on the wireless 'to comfort the sick, the suffering and the lonely'. Perversely, her letter appeared in an edition whose distribution was badly affected by the General Strike, but she persisted, even organizing a nationwide petition, to which 5,000 people added their signatures. Although reluctant – the then head of 'services and religious addresses', J.C. Stobart, wrote, 'I find it hard to gauge the strength of this demand' – the managing director, John Reith, agreed to a modest experiment. A 15-minute service would open the day's broadcasting, at 10.15. Miss Cordeux had favoured an evening service, and wanted half an hour, but she had the wisdom to accept the compromise and believed that the public response would turn this modest innovation into a permanent feature of the broadcasting landscape. Even she could not conceivably have guessed that it would still be there, substantially as she had envisaged it ('a little sacred music, hymns, a brief reading or address') into the next millennium – by some distance the longest-running programme broadcast by the BBC.

So we were burdened with the weight of history as we crossed the road from the Langham to All Souls', clutching Hubert's instructions, a Bible and a copy of *New Every Morning* to lead the nation in prayer. In one way, it was a pleasant enough duty in those days, because no original thought or planning was required, beyond the ability to read a stopwatch and to come out on time. Once one had mastered the art of reading the Lord's Prayer at one of its acceptable variety of speeds (I could do anything between a brisk 24 seconds and a reverent 36), and had timed all the various blessings so that an appropriate one could be chosen according to the clock, the rest was fairly routine.

But while the actual broadcast usually presented few problems, the fact that it was live, and from a church open to the public, meant that we were often taking our broadcasting lives in our hands. John Lang, for instance, was once persistently interrupted by a man in the gallery of the church, who kept shouting that he was 'Jesus Christ'. John, being the man he is, tackled him afterwards, and got punched on the nose for his pains. He then, brave man, pursued his attacker along Upper Regent Street, finally cornering him near Oxford Circus, whereupon the man attempted another blow. The passing constable who intervened was rather taken aback to discover that the two warring figures he had separated were, respectively, a man claiming to be the head of religious broadcasting (who was bleeding profusely from the nose) and another – apparently unharmed – claiming to be Jesus Christ.

On one occasion I was taking the service when a tramp who had concealed himself underneath newspapers on a pew in a dark corner of the church emerged just as the red light flicked on. He began to tell the BBC singers, in unparliamentary language, what he thought of the noise that had aroused him from his slumbers. I paused at the end of the introit, not sure what to do, as the invective continued. After a few seconds, the commissionaire, who was outside the door, and meant to be guarding against this very eventuality, burst into the back of the church and with a great clattering of swing doors the offender was ejected, still mouthing obscenities. Christine, listening at home, heard all the muffled shouting, banging and slamming, but said the highlight was what followed. True to my script, and in my very best daily service voice, I told the bemused listeners that, 'The theme for today's service is "The Peace of God".'

Some of the minor disasters on the daily service were self-inflicted, of course. One young producer on attachment from local radio was eager to have a go, as he put it, at presenting the service. The system was explained to him, and he duly gathered what he assumed were the necessary books – *New Every*

Morning, *The BBC Hymnal* and his own Bible – and made his way across to All Souls' with plenty of time to spare. When he came to look up the reading, however, he discovered a problem. The sheet told him he should read Wisdom of Solomon 5:1–8, a passage about the vindication of the righteous man. The trouble was, he couldn't find a book called 'Wisdom of Solomon'. It is, of course, to be found in the Apocrypha, which isn't included in most English editions of the Bible. But he did find a book called 'Song of Solomon', a sufficiently close title to suggest a minor typing mistake in the office, so he turned to that and got himself ready to go on air.

Unfortunately there wasn't time for him to read carefully through Song of Solomon 5:1–8 before the broadcast began. Doubts first began to enter his mind when he found himself in the middle of a passage of quite dramatic eroticism, and completely took over as he read 'My beloved thrust his hand into the opening...' The first phone call probably reached the BBC switchboard a few seconds later, but being a determined soul and knowing nothing of that he soldiered on to the rather abrupt end ('I am faint with love'). Soon after, though we were assured the two things were unconnected, we stopped reading from the Apocrypha in the daily service. One imagines that as well as those quick to complain were others who were digging out a long-ignored copy of the Bible to savour these unexpected sexy delights.

Over the years other things about the content of the daily service changed, as was inevitable. Eventually we abandoned *New Every Morning* – if ever a title could have been sued under the Trades Descriptions Act that was it – and early in the eighties introduced once a week what was called an 'Act of Worship' (a subtle distinction), which incorporated recorded music and gave the presenter more opportunity to reflect and even pray about the day's news and events. I am glad to say the service, which remains live, 15 minutes long and in a morning slot, is still with us, though it usually comes from a church in Manchester, where the religious programmes department is now based. I hope Miss Cordeux feels that her persistence and determination over 70 years ago is still paying off.

It was not only on the daily service, of course, that broadcasting gaffes occurred. There was, for instance, a memorable recording of compline, presented by Father Pat McEnroe. This was a 15-minute service for Sunday nights, sung by the BBC singers with the prayers and responses taken by a member of the religious broadcasting staff (on the time-honoured principle of 'staff no fee'). It was usually recorded on a Sunday afternoon, when most of the singers were free of other engagements, edited – where necessary – and then sent to the tape library for transmission that evening.

On this occasion the first take was a disaster of fluffs, missed entries, wrong notes and extraneous noises – such things do happen, of course. Half-way through it the studio manager suggested via the headphones that Pat should soldier on to the end, so that at least they could get a timing on it, before doing the whole thing again. Pat agreed, and they lurched their way through to the final prayer, which he ended, with relief, with the additional blessing, 'Thank God that's over!' They then did the recording again, this time, predictably, without a single hitch.

Pat went home to his flat, and later that evening switched on to hear himself leading the nation, or at least that part of it tuned to Radio 4, in prayer. They were barely a minute into the programme when he realized with shock and horror that the wrong tape was being broadcast. Somehow the unedited version had gone for transmission. He tried vainly to get through to the Radio 4 continuity suite in time, and finally had the mortification of hearing himself muttering at the end, with what sounded like grim satisfaction, 'Thank God that's over!'

Another late-night devotional slot also had a memorable gaffe. *Lighten Our Darkness* was a 10-minute programme intended to prepare radio listeners for Sunday. It went out, in those days, at 10 o'clock, early enough to catch even the most fragile of would-be worshippers before they hit their pillows. It followed a half-hour comedy programme, and there was no doubt that the junction between vulgarity and piety didn't always operate smoothly. One of our more daring producers decided to introduce this particular recording of *Lighten Our Darkness* in a way that would ease the transition, prefacing the usual godly greeting with the harmless observation 'Well, that was a lot of fun, wasn't it!' It would have been a good idea, but for one of those thousand-to-one mischiefs which seem to haunt broadcasting studios. A plane had crashed, and a newsflash was inserted between the two recordings. Many listeners were distinctly not amused to hear the presenter of *Lighten Our Darkness* observe that this tragic information was 'a lot of fun'. As can be seen, we certainly did our bit in religious broadcasting to keep the BBC switchboard staff and the duty officer on the alert during what would otherwise have been the dead hours of radio transmission.

It was during my early days at the BBC that the Arts Centre Group came into being. Back in the sixties I had employed at *Crusade*, as an itinerant salesman, the rather eccentric talents of a young actor, Nigel Goodwin. He had been converted, pretty well out of the blue, at a tent mission on Wimbledon Common – I think I've got the facts right – and was 'resting' between engagements, in the time-honoured manner of the acting profession.

Nigel, who had made a reasonable start to an acting career, with a number of parts on television as well as on stage, fell under the influence of L'Abri early in his Christian experience. This was the centre in the Swiss Alps run by Francis Schaeffer, an American pastor-philosopher of an unusual kind. Schaeffer had set himself a daunting agenda: to change the whole direction of modern culture, which he saw as deeply flawed by existentialism.

Schaeffer was in many ways a typical American biblical literalist, but unlike most of the others he read books other than the Bible, listened to music, went to the theatre and watched films. In other words, he was a literate, articulate and cultured man of his time, not quite the flavour of the environment in which he had grown up. Indeed, he vigorously rejected what he called 'Ugly Evangelicalism' – the cult of brutish buildings, crude and unkempt chapels, ghastly music and thoughtless worship. It was easy to see how he struck a chord with many younger Evangelicals from western countries, who felt that their faith had isolated them from the beauty and splendour of much of the world around them. At L'Abri there was good music, drama, and animated discussion of poetry, plays and visual art. In the sixties and seventies, it became literally a 'haven' – *L'Abri* is French for 'the shelter' – for thousands of young Christians, among them the aforementioned Nigel Goodwin.

He took the bait, hook, line and sinker. This was what he wanted to hear: not only that it was 'all right' but positively commendable to be an actor, a musician, a playwright, an artist – provided you worked to an agenda consistent with the purpose of the Creator. That was the Schaeffer distinctive. For him, much modern art was simply negative and destructive, a flight from reason. He categorized it as 'upper storey' – located not in the real, created world but in a fantasy world without meaning, shape or purpose, and therefore under divine judgment.

He backed this up with an approach to scripture which seemed strangely at odds with his understanding of the divine gift of creativity. For him, the first 12 chapters of Genesis – from the story of creation to the tower of Babel – were, and had to be, rooted in what he called 'space-time history'. If they were not, within his definition, 'real' events, then everything else in the revelation of scripture lacked a rational basis. I once asked him if 'true truth' (a typical Schaeffer tautology) could not be conveyed through poetry, image and allegory. He thought for a moment, and then agreed that it could. So why, I asked, couldn't the opening chapters of Genesis encompass that kind of literature? He rejected the notion outright. If those chapters were not truth, in the historically verifiable sense, then for him the whole

Christian 'system' – the divine 'universal' which made sense of the human 'particular' – would fall apart.

I met Francis Schaeffer several times in Switzerland, because Hodder and Stoughton paid me generously to re-write several of his books in readable English. Working from audio tapes of his lectures, I did it and enjoyed it just as I enjoyed sitting in one of his seminars at L'Abri, or crossing swords with him in serious discussions. Several of the books became religious best-sellers, notably *Escape from Reason*. However, unlike Nigel and a number of his contemporaries, I was never able to accept the whole Schaeffer 'package'. Nevertheless, I was glad that he had come along to rescue many young Evangelicals from the miserable, culture-starved regime into which they might otherwise have been trapped. And beyond doubt some of the most influential Christian writers, artists and producers of the following decades owed much to the influence of Schaeffer and L'Abri.

This is not really a digression, because L'Abri, and what it stood for, was probably the starting point of an idea which Nigel Goodwin had been ardently promoting for some time – the notion of a Christian 'arts centre' in London, where issues such as these could be debated, work encouraged and a meeting place created where Christians in the world of the arts, the media and entertainment could gather, and also to which they could invite friends and colleagues.

It would have remained a pipe-dream had not Cliff Richard warmed to the idea. As a result, a meeting was called in 1971, which took place in the lounge of our home in Finchley. Among those present were Ronald Allison, Nigel Goodwin, Cindy Kent, Bill Latham, Christine and myself – and Cliff. We were all fired up with the possibilities of such a venue, and of an organization – not too structured – which could encompass the growing number of Christians who were working in hitherto alien territory, the world of the arts and the media. We had the ideas and, happily, Cliff had the financial resources. That evening the idea was born of the 'Arts Centre Group', a Christian project to infiltrate the world of the arts with the truths and insights of the gospel. We all agreed that it should have a broadly Christian basis, though not as narrowly defined as the L'Abri one. We formed a committee (most of us who were there that night) and asked Nigel, who was clearly destined to be the 'executive officer', to start looking for suitable premises.

Being the person he was, he came up with two: a country mansion in Essex, for quiet contemplation and 'retreat', and a 'working centre' in Kensington, just off the famous High Street. Eventually, after some bargaining, the former was purchased and the latter leased. A young Anglican clergyman and his wife, Jack and Pauline Filby, were installed as wardens of the Essex base, called 'Batailles', and Nigel took up residence in the West London premises.

To be honest, 'Batailles' never worked out. It was probably too far from London (or anywhere else, really) to be much use for short stays, and we had inadequately defined precisely what its role was to be. On the other hand, Hornton Place became a genuine centre for Christians in the 'business', as well as for arts and media students, and the membership of the ACG rapidly grew to 400 or 500. It was a classic example of the 'problem' of having more money than sense – not one that most of us who were involved had ever experienced. Fortunately, we learnt very quickly, and our excellent solicitor friend, David Thompson, was quick to point out a few home truths.

Consequently, within a year or so 'Batailles' was sold, and shortly afterwards far more appropriate London premises became available, thanks to the good offices of the diocese of Southwark. They had an old vicarage, now redundant, in Short Street, just behind the 'Old Vic' theatre near Waterloo station. It was absolutely ideal for the ACG, with a church adjoining, a neat little courtyard behind and a good-sized room for meetings, exhibitions and so on. Again, membership rose, even though we were careful only to admit people who were genuinely and professionally engaged in the arts, media or entertainment business, or were full-time art or media students. By the time we had our inaugural service, in 1972, the membership was well over 600.

That was quite an occasion, with Donald Coggan, then the Archbishop of York, taking part in a splendidly creative service, with particularly memorable music. The ACG stayed in those premises until, eventually, the extremely generous lease ran out and the movement decamped a few miles north across the river, back to the Kensington area, just off the Portobello Road, where it continues to flourish.

Quite early in my BBC career a crisis arose over *Thought for the Day*, as it was now called. In its new incarnation it was live and very much part of the *Today* programme. Consequently speakers were encouraged to tackle topical issues. This was meat and drink to the current producer, Roy Trevivian, a politically radical priest but a highly gifted broadcaster. Roy had turned 'pushing back the acceptable boundaries' into an art form, causing his boss, John Lang, sleepless nights, but also making some of the best and most popular religious programmes ever to be broadcast on British radio.

On this particular occasion, parliament was due to debate later that day a new clause to the Immigration Bill, which would introduce the principle of 'patriality' – admission would be permitted if a person's parents or grandparents were British. Colin Morris, one of the country's leading Methodists, then freshly back from many years in Zaire, was due to speak on *Thought for the Day*, and chose to tackle this sensitive topic. It probably wouldn't have mattered had he done it in the usual cautious way, with plenty of 'some people think' and 'but others would say' sort of phrases. Being Colin, and doubtless egged on by his old friend Roy Trevivian, he came up with a masterly, witty, incisive and utterly devastating critique of the proposed Bill, pointing out that under its terms Jesus of Nazareth, for one, would be permanently excluded from these shores. I heard it while sitting on the edge of my bed, and knew trouble was in store, partly because protocol at that time excluded one-sided coverage of issues currently being considered by parliament, and partly because it was a full-frontal attack on government policy, with no opportunity for reply.

So it proved. By the time I got in to work a meeting of the Department had been called. From the director-general downwards, there was shock and horror. How could religious broadcasting do such a thing? What defence could we offer to the charge of blatant political bias? Roy, of course, was completely unrepentant. He demanded that we each say whether we would, or would not, have permitted Colin Morris to say what he did. Mercifully, John Lang ruled that as I was so new to the department, I was to be excused from answering. Most of those who did prevaricated. Yes, they agreed, it was an outstanding piece of broadcasting, but clearly flouted the rules. Some said they might have been tempted to let it through, as a brilliant example of Christian polemic. Most said that they would have tried to tone it down, or sought advice from further up the chain of command.

In the end, nothing much happened, of course. No one was fired. But Roy's brilliant career in radio had taken a fatal turn, and it has to be said that his sense of betrayal – which he saw, rather typically, as an instance of the 'old boy' public school network pulling together against the 'non-conformist' – destroyed his confidence and eventually his health. He left the BBC for a job in Central Africa, which turned out to be a personal disaster, and retired from broadcasting and from public life a sick man.

It is interesting that Colin Morris, on the other hand, went from strength to strength – president of the Methodist Conference, frequent and popular broadcaster on radio and television, and eventually head of religious broadcasting, no less! Colin's working-class and radical qualifications are every bit as genuine as were Roy's. The difference lay, I suppose, in the temperament and character of the two men, and also – revealingly – in the subtle difference between the role of a producer and a performer. Performers can try to push back boundaries as much as they like. Producers, on the other hand, are there to stop them going too far.

The most important event in my own life at this period, beyond doubt, was the sudden death of my mother. She dropped dead while opening the door to the milkman. She fell in such a way that he couldn't get the door open, and it required the combined efforts of him and a neighbour to get into the house and send for help. In fact, she had died instantly.

Christine rang me at work with the news, and in something of a daze I drove out through the familiar roads of inner north London to my old home in Sylvan Avenue, Wood Green. My elder brother, Geoff, was already there, and soon mum's vicar, Fred Pickering, arrived to have a prayer with us. A glass of whisky with the neighbour seemed a suitably convivial way to mark the end of a long and basically happy life – an end celebrated in a lovely funeral service at St Cuthbert's.

The death of a parent is a peculiar experience, and the death of the second parent, so that one is suddenly aware of the removal of a great chunk of the past, is even more so. My father had died, of course, slowly, so that we had time to come to terms with it. Indeed, his general health had never been robust, so I suppose we always lived with the possibility of his death. But my mother, who was 81 when she died – and made her first flight across the Atlantic to visit her American relatives when she was well into her seventies – had seemed fairly indestructible. Our children had been very dear to her, and they missed her, of course, but very young children have an amazing ability to take mortality in their stride. Strangely Adrian, who was just three and barely aware of what had happened, went through a period in which he was afraid that he would stop breathing and die. It is probably just as well sometimes that we don't know what is going on inside a child's imagination.

Those early years at the BBC, probably up to the end of the seventies, were in many ways the twilight of an era. In 1972 we celebrated the fiftieth anniversary of the founding of the BBC, and I remember thinking how little in its essential character had changed in that half a century. Of course, outwardly, broadcasting had been transformed, with the advent of television the catalyst for much else. But attitudes of mind are less easily changed.

I was commissioned to compile a long-playing record (and that sounds quaint today) marking 50 years of religious broadcasting, which meant some delving into written archives. In the religious broadcasting papers I found a minute of a board of management meeting in the mid-fifties at which a senior BBC figure argued seriously that television was a fad which would never last. At that time radio was commonly described as the 'senior service' – rather like the Royal Navy. In that case, television was clearly the RAF, the new boys on the block who would eventually take things over and win wars virtually on their own. But such is the innate conservatism of an organization like the BBC that there were still people in the seventies who regarded television as a cheeky upstart, and who still believed that radio was the only serious kind of broadcasting.

That may account for the vast resources which were poured into Broadcasting House. It may well be that things have now gone too far in the other direction, but in the seventies radio was undeniably overstaffed. If a 10-minute feature was being recorded for Radio 4, for instance, and it included even one short, taped insert or a snatch of a gramophone record, not only would an hour's studio time be routinely booked, but as well as the producer, his or her PA (to time it on a stopwatch) and a studio manager, there would have to be a second studio manager on 'grams', to push the button which would play in the tape or record. The technology existed to do all of this from the studio desk, but rules agreed between the union and the Corporation dictated levels of staffing for all programmes. And woe betide the producer who dared to push a button or wield a razor blade to make an edit, no matter how simple. I was once seriously threatened with dismissal when I was caught cutting tape in a preparation studio.

It was not only in the studio that we all fell over each other. The life of a radio producer, especially one working for Radio 3 or Radio 4, was idyllic. Broadcasting House – 'BH' to its habitués – was one of the best clubs in London, combining the atmosphere of a university senior common room with the amenities of a high-class country hotel. The restaurants around Oxford Circus were full at lunchtime of BBC producers lunching their guests at the Corporation's expense, and the BBC Club in the Langham was crowded with jovial people downing good wine at a fraction of the usual bar prices. The corridors of BH were lined with trollies carrying refreshments to revive the flagging spirits of producers and contributors, worn out with the sheer weight of their own witty conversation.

I would not want anyone to think that this is a complaint. Like everyone else, I enjoyed the atmosphere, which was intellectually challenging and in its own way professionally demanding. Programmes – even ones with minute audiences – were ruthlessly assessed, especially at the weekly programme review board, and praise was not lightly handed out. All of us, from the top to the bottom, felt that we were working for an important part of the national culture. It still gave something of a thrill to be able to say at a party that you worked 'for the BBC'.

But in hard truth the palmy days of radio were drawing to a close. Sooner or later harsh reality would demand that a stern eye be turned on working practices, programme budgets, studio costs and so on. It was clearly odd, to say the least, that the two radio channels with the smallest audiences, Radio 3 and Radio 4, swallowed the lion's share of the resources, while the networks which had by far the largest audiences got by on a shoestring. Partly this was because those who ran the Corporation, including the governors, seldom listened to the popular stations, reserving their radio listening for the *Today* programme, *The Archers* and

Desert Island Discs on 4, and concerts on 3. Most of them would have been genuinely astonished to learn that the average evening concert on Radio 3 would have an audience of around 50,000 people, scattered across the United Kingdom. By contrast, Radio 1 at that time frequently had audiences of several million, as did Radio 2, especially in the morning.

I remember John Lang remarking that when he first came to the BBC and saw the audience figures he could hardly believe his eyes. Surely the figures for Radio 3 must be wrong? After all, most of his friends listened to it all the time.

In fact, public perceptions of listening figures on the radio are often wildly inaccurate. Newspapers frequently refer to the '5 million' listeners to *Today*. Frankly, 'in your dreams', Mr Humphreys. At the peak of its popularity, before the days of Radio 5 Live and breakfast television, it may occasionally have hit something approaching that figure, but not in recent years. In 2000, the 15-minute segment leading up to the 8 o'clock news (which includes *Thought for the Day*) had 2.5 million listeners and the rest of the sequence rather less than that. The strength of the programme, of course, is that however small the audience is, among them are 600 MPs, all longing for a call to take part. Also listening intently are the producers of the day's radio and television talk shows and news sequences, and the editors of most newspapers, desperately looking for titbits and ideas to while away the dread empty hours or fill the vacant columns.

In fact, the whole news 'business' is deeply incestuous. The production team of *Today* wait anxiously for the first editions of the morning papers, not so much to discover the news but to see which items are making the lead stories. Nobody wants to look an ass and go for broke on a story everyone else is ignoring. But then, later in the day, newsrooms up and down the country will bin other stories because '*Today* didn't carry it'. This partly explains why what in world terms is a parochial story may become the main lead not only in the morning papers but also on *Today*. Once or twice, in recent years, I have offered a topic for *Thought for the Day* which I felt arose directly out of a contemporary concern, only to be told that 'it's not in the papers' – as though that automatically means that it doesn't really matter. It is in this way that the news agenda is distorted – I hesitate to say 'manipulated', because that would involve a degree of commitment or forethought, which have never struck me as prime virtues of most news editors.

This is not at all the same as to say that journalists 'don't care', or that the news passes by or through them leaving them untouched. I remember well the day in 1981 when a gunman tried to assassinate the pope in St Peter's Square, and for a time it seemed that he might have succeeded. I was sitting in my office on the second floor of BH when there was a knock on the door and the Radio 4 duty newsreader came into the room. I had known her quite well for several years, but I had never seen her so obviously shocked. She asked if I had heard the news, which I hadn't. She told me about the attempted assassination, and then sat on the office settee, close to tears, and repeating several times 'How could someone do that sort of thing?' She then added, significantly, 'People can't imagine what it feels like, bringing news like that to the public.' I suddenly saw that her role was not unlike that of the police officer who has to call at a home and tell someone that a member of the family has been killed in an accident – but on a vast scale. From that day, I have regarded newsreaders with fresh respect.

However, I have enough of the journalist left in my veins also to understand the surge of adrenaline that shoots through the newsroom when a really major tragedy strikes. I went into BH on the Sunday that Diana, Princess of Wales, died in the car crash in Paris. Although I had not been in the building for several years, I could smell the excitement in the air, and as I worked with the producer, Beverley McAinsh, on an hour-long live programme for Radio 4 that evening, I shared it. It would be dishonest to say that it wasn't intensely exciting, in the way that I imagine driving in the Monaco Grand Prix could be. The problem, however, is obvious. At what point does the story take over, and the human concern and sensitivity for individuals' feelings go by the board?

In fact, apart from the *Sunday* programme, which was in any case a gentler affair than its modern successor, and a stint as producer of *Thought for the Day*, most of my time as a radio producer in the seventies was occupied in making feature and documentary programmes for Radio 4, or music programmes for Radio 2.

The music programmes were a novelty for me, but one I enjoyed enormously. The major one was called *I Believe in Music* – the title of a well-known pop single – and was presented for a long while by Dana, the young Irish singer who burst on the scene by winning the Eurovision Song Contest as a fresh-faced teenager from Derry. Since then she had created a successful career in show business, with several chart albums and singles to her name, and was a popular stage performer on tour, especially for summer seaside shows and Christmas pantomimes. Unlike Cliff, who was never known to anyone by his birth name, all her friends and family called her Rosemary – Rosemary Brown. I approached her because I knew she was a practising Catholic Christian, and it seemed to me that she had all the essential qualities of a good Radio 2 presenter.

All of which was true, in addition to which she was a delight to work with. She always came to planning sessions with lots of ideas of suitable record tracks, and could see ways in which they could be spun together to make a coherent presentation of a theme for a gently religious programme. Her spoken voice was as attractive as her singing one, and she had an impish sense of humour which came across well on the air. As may be gathered, I felt I had found a 'natural', and was only sorry that other commitments meant that she couldn't present the programme all through the year.

Working together does create a kind of mutual dependence which is the true creative chemistry of broadcasting, and I think it is true to say that Rosemary and I worked together well. She was going through quite a difficult time in her life. She had a steady boyfriend, Damien, whom I met several times. He lived in Ireland, where he ran a hotel in County Armagh. He had had a drink problem, which was not a good thing for someone working in the licensed trade. He seemed a gentle and warm man, but Rosemary's family felt very strongly that he was not a suitable husband for their talented and attractive daughter. Family meant a great deal to her, and things had become quite tense, especially as her father was suffering from a heart condition and she did not want to upset him needlessly.

All of this we shared after our recording sessions. I can remember the day when the first breakthrough occurred. Rosemary came into my office, sat down and said, 'Damien rang me last night. He said something very strange. He said he'd been to a Christian conference and he'd accepted Jesus Christ as his personal Saviour. What do you think that means?' I did my best – after all, this was hardly unfamiliar language to someone of my background – but in any case she quickly learnt for herself. Damien came over to explain, but the best 'explanation' was the obvious change in him. He was positively alight, bursting with some new energy and understanding. He told Rosemary what had happened at the conference, which was a gathering of charismatic Christians in the Republic, mostly like himself, devout Roman Catholics. As they prayed and sang, he simply felt that God was speaking to him, directly, personally. And in a direct and personal way he responded. It was a life-changing encounter with God the Holy Spirit, in theological terms, or a 'born-again conversion', in the language of the tabloid newspapers. Anyone could see the difference, as Rosemary's family did. She not only accepted with great joy what he had told her, but in the process also felt her own faith – which had always been a deep and real thing to her – warmed. Within a few months they were married.

Rosemary for some reason owned an extremely large Volvo estate car, without power-assisted steering, a refinement which was in any case quite rare back in the seventies. She used to drive it in from her home in Wembley to Broadcasting House, where we reserved a parking place for her in the underground BBC car park. This was a labyrinthine maze of pillars and bits of wall, marked out with white lines to delineate the alleged parking spaces. Few of us who ever parked there emerged unscathed, and it had been known to reduce mature drivers to tearful despair. Of one retiring head of light entertainment, it was said at his leaving party that not one pillar in the Henry Wood House car park would be without a memento of his career.

It was into this car park that Rosemary drove her oversized Volvo for the first time. Somewhat surprisingly, she managed to park it. The difficulty came when she wished to leave, because by then another car had parked rather too close to hers, and extricating her vehicle proved both exhausting and frustrating. Eventually she gave in, made her way to reception and phoned my office. 'David,' she announced, 'you will have to come and get my car out of the car park'. I could offer no excuse, so made my way down to the depths under Upper Regent Street, where I wrestled with this tank of a vehicle before finally manoeuvring it out of its bolthole.

Partly as a result of that experience, the next time she came up for a programme she decided to park on a street meter near Broadcasting House. On this occasion the phone call from reception was even more urgent.

'David,' she said, 'I've parked on a meter.'

'Good,' I replied, 'see you in the office'.

'No,' she insisted, 'you don't understand. I've parked *on* a meter'.

And indeed she had. The meter looked a poor thing bent flat under the rear wheels of the Volvo. However, there are advantages in being dark-haired, brown-eyed, petite and persuasive – not to say Irish – a combination which miraculously gathered a small army of willing men who literally lifted the car off the apparatus and even managed to restore the meter to something like its normal posture. Rosemary was effusive with her thanks. 'Aren't people so nice,' she remarked, as we made our belated way to the studio.

Dana continued as our most regular presenter of *I Believe in Music*, even through a period when she couldn't sing because of a serious problem with her larynx, but her 'deputies' were also pretty good – Cliff Richard, for one series of 13 programmes, and Mary O'Hara, the singing ex-nun, for another. I have always followed Rosemary's career since with interest and admiration – not many pop stars of the seventies ended up as credible candidates for their nation's presidency, and none, that I can think off, eventually made a mark in the United States as a television presenter – in her case, of a very popular Catholic programme.

The Sunday breakfast slot occupied by *I Believe in Music*, and later by the highly successful and long-running series *Good Morning Sunday*, came into being partly because the network controller wanted to move our existing religious programme from its mid-morning placing. At the later time there had been for 20 years or more the *People's Service* – an odd title, really, smacking of a Marxist agenda, but actually an attempt to describe an act of worship that wasn't liturgical or traditional, but unashamedly 'popular'. Roy Trevivian had given that programme a fresh impetus in the early seventies, and for a time a very large audience, running into a couple of million at times. But now even that format was beginning to sound rather dated and 'churchy' for Radio 2. It was replaced for a while by a half-hour which was called *Gospel Road*, in which a variety of presenters offered 30 minutes of popular sacred music and some Christian reflection as an interlude in Pete Murray's morning show.

Several of the producers had a turn at producing this, and I did it with a man who was to become a significant influence in my life, Bill Westwood. He had just come to London as Bishop of Edmonton – my own area of north London – and brought with him a good deal of broadcasting experience gained in Norfolk, where he had been a vicar. Bill was made for Radio 2 and took to the format, the network and the audience like a duck to water. He also got on notably well with Pete Murray, which was a great asset to the programme.

We would choose the music between us, mostly records, though occasionally using taped music recorded specially for *Gospel Road* by church groups. On one memorable occasion Bill had opted to include The Bachelors' hit 'I Believe' (that will indicate the intellectual and musical level of the programme very well). He cued it in and the record began in the normal way, but almost immediately began to slow down. At first the studio manager and I just hoped that the fault would right itself, but these kind of problems seldom simply go away. In this case, it got steadily worse, until it was obvious that the tortured bass trio emanating from the speakers would have to be put out of their misery. I just had time to warn Bill that we were fading the track, but that was sufficient for him to talk confidently over the fade. 'There go The Bachelors,' he said, 'sinking away but still believing.'

Sometimes we went out on location to record inserts for *Gospel Road*, and at Bill's suggestion we included a visit to Tottenham, calling in at the parish hall of St Paul's Church, right next to the Spurs' football ground. Pete Murray was with us, and Bill suggested that we creep into the back of the hall and see what was going on. In fact it was a bingo session, but our entry did not go unremarked. The caller – a lady in a flowery dress, of commanding mien – beamed at us as we stood nervously near the door.

'Ladies,' she said, 'we are privileged to have three unexpected visitors – one, I know, is the Bishop of Edmonton, but I'm afraid I don't recognize the other two gentlemen.' As the 'other two' included one of the best-known broadcasting faces of the decade, Pete Murray was reminded of this little incident whenever he met Bishop Bill subsequently.

During my years as a radio producer I met many

impressive people, some funny ones and a few – thankfully, not many – who were downright unpleasant. Some of the ones who made the deepest impression on me, for one reason or another, are discussed in the next chapter, but there were others whom I met briefly but who nevertheless made a great impression on me, or are remembered for particular things that happened.

For instance, I worked a few times with Jimmy Savile, on a programme called *Speakeasy* which Roy Trevivian had devised. It was a talk show, just about the only one on Radio 1, and combined a couple of items from a live band with a studio discussion on a religious or moral topic with a young audience chaired by Jimmy. He did this with tremendous aplomb, always coming in with the shrewd question at the right moment, and seeming to show an extensive knowledge of the fields of ethics, morality and religion. In fact, he was like a ventriloquist's dummy (though a highly sophisticated one). Roy, in the control room, would bark 'Ask him about contraceptive counselling.' Quick as a flash, Jimmy would cut in on the surprised speaker. 'That's all very well, but what about contraceptive counselling?' Jimmy didn't know, but Roy did, that the speaker had been hoping nobody would ask him that very question, realizing that it was the weak spot in his argument. Jimmy, as presenter, got the credit, of course – and fairly so, because he would also have got the stick if he had been barking up the wrong tree. But the producer's skill was also vital. It was a superb example of a creative relationship of total confidence between producer and presenter. In truth, the two men – the Anglican priest and the cigar-smoking and eccentric Roman Catholic – seemed made for each other.

Not, though, it must be said, in their personal approach to religious faith and belief. I once listened bemused as Jimmy Savile expatiated at length in the BBC canteen on the reasons why St Peter wouldn't dare bar him from heaven. '"What do you mean, he's led an immoral life?" God would say to him. "Have you any idea how much money he's raised for charity? Or how many hours he's put in as a porter at that hospital? Get them doors open now, and quick!'"

Equally, I remember the singer/actress Toyah Wilcox, whom I only met once, when she was on Radio 1's *Talkabout* – the successor to *Speakeasy* – which I co-produced for a time. She was then at the height of her popularity as a singer, with something of a punk image, and I expected her to do what most of the pop stars did, which was avoid any contact at all with the punters and make her getaway in a big car as soon as she could when the programme ended. But Toyah sat chatting to the young people in the studio audience, genuinely relating to them and taking an interest, and stayed until we had to insist on clearing the studio. For me, that's the difference between being a big star and a big person.

In a very different way, I remember two distinguished churchmen. Cardinal Heenan was Roman Catholic Archbishop of Westminster when I first joined religious broadcasting. Earlier in his career he had been a considerable broadcaster in his own right, but his appearances at the microphone were now quite rare. On this occasion I was producing a short talk by him – it may well have been a recorded *Thought for the Day*, because in those days it was occasionally recorded to make it easier for distinguished churchmen such as cardinals and archbishops to take part. Cardinal Heenan was clearly suspicious of our intentions. He wanted to know exactly how long we wanted his talk to be, and then enquired sharply about the editing of it. He didn't seem terribly reassured when I told him that if it needed any editing I would be doing it. We had a run-through first, and the Monsignor who had accompanied him was quick to spot a mispronunciation: 'Didache, with a hard ch, I think, excellency.' It was the obsequious 'I think' that appealed to me – that, and the fact that the cardinal wasn't sure how to pronounce the Greek word for 'the teaching', a thoroughly human failing, I thought.

Michael Ramsey, while Archbishop of Canterbury, also

came into the studio to record a *Thought for the Day*. He arrived in a rather battered Morris Minor driven by his wife, and squeezed his purple-cassocked frame out of it on to the pavement in front of Broadcasting House. The uniformed commissionaires, who had been told to prepare for the arrival of the archbishop, were taken aback by this, but relieved when I darted forward to greet him and introduce him to the waiting BBC luminaries. We then descended to the studio in the basement, where Dr Ramsey accepted the offer of a cup of coffee, which arrived, in true 1970s style, accompanied by an impenetrable triangular container of cream. The idea was that you peeled off a tiny strip and then squeezed the contents into your drink. The whole procedure was fraught with potential hazards, and before any of us could get from the cubicle into the studio, where the archbishop was sitting at a table before the microphone, the inevitable had happened. Presumably Lambeth Palace didn't offer much practical experience of individual plastic cream containers. After a brief reconnoitre with its engineering, Dr Ramsey did what most people did on their first encounter with the thing. He pulled on the strip while squeezing the container. The result was always the same, but much more disastrous if one was wearing a purple cassock.

The least worried person by all this was the archbishop, who proceeded to record his talk, complete with the constant 'errs' and 'umms' that were his trademark. I took the precaution of recording a minute longer than usual and then left the studio managers to remove the extraneous vocal noises. There were two results of this. The first was a talk by the archbishop of quite unique fluency (indeed, so fluent that some doubted if it was really him at all). The second was a tape consisting entirely of his very beautiful 'umms' and 'errs', which became a classic of the departmental archives.

I have already mentioned Mary O'Hara, the folk singer who presented several programmes in our series of *I Believe in Music*. She had been a nun in an enclosed order for many years, but achieved considerable fame when she left the convent by taking up a successful career as a singer. She was a striking woman, quite tall and elegant, but with what one would call, I suppose, a small, even vulnerable, voice. She remained a devout Catholic, and accepted our invitation to present the programme, arriving (as one would hope) with many ideas for records and songs and writing a thoughtful script to link them.

However, my main memory of her is not her skill either as a singer or presenter, but for giving me a major shock on a live broadcast. We had had our rehearsal and were waiting to go on air. We were also, of course, listening to the previous programme on Radio 2. As it drew to a close, I pushed the talkback button to check that all was well in the studio, but got no reply. I looked through the soundproof glass window, but my presenter was nowhere to be seen. I stood up and scanned the corners of the studio – no sign of her. Had she had a sudden attack of nerves and fled to the ladies? Or, worse, felt a sudden, insistent call to return to the convent? I left my seat and rushed into the studio, to find Mary stretched out flat on the floor, hands folded in the 'coffin' position on her chest, eyes closed, totally cut off from the panic going on around her. I said, with some urgency, that there were 30 seconds to transmission, at which she opened her eyes, slowly swayed forward from the hips and then raised herself to a standing position. Without a word she took her place at the microphone, and when the red light came on embarked on the programme with quite supernatural calm.

Live broadcasting inevitably has these moments of panic, and those who survive best are those who can cultivate a sense of detachment. James Alexander Gordon, who is best known to my generation as the man who has read the football results on *Sports Report* for what seems like half a century, likes to tell the story of the midnight news bulletin on Radio 2 when he had to cope with a drunken newsroom sub and a fire in the studio both at the same time. In fact, the two were connected, because the sub, who had brought him the news seconds before he was due to go on air, had stayed playfully to set fire to the bottom of the script as he began to read it. James used the glass of water conveniently provided for announcers' dry throats for rather more urgent purposes and managed to put the flames out, but not before the weather summary, which was to end the bulletin, had gone up in smoke. When he got to the weather, James muttered something about 'changeable' – a good, all-purpose summary of the British climate, I suppose.

The programme slot occupied by *I Believe in Music* – breakfast time on Sunday morning – was a good one for a programme of this kind, but didn't, at that time, offer a potential audience as big as the one we had lost with the *People's Service* and its replacement, *Gospel Road*, later in the morning. I know that our departmental head at that time, Colin Semper, was involved in lengthy negotiations over these placings, but the arguments for religious broadcasting that had cut ice in the Reithian era no longer carried quite the same weight. What mattered more and more was the number of listeners, and whether the programme fitted the controller's desired 'profile' of the network. In fact, the eventual 'trade-off' was a much longer, live Sunday morning programme, entitled *Good Morning, Sunday*, which, under some enterprising producers and two popular presenters, Roger Royle and Don Maclean, was to survive and flourish into the new millennium.

This was the beginning of the new era in broadcasting, one in which religion had to compete on no better than level terms with every other kind of programme (and sometimes, especially on television, not even on level terms). There was still plenty of religious output, but probably for the first time I began to realize that the broadcasting environment was changing, even if for the present slowly and gently.

Such matters of broadcasting politics concerned me very little at the time, I must confess, though they were later to haunt my days. During the rest of the seventies and into the early eighties I enjoyed my work as a radio producer, even picking up a couple of national awards for programmes and series, and being gradually promoted, in the BBC way, from producer to senior producer to the grand title of 'Editor, Religious Programmes, Radio'. I felt that here was a job I could do quite well, and even help others to do. And I could not see any other future, in terms of work, than BBC production through to retirement at 60.

MANAGING RELIGION

Once again, I was wrong. That is to say, my supposition that life at the BBC would from now on be a gentle canter to retirement, with a reasonable pension at the end of it, was inaccurate. Instead, I ended up, almost without realizing it, as 'Head of Religious Programmes, Radio' – HRPR, in the strange jargon of the Corporation – and finally 'Head of Religious Broadcasting' (HRB).

I say 'almost without realizing it' because, like most of the other career shifts in my life, it was more a matter of 'greatness thrust upon me' than 'achieving greatness'. It is true that I had twice applied for the post of radio head, first when John Lang left and then again after Michael Mayne's time in charge. Both times I was urged by influential people in the BBC to apply, and both times I failed to be appointed. I had no quarrel with that, though I admit I felt rather annoyed with myself for having succumbed to various voices that had influenced me to apply. I was happy doing what I was good at, which was producing programmes, and not very sure that the cut and thrust of BBC management was quite my forte. Colin Semper, on the other hand, who was appointed in Michael Mayne's place, took to it with enthusiasm, networking away with senior colleagues, arguing the case for this series and that, and generally charming the birds off the trees.

Of course, eventually he got bored with this role, too. He had once admitted to me that he would find the offer of a deanery irresistible, and so it proved. Actually it was the post of Provost of Coventry, which was much the same thing. Off he went, and within a few months he had got Jaguar cars (or was it Rover?) sponsoring the cathedral clergy, raised some vast sums of money and got any number of ambitious projects off the ground. The move was not a happy one for him domestically, however, and within a few years he was back in London as a residentiary canon of Westminster Abbey, where his former colleague at the BBC, Michael Mayne, was by now the dean. From all this, it is possible to see the 'style' of management at Broadcasting House, and especially in religious broadcasting, at that time.

When Colin Morris, who was then HRB, suggested I should apply for the post of HRPR, I demurred. Twice bitten, I felt, was twice shy. In any case, I wasn't sure that my ego, rather more fragile than some people supposed, could survive another rejection. There were several plausible candidates, some from inside the BBC and some from outside. However, since the last board for this post, I had at least had some experience of management at a lower level, in my role as editor, religious programmes. I had taken to attending the weekly review board whenever Colin wasn't available – a chore I enjoyed, to be honest – and I found the then controller of Radio 4, Monica Sims, a source of encouragement and wisdom. She was a woman with a wealth of experience in the BBC, as a very successful television producer, then as head of children's programmes and now as CR4 (in the BBC nomenclature). In addition to this general support, she asked me to go to the Prix Italia, the foremost international radio awards, as one of the BBC's 'observers'. This meant a delightful week in Capri, of all places, accompanied by Christine, with the chance to listen to some of the very best output from European radio and exchange experiences and opinions with leading programme makers from across the continent. It also gave me the chance to get to know one or two of the other BBC people attending, most of them senior figures in production or management.

The other extension of my broadcasting experience was an attachment to television production. This was something of an eye-opener, because although I had had quite a few years' experience writing for television and presenting programmes, I had very little idea, to be honest, what an incredibly complicated and labour-intensive process television production is. I worked as producer on a programme called *Choices*, which was an audience participation studio discussion. Chairing the programme was Libby Purves, best known in those days as a radio presenter, but tackling a major television series for the first time. Handling an audience of over a hundred people, who were free to participate simply by raising a hand and catching her eye, and also trying to shepherd a panel of articulate and sometimes aggressive members, was a baptism of fire. We all thought she did very well indeed, but the television review board astonished us by spending most of the time dedicated to discussion of the programme's quality by arguing as to whether she should or shouldn't wear her glasses. It was a revealing introduction to the different values which television tends to bring to broadcasting: the image is all.

The other difference I immediately noticed was how desperately seriously everything is taken. For instance, there was a quite embarrassing debate about whether my name or the other producer's should take the lead in the credits. I think he was genuinely surprised when I said it made absolutely no difference to me.

In Broadcasting House in those days the conversation in the lifts or the canteen was about almost anything except work, whereas in Television Centre nobody ever seemed to talk about anything else. Remarkable shots, unusual film locations, intransigent performers and brilliant set designs were the ordinary stuff of conversation. And so were budgets, endlessly – how we saved money, how we spent money, how we screwed a few thousand more out of the departmental funds. In fact, of course, television is ruled by money, partly because the whole thing is so wretchedly expensive. If you make a mistake on a radio recording and it has to be scrapped or re-recorded, the loss may run to a few hundred pounds. For television, that figure instantly becomes thousands, probably tens of thousands. So it is perhaps understandable, even commendable, that those charged with spending these vast sums do it carefully and seriously.

However, as may be gathered, it was not an atmosphere which I found very congenial. A radio production team is three or four people, a television one is 40 or 50 – and each member of that team comes to the task with a completely different agenda. The lighting man sees the lights, the make-up artist the make-up, the designer the set, the vision mixer the pictures, and so on. Only the producer, to be honest, has to see the thing as a whole, and that can be a very unpopular responsibility. Of course, a good production team pulls together, in one sense, and over a series a sense of camaraderie can be built up, but very often there is little sense of loyalty to a particular programme, beyond ensuring that one's own contribution to it enhances one's career rather than damaging it. To be honest, it was a relief to get back to radio – even though the first thing that faced me was to be the board for the head of department job.

I was relieved to see that Monica Sims was to be on the selection board, along with Colin Morris and one or two other senior BBC people. These boards follow a fairly set pattern, the whole thing conducted with immaculate courtesy, yet with a cruel determination to expose a candidate's weaknesses. I knew all of the board members quite well, but couldn't be sure whether that was a help or a handicap.

At any rate, I was well versed by now in the art of taking rejection on the chin, so I went home that evening slightly surprised but not disappointed that no one had rung me in the office to tell me who had been appointed. Perhaps the post-interview discussion was going on into the evening.

However, later that night Colin Morris phoned. He asked me how I thought I had done (an unanswerable question) and then congratulated me on getting the post. I broke the news to Christine, still scarcely able to credit that it had happened. I would be the first layman to head the department in its history, so far as I can tell, and one of the very few to have been educated entirely in the state sector.

I suppose it could be said that I took over religious programmes when they were probably at their all-time apogee. Certainly I remember several times making the point at public meetings that there had never been so much religious broadcasting on the BBC at any time in its history. On network radio there were over 600 hours of religious programmes a year, and something like 120 hours on television. And this output was not broadcast at the margins of audience appeal, but in the mainstream of programming. We had a large staff of producers, many of whom were extremely talented, and in many cases coveted by other production departments, and our programme budgets were adequate.

There is no doubt that the general morale of religious broadcasting had been boosted by the arrival of Gerald Priestland in the mid-seventies as religious affairs correspondent. Douglas Brown, his predecessor in the post, was a wise and respected broadcasting journalist, who had done a good deal to drag religion into the newsroom. But Gerry Priestland was nothing less than a broadcasting legend. He had held all the top jobs in BBC News – Delhi correspondent, Saigon during the height of the Vietnam war, Middle East correspondent and finally, the crown jewel of the whole news operation, Washington correspondent. His voice was known and respected wherever the BBC was heard.

When he finished his time in the USA Gerry came back into the kind of situation journalists dream of. What would he like to do? Which of the home correspondent posts would he prefer? And, while he was deciding, would he like to try something they had been toying with for some time, a 'leader column' spot at the end of the *Nine O'Clock News* each night?

That particular assignment was probably the only 'failure' in his whole broadcasting career – not because he didn't do it as well as anyone could possibly have done, but because the task was impossible. Broadcast news is not like a newspaper, where the reader expects a slant, a point of view, even a political agenda, to colour its treatment of the news. The BBC stood for utter impartiality: what its proponents liked to call 'straight news'. I can remember Gerry over lunch one day pouring scorn on the whole idea of 'straight' news, just as he ridiculed the idea that any journalist could get at 'the truth' (as in, 'We were determined to get at the truth behind this story'). Nevertheless, he allowed himself to get drawn into an experiment which was, on his own arguments, doomed to failure. By definition, the BBC does not have an 'opinion', a 'slant' or a 'political agenda'. If it had, it would lose its hard-won credibility as the provider of reliable news – not necessarily 'the truth', but at any rate as near to 'the facts' as can be got.

Slightly bruised by the *Nine O'Clock News* experience, Gerry was finally able to tell the BBC bosses which home post he would like to have. On his track record one might have thought it would be political correspondent, but in fact he told them, to their utter and publicly admitted astonishment, that he would like to be religious affairs correspondent. This was a relatively new position, to which Douglas Brown had been promoted after several years as religious affairs reporter (the subtleties of nomenclature disguise an enormous gulf of status).

In fact, when I joined the BBC no such post existed at all, for the simple reason that there wasn't any religious news – at least, none got broadcast. It was a sign of the times that during the early seventies, while churchgoing may still have been on the decline, the interest in religious news and opinions was on the increase. In 1970 there was no regular treatment on BBC radio or television of religious news or issues, no dedicated religious reporter or correspondent, and very little coverage of religious events or personalities in the recognized news outlets. That began to change with Douglas Brown's appointment and with the arrival of *Sunday* on Radio 4. It was, of course, immensely helped by a positive spate of good religious stories – controversy over various schemes for unity between churches, the proposed revision of the Church of England's services, the visit of the Pope to the British Isles and of the Archbishop of Canterbury to the Vatican.

But what did most to advance the cause of religious news was the advent of the General Synod of the Church of England, ridiculous as that may seem to some. Suddenly, the Church in England had what the Church of Scotland had possessed for centuries, a national debating chamber. When Synod debated hanging, its proceedings were covered extensively on the general news. When it debated nuclear disarmament, the whole debate was carried live on BBC radio and television. What surprised many dispassionate observers who watched or listened to the broadcasts was the quality and charity of the debate. Opinions and beliefs were strongly expressed, but with none of the childish abuse and ridiculous background noises that people had come to associate with the proceedings of the House of Commons. The department was even invited to produce a regular 20-minute report for Radio 4 on the proceedings of Synod whenever it was in session, a task that first Douglas Brown, and then Gerald Priestland, accomplished with professional skill and, in Gerry's case especially, an eye for the colourful descriptive phrase.

Gerald's arrival in the department – he was based with the religious radio team, but spent a lot of time in the newsroom – was a great lift to morale. For several years he was a regular presenter of *Sunday*, where I came to appreciate his mastery of the broadcasting craft. He was not an easy man to produce, needless to say, but even the battles were entertaining. His two long series for Radio 4, *Priestland's Progress* and *The Case*

Against God, were broadcasting milestones, attracting (by radio standards) enormous audiences and, in the case of *Priestland's Progress*, over 20,000 letters from listeners.

The team that worked on both series was one that was calculated to give any management a few headaches, to offset the warm feeling induced by public and professional applause. To marry, as we did, Gerry Priestland with an equally single-minded and perverse producer, Chris Rees, was to ask for trouble. Neither had the slightest concern about things like budgets, schedules or BBC politics. They seemed able to focus their entire (and very considerable) energies on the one business of making the programmes according to the creative vision they felt they had 'received'. In pursuit of this they knew no obstacles and would brook no interference. I still bear a few scars, but the result was radio of a quite outstanding kind – radio which, I feel, surpassed anything that television could have done, because it was all about words and ideas, imaginatively woven together into a rich fabric of sound.

Like many of the older school of BBC journalists, Gerry had elevated the technique of filling in a 'T&D' claim to an art form. T&D was, to put it simply, expenses (travel and duty), but it was regarded by many as a kind of general supplement to the meagre pittance they were paid by the Corporation. Indeed, one of our television producers told me that he made more money each year from T&D than he did from his salary. Gerry's forms presented me, as his manager, with a number of headaches, as I was required to authorize the payment as genuine reimbursement for expenses. Being an honest man, he never actually claimed for anything that he hadn't incurred. It was more the nature of the expenses which posed managerial dilemmas. Any meal involving Gerry and his producer necessitated wine, and not just any old wine, nor minute quantities. Hotel stays always seemed to require quite a lot of room service, phone calls, taxis and such like. When I protested that the budget couldn't stand it, he would look at me disdainfully and say, 'The BBC can always afford it.' There truly was the voice of the 'old' Corporation, the one for which he had worked since leaving university. I have to say that he found in Chris Rees not only a brilliantly creative producer but an apt pupil in these dark arts. No hired Cortinas or Astras for him: it was top of the range BMWs and Mercs, every time.

Gerry told us, with admiration, of one of his colleagues in the newsroom who, years before, was sent to cover an incident in the Thames estuary involving a ship in trouble. To save money, he had hired a rowing boat to approach the vessel and do his radio newsreel report. When he put in his T&D claim, however, this had mysteriously expanded into a motor launch, hired (in the teeth of furious competition) at enormous expense. Unfortunately for him, his rowing exploits had been briefly caught on the television news cameras and his line manager had seen it. He was sent for and asked, not surprisingly, why he was claiming for a motor vessel when he had appeared so publicly in a simple rowing boat. Instantly, the reporter asked for his T&D form back and spent a moment or two correcting it, finally handing it back to his boss. It now read, 'To hire of motor vessel £50, to hire of rowing boat required in order to reach motor vessel £10.'

Chris Rees was by no means the only gifted producer in the religious radio team. It would be invidious to list them, but among the mostly young men and women we had gathered together were several who went on to notable careers in broadcasting – several, such as Angela Tilby, John Forrest, Hugh Faupel and Michael Wakelin, to television, others to management posts in broadcasting, or to the independent production companies that came into being with the changing climate of the nineties. Not all of the best producers were based in London, either. Increasingly the regional production centres were taking on projects far beyond the original notion of producers who would arrange and broadcast 'talks and services' from the various English regions. In Wales and Scotland, too, there was an upsurge of creativity in religious radio during the eighties. I doubt if there was a better discussion programme on any of the networks than Radio Wales' *All Things Considered*, made by our religious broadcasting colleagues in Cardiff.

So these were heady days for radio religion, but for those who could read the runes there were disturbing signs, even if as yet, clouds 'no bigger than a man's hand'. It was easy to detect what I called 'unhelpful presuppositions', such as that religious programmes needed special 'protection' because of their 'minority status'. I would sharply point out that by that argument one should 'protect' the football output then on Radio 2, because the religious constituency was demonstrably larger than the number of people who went to watch professional football. I felt that our only defence was the enthusiasm and appreciation of our audiences, but that on those grounds we were much more secure than virtually the whole of Radio 3, the handful of children's programmes or *Today in Parliament*.

It was interesting to be involved in the constant debate about *Thought for the Day*. One couldn't deny that the whole idea of a spot in the BBC's flagship current affairs programme dedicated to a religious view of the world was a broadcasting curiosity. Indeed, it was hard to think of a similar programme anywhere else in the world. But the suggestion that *Thought for the Day* only survived there because of some Reithian principle about 'Christianizing' Britain, or that it depended on religious string-pulling behind the scenes, needed to be vigorously countered. *Thought for the Day* was there because the audience wanted it. True, surveys showed that there was a small minority of listeners who somewhat resented it – but nowhere near as large a number as those who deeply resented the sports slot, which had two placings in the *Today* sequence, and nowhere near as large as the number who said that they appreciated and enjoyed it. In other words, there was no broadcasting reason to drop it, even if it were true that, had one been starting with a blank sheet of paper to devise the *Today* programme in 1985, one wouldn't have thought of placing a religious comment slot just before the 8 o'clock news.

It was much the same with the daily service. I knew that a succession of controllers of Radio 4 had wanted to shift it, feeling (and being told by their departmental assistants) that it was an audience loser in the middle of the morning schedules. Again, it was hard to argue the case for a live act of Christian worship right in the middle of the morning output of the nation's senior talks network, but the fact was that it was there, and didn't lose audiences. It is true that the audience fell after it, which may mean that a different audience tuned in for the daily service and then, devotions over, switched off the radio and made for the garden or the conservatory. But, again on strictly broadcasting grounds, there were no convincing arguments for dropping it.

That didn't prevent several CR4s from trying, not to drop it entirely, but to move it either to a different time or to one or other of the two wave-lengths which Radio 4 had available to it. In the end, inevitably I suppose, they won, so that for some years now the daily service has been broadcast only on long wave, and earlier, at 9.45 – not so very far from the slot it first occupied 70 years ago! That meets the needs of the dedicated listener, of course, but largely rules out the element of serendipity, as Monica Sims called it, which makes radio listening – especially to Radio 4 – such an eccentric delight. I mean the accidental 'coming across' a programme which you wouldn't have tuned in for, but which proves a joy. I can say that over the years a number of people have had life-changing encounters with God, no less, through 'happening' to hear the daily service. Indeed, I can think of one woman who is an ordained Methodist minister today, whose faith journey began back in the seventies when she happened to hear the daily service and was arrested – for once, it seems the right word – by a passage which was being read from the Bible. As a result, she decided to try church the following Sunday. The nearest one was Methodist – and the story went on from there.

It would be wrong to suggest that radio management at that time was anti-religion. Several of the most senior people, including David Hatch, the managing director, were immensely supportive. I think things were rather different in television, partly due to the highly exposed nature of the medium. Viewing figures were pored over like the entrails of a bullock to detect signs and portents. And there was, and is, a widespread feeling that religion, along with a number of other 'serious' issues, is unsuitable for mainstream popular broadcasting, but should be accommodated in some specialist and targeted area of output.

But while there was little antagonism to religious programmes as such on the radio, there was a very significant shift of emphasis taking place. In the seventies it was still assumed, and publicly argued, that it was the BBC's duty to uphold and promote the best aspects of British culture, including the Christian faith which has so deeply shaped it. This belief went back to John Reith, it is true, and was often dubbed 'Reithian'. But the principle is carved into stone above the doors in the entrance hall of Broadcasting House, where words of St Paul from the epistle to the Philippians are quoted. The first governors pray to Almighty God that those things which are 'pure, true, lovely and of good report' might be the fruit from the seed broadcast from this building. Those words, etched there in 1928, echoed the views of Reith, it is true, but they were also the common denominator of BBC policy right up to the era of Carleton Greene in the sixties. There were still many people, especially in radio, who would have made them the touchstone of our broadcasting policies.

The differences that were beginning to surface did not arise from a root and branch rejection of that position, but by a redefinition of British culture. By the seventies we were all aware of the presence in Britain of huge numbers of people for whom the Christian faith, even if at second, third or fourth-hand, was not the hallmark of their culture. These were people of an Islamic, Hindu or Sikh culture. To them one would have to add the small, but influential, band of humanists and Marxists, who would emphatically not see broadcasting in terms of underpinning a Christian culture. In other words, we were entering a new world, or at any rate a new Britain, which had no one defining culture and certainly no agreed set of beliefs and values. One sensed the first tremors of this earthquake, and there was no shortage of voices warning about the threat it posed to 'Christian values', but the scale of the revolution, when it came, surprised me.

As head of religious programmes I was aware of a growing pressure to provide more opportunities for members of the minority religious groups to broadcast to the general public. BBC local radio already provided programmes within target areas for language and culture groups from the Indian subcontinent and Arabic lands. But the challenge was to create a platform from which they could contribute to the religious life of the nation as a whole, not simply to reinforce a ghetto mentality. This proved harder in execution than in prospect, partly because some of these groups had no particular desire to broadcast beyond the confines of their own people, and partly because it was hard at first to find broadcasters capable of attracting and holding a mainstream audience.

The Jewish community provided a model, of course. They had been involved with broadcasting from its early days, including religious programmes, and in a sense they provided a model for the way in which Islamic, Hindu and Sikh broadcasters could also take part. However, Jewish people had been part of British life at the deepest level for many hundreds of years. English was in most cases their native language. They were at home with the idiosyncracies of the national character. It would take a truly remarkable person to achieve in a decade what had taken them so long, and been so painful a progress.

Happily, it was not all that painful, and it didn't take hundreds of years. Among the first of the broadcasters to break through in this field was Indarjit Singh, the editor of the *Sikh*

Messenger. Indarjit is a true journalist, at home with words, a master of English idiom and a man with a nice sense of humour – one might say, without being patronizing, an English sense of humour. I liked his story on *Thought for the Day* of a traffic jam on the Paris *périphérique*, when the cars were stuck immovably in a sweltering heatwave. Most people got out of their cars, as Indarjit did, wearing his *patka* (turban), and surveying the scene. The driver of another car with British registration plates 20 yards away approached him, addressing him in a homely Brummie accent. 'Bloody foreigners,' he said conspiratorially, 'No idea, have they?' At that moment, Indarjit felt he had arrived as a true 'Brit'.

Others followed along the path pioneered by such Jewish luminaries as Hugo Grin, Dr Jacobovitz, Lionel Blue and the present Chief Rabbi, Jonathan Sachs, for my money one of the very best broadcasters of any kind on the radio. The quality of their contributions softened the blow for committed Christian listeners, but there remained a groundswell of complaint that 'things aren't what they used to be'. The hard truth was that they never would be again.

The pressure on religious broadcasting to become more genuinely multi-credal arose only partly from the increased number of adherents of non-Christian faiths in Britain. More profoundly, it was part of the general shift from traditional values in society as a whole. After all, most of the proponents of these views were no better disposed towards Islam, say, than towards Christianity. But it was the Christian church that was seen as one of the bulwarks of 'old' Britain, a Britain which needed to be dismantled before the 'new' one could be built.

All of this had begun, I suppose, with the sexual revolution of the sixties. The men and women of that generation were much more aware than those who followed them that they were breaking taboos which were centuries old and rooted deeply in the nation's cultural and religious values. Many of them were consciously in rebellion against a religious – usually Christian –

upbringing, and carried with them an air of bravado about it. That generation of young men and women were now older and occupying many of the positions of influence in society, perhaps especially in the media. It was hard to expect them to support a way of life and a set of beliefs which they had deliberately rejected 10 or 20 years earlier. The result was a strangely contradictory approach, in which they appeared to be extremely liberal and broad-minded towards everybody except those who retained 'old-fashioned' religious values and beliefs. Towards them there was an almost irrational prejudice, so extreme in some cases as to sow the thought that there is no one on earth as utterly illiberal as the thorough-going liberal.

In terms of religious broadcasting policy, this shift of emphasis meant that programmes were to reflect what the Central Religious Advisory Council (CRAC) called the whole spectrum of the nation's religious life and beliefs, which were then defined as 'predominantly, but not exclusively, Christian'. I am not sure that the same definition would be taken to apply in the new millennium, when religious programmes are quite consciously reflecting a 'spirituality' or 'religious exploration' that goes far beyond the confines of any of the organized faiths, and indeed rejects any kind of formal belief system. This, it would be claimed, is the predominant 'religious climate' of modern Britain. The traditional faiths, including the Christian churches, are seen as a minority, whose beliefs and concerns are proper topics for broadcasting, but deserving of no special protection or promotion.

This seems a very long way from the beliefs of the founding fathers of the BBC, of course. However, John Reith himself sowed the seeds of later moves to use broadcasting as a means of shaping (rather than reflecting) the prevailing culture. His agenda was quite open: to promote through the BBC an 'optimistic, manly Christianity, without dogma'. Just to look at the words he chose is to see the 'flavour' of religious broadcasting, certainly up to the second world war. BBC religion was 'broad', positive, traditional and patriotic. It succeeded in excluding evangelicals almost totally, and permitted Roman Catholic participation only under the severest constraints. From the earliest days the Jewish faith was allowed the occasional broadcast talk – at Passover, for instance – but in truth its approach was sectarian. The description would have shocked those in charge of broadcast religion, but the facts are indisputable. The 'establishment' held sway, and those, from any quarter, who would have disturbed the status quo were simply not invited to the party.

This genteel, polite and moderate version of the Christian faith predominated for two decades, at least. It can be found in the records of all the great religious broadcasters of that period, from G.H. Elliott to Dean Inge and from 'Tubby' Clayton to Dick Shepherd. One searches in vain for the dissenting voice until William Temple came on the scene, to be followed by the orthodox – dare one say 'dogmatic'? – genius of C.S. Lewis. In fact, the war years, when those two were enormously influential broadcasters, saw the first beginnings of a more robust kind of BBC religion. This recognised that many people were not from a genteel, well-educated, middle-class background. They were not brought up on school prayers, daily matins or choral evensong. They had religious needs, and they had religious beliefs, but they were altogether more earthy. Their root and heart was in the feelings rather than the intellect, and their search for the divine was along paths trodden by friends, relatives and neighbours, rather than academics and well-spoken clerics.

It was a recognition of this that brought about the introduction of the *People's Service* and a *Sunday Half Hour* of hymn-singing on the Forces Programme, and even, at a different level, of Dorothy Sayers' play-cycle *The Man Born to Be King*. Chaplains in the Forces were among the first to discover that the 'ordinary' man of the 1940s was largely ignorant of the teachings of the Christian faith, while clinging, in a slightly detached way, to various remnants of its culture. C.S. Lewis'

Broadcast Talks – later published as the best-selling book *Mere Christianity* – and *The Man Born to Be King* were, in different ways, attempts to remedy that ignorance. In the event, the former was probably slightly too cerebral, and the second (in contemporary culture) slightly too shocking, to be entirely successful, but both were landmarks in religious broadcasting history. The old era of religious broadcasting, built almost exclusively of devotional talks and high-class broadcast services, was coming to an end.

From all this it will be seen that religious broadcasting has never been 'agenda-free'. John Reith had his agenda, and the broadcasters of the war years had theirs. In the post-war years the religious scene began to shift dramatically, with a general decline in churchgoing and a growing dissatisfaction with what was seen as the 'old regime'. The BBC was still largely run by a cabal of ex-public school men, culturally isolated from the general population, but this could not continue indefinitely. Both inside and outside the Corporation voices were raised in support of a different approach, and though an organization like the BBC takes reluctantly to it, once change begins it has a kind of inevitability about it. The sixties were just such a period of change, and my arrival at Broadcasting House more or less coincided with the point at which that change had become irreversible.

Part of it was this determination to break the hold of the 'establishment' on public service broadcasting. As I have said, the Church (and especially the Church of England) was seen as a bulwark of that establishment. Consequently, people who in other circumstances would have regarded Islam or Hinduism with great suspicion were urging religious broadcasting to welcome them into our output, and at the same time to transform most of our other programmes into areas for open exploration of the religious search, rather than reflections of an established Christian culture.

Personally, I had little problem with that. There was

enough of the evangelist in my soul to believe that the religious search, honestly and openly pursued, would eventually lead people to the truth as it had been revealed in Jesus Christ. Indeed, religious broadcasting embarked on a number of projects which followed exactly that agenda, such as *Priestland's Progress* and the *Case Against God*, and two later series by the splendid Brian Redhead, one on church history and the other on the Bible.

But I also knew that thousands of people depended on BBC radio for support and encouragement in their Christian faith. They were the devoted listeners to our Sunday services, the daily service, *Prayer for the Day* and *Pause for Thought* and the several other devotional slots in the weekly output. Far from being unpopular, these had a loyal and enthusiastic following, and I couldn't see why these people, licence payers and citizens as they were, should be deprived of them on what seemed to me arbitrary and doctrinaire grounds.

Two areas of the BBC were especially vulnerable to this movement, BBC local radio, and the World Service. In both cases, it was understandable that there were circumstances in which actually to promote the Christian faith, or deliberately to ignore religions such as Islam and Hinduism, would be utterly wrong. Some BBC local stations were situated in areas where a large part of the population were Muslim or Hindu, and there was every reason to reflect that fact in their religious output. Equally, on a world scene, there were huge parts of the world, and whole nations, where Christianity was a minor influence and where one or other of the major world religions held sway. In those circumstances, only a multi-faith approach could be justified.

However, in some cases, what seemed to me quite unreasonable demands were being made. I recall being involved with a situation at Radio Leeds where the advisory council felt that the religious output should be split equally between the religions of the immigrant communities and Christianity. At first sight this seemed reasonable, but in fact it was heavily loaded against the culture of the majority of the population, who were not Muslim, Hindu or Sikh, but would have described themselves as 'Christians'. The fact that most of them were non-churchgoers was irrelevant – after all, most of the Hindus were non-templegoers, too. If we were fairly to reflect the different cultures in that city, we would have to work on the assumption that most of the 'host' community were culturally Christian, just as many of the immigrant community were culturally Islamic or Hindu. That would give a breakdown of output in the Leeds catchment area of perhaps 70 per cent 'Christian' to 30 per cent 'other faiths'.

Similarly, over the country as a whole, the same approach would mean that something less than 10 per cent of total religious output should reflect the beliefs and culture of the non-Christian religions. I wouldn't deduce from this that 90 per cent of it should be Christian, but that the rest could be split between programmes reflecting the human search for spirituality and religious understanding (in a general way) and programmes explaining and examining the Christian faith and reflecting its life and worship. It seemed to me then that a solution along these lines would have been fair and equitable, and also sound policy for a public service broadcaster. However, it proved more difficult to implement, partly because of a growing disinclination to 'clog' the radio networks with regular strands of worship programmes, and partly because in the prevailing liberal climate it sounded like an elaborate attempt to preserve the Christian stranglehold on broadcast religion.

The World Service was a special case, of course, and not one over which I had any direct control. But I admired the way in which the small team of religious producers at Bush House managed to keep religious issues in the mainstream of the output, as indeed they are in the mainstream of life in many parts of the world. At that time the redoubtable Pauline Webb ran the small external services religious team. Later I was to admire the work of Tim Dean in much the same role. My only hesitation was about so-called 'multi-faith' services, which at one time seemed likely to become a feature of World Service output. I confess that I disliked them heartily.

I attended one, broadcast from St Martin-in-the-Fields, London, which I found really quite offensive. No one could question the good motives of those who had planned the 'service', but it seemed to me to be based on a premise which was essentially unacceptable both to Christians and Muslims, in that it assumed that we all believed fundamentally the 'same' thing, or at any rate believed in the 'same' God. This seemed to me insulting to those who held a monotheistic view of God – one can imagine what the Hebrew prophets would have made of it! – and demanded more than they could possibly deliver of Buddhists, who don't believe in a 'God', in that sense, at all. So we all sat there listening to readings from the various scriptures, carefully chosen to avoid offence, under the shadow of the church's cross and in front of the altar where week by week Christians celebrated the 'one sacrifice for sins for ever'.

That particular service helped to clarify my own thinking about a multi-faith approach to broadcasting. I decided that I was happier to see religious broadcasting as a large and open platform, on which all manner of good things were displayed with equal prominence. All who wished to participate were expected to treat the other participants with respect, but to take part did not imply any kind of approval of others' beliefs. How could it, when by definition a Muslim believes that the final and definitive revelation of the truth of God is the Quran and a Christian believes that Jesus is uniquely the revelation of God to humanity. Yes, there is a 'religious approach' to life, which recognizes that there are values and truths about human existence which go beyond the purely material and mechanistic. We may call this, if we wish, a 'spiritual' dimension. But that is not at all the same thing as saying that everything that goes under the banner of 'spirituality' is either true or necessarily good, and each of us must be free not only to assert what we believe, but to have freedom not to agree and not to believe. Religion, in other words, is simply a description of a phenomenon of human experience. Anything claiming to be a 'religion' may be true, or partly true, or false, or partly false. It is not the role of a broadcasting organization to decide which is which.

Working from this premise, I felt that we achieved a reasonable mix of programmes in religious output on network radio. It took a while to discover broadcasters from some of the ethnic groups who were happy to take part in programmes, and to this day there is an obvious shortage of Muslims who are willing or able to address the broader audience from the standpoint of their own clearly defined faith. It is also a fact that a number of the mainstream religions are simply not interested in sharing their worship or faith experience with the general audience.

But the response to programmes exploring that wider search for spiritual meaning which I described proved to be highly popular. One of our young producers, Beverley McAinsh, made a programme for Radio 4 called *Only Connect*, which was about various avenues into spiritual exploration. I suppose, to be brutally honest, I found it all a bit 'touchy-feely', but the audience clearly found it deeply satisfying. At least, out of a total listening audience of about 100,000 (a good evening 'reach' for the network) no less than 800 took the trouble to write in for more information, or simply to pass comments on it. That, incidentally, is one of the distinctive features of radio listening, compared with television viewing: the audience do not regard themselves as 'spectators' but as participants.

I have already mentioned CRAC, the Central Religious Advisory Council. This was set up in the early days of the BBC to provide some degree of liaison with the various churches and to offer, as its name implies, advice to the Corporation over its religious broadcasting policies. When ITV came into being in 1957, they also became involved, and as the religious scene changed, so CRAC's membership enlarged to encompass members of other faiths – Jewish, Hindu, Sikh and Muslim. All of the members were appointed not by the religious bodies themselves but by the broadcasting organizations, and they met alternately on BBC or ITV premises. By tradition, an Anglican bishop chaired CRAC, which was serviced for a long time by the BBC's department of corporate affairs.

As head of religious programmes, radio, I had to attend CRAC, of course, and present a brief report. I had expected to discover a body positively steaming with outrage, or perhaps riven with internal dissent. In fact, it was all extremely parliamentarian, except that virtually nothing proposed by the broadcasters was ever rejected, and criticism of their programmes was muted – possibly because on the whole they had not bothered to listen or watch. To be honest, it was a typical piece of clever public relations, providing a veneer of public consultation while ensuring that the professionals were left to get on with what they thought they knew about.

At times one felt that CRAC must surely stir itself – over the abolition of the 'closed period' for religious programmes on Sunday evenings, perhaps, or when BBC television began to cut down drastically on broadcast services, or – later, in 1990 – when the decision was taken to move the religious department to Manchester. But no. Wined and dined at the broadcasters' expense, and possibly slightly flattered to be there at all, or possibly completely out of their depth in this world of mandarins, tribal chiefs and spin doctors, they tended to nod what passed for approval. The members of the so-called 'minority religions' – apart from the highly articulate Jewish members – seldom expressed an opinion about anything that did not directly affect their own constituency, while the men and women from the Christian churches gazed helplessly at the mountains of background papers, or watched videos of carefully selected prize programmes, or sat through slick presentations by producers who had spent an inordinate amount of time spinning the wool that was about to cover their eyes.

I suppose that sounds quite cynical, coming from someone

who was for six years part of the process. But it was a cynicism, if that is indeed the right word, born of a long apprenticeship in programme offers meetings and review boards, at all of which the same elaborate games were played. Excellent people sat on CRAC. The chairmen took their role seriously and conscientiously, in line with the brief presented to them by the secretariat. And just occasionally someone would ask a truly awkward question, usually countered with all the straight-faced solemnity of a Whitehall aide briefing a troublesome minister. But we all soon learnt not to rely on CRAC as any kind of port in a broadcasting storm. It was more like a pleasure steamer adrift in mid-channel blissfully unaware of its real situation.

All of this might imply that managing BBC religion was a stressful role fraught with opposition, problems and difficulties. Actually, it wasn't like that at all, mainly because in the early eighties most of the senior management in radio were on our side. David Hatch, the managing director, was both a friend and a supporter, though not sparing in criticism – brutally expressed – when he felt we had deserved it. I have already mentioned Monica Sims, who was also uniformly supportive when she was CR4, and also when she moved from there to be director of programmes. Ian McIntyre, who moved from CR3 to take over as CR4, was an eccentric, in broadcasting terms: a man who managed to tear the *Today* programme into separate pieces, divided by two segments of 30 minutes which he called *Up to the Hour*. To attempt such a move in the teeth of furious opposition from the very powerful *Today* team was astonishing. To bring it off beggars belief, though the blood on the walls of sundry offices on the third floor was reported to be real and warm. The experiment lasted exactly the same length of time as Ian's tenure of the controller's post, and probably hastened his departure. However, so far as religion was concerned he was a supportive manager, though, like David Hatch, a withering critic of anything he deemed second-rate, ill-conceived or sloppily produced.

In fact, he and his friend George Fischer, who was head of talks and documentaries, were the scourges of nervous producers, and even tyro heads of department, at the weekly review board. The criticism, however, while often cruel, was also always witty and elegant. If they cut you up, at least they did it with style.

My favourite McIntyre moment at a programme review board concerned an edition of *The World Tonight* which we were considering. As ever when a programme from news was being discussed, but especially if the news bosses thought there might be cause for concern, an enormous mafia of apparatchiks were filling the seats around the oval table. Ian noted their attendance with grim delight, and then sat poker-faced through their interminable explanations for whatever it was that had been indefensibly awful about this particular programme. When they had finished, there was a moment's silence, as we all took on board that the case for the defence had ended, and then he spoke.

'Why not', he suggested in a gently helpful tone of voice, 'simply plead guilty but insane?'

Religious broadcasting had a few programmes on Radio 3, notably *Choral Evensong*, broadcast live and at great expense from a cathedral or 'major church' every week. It was a delightful piece of broadcasting, and it pleased me that it was one of the highlights of Christine's working week, as she created a pause in her working routine as a health visitor, and of my father-in-law, who sat with a cup of coffee in his cottage in Suffolk keeping a note of the hymns, readings and anthems for his private records. But I would have to say that there was no other programme in our entire religious output that cost as much per listener as that one. An unkind colleague once worked out that it could well be cheaper to offer our 'core' listeners a free cassette of the service each.

We had tried over the years to get a foothold for religious ideas and topics on Radio 1, the BBC's largest radio audience by a long way in those days. We had achieved brief successes in the seventies, some of which I had had a hand in, but it was hard to create anything that would please both the controller and his very critical audience, who basically wanted Top 20 music by day and 'specialist' music by night. One of my producers, John Forrest, came up with a brilliant idea which linked together snatches of speech – on a theme – with recorded music. It sounds predictable, but in fact it was imaginative and thoughtful, while matching the general air of noisy irreverence which gave Radio 1 its 'feel'. Later, and on the back of that, we were able to commission a completely new work by Adrian Snell, a kind of rock oratorio. It cost an enormous amount of money, in radio terms, but it did make a memorable piece of broadcasting.

For a year or two I produced, for much of the time with Sue Davies, one of the most creative producers I have ever worked with, a Radio 1 programme called *Talkabout*. This was the successor to *Speakeasy*, and combined a couple of pop or rock records with an hour's live conversation between an invited audience of young people and two or three studio guests. Our presenters during this period included the eccentric Jonathan King and the highly gifted, but sadly flawed, genius of Adrian Love.

Adrian presented us with a problem new to me as a broadcaster. He was a gentle, intelligent and charming man while he was sober, but even a small quantity of alcohol seemed to have a devastating effect on his character and his competence. He was, in other words, an alcoholic. Working with him, and forming a genuine liking for him, it was desperately sad to see how pernicious this problem was. Like many heavy drinkers, he was highly skilled at covering up the more obvious symptoms – breath, slurred speech and so on – but the brain simply refused to co-operate in these stratagems at times.

The crunch came on a broadcast from Belfast, with an audience of Catholic and Protestant sixth-formers. We flew over in the early afternoon, and when we were leaving the airport

Adrian suggested that, as this was his first ever visit to Northern Ireland, it might be a good idea if he took a taxi ride around the city just to get the feel of the place. This was, of course, during the height of the 'troubles', and the object of our programme was to discover what common ground there might be between young people across the community divide. Foolishly, with hindsight, I agreed to his request, and he set off in a separate taxi, promising to be at the venue for the broadcast in good time.

That part of the promise he kept, more or less. But when he arrived it was obvious that he had not only researched the ghettoes and green lines of Belfast but also the bars. He tried to explain that he intended to visit first a republican bar and then a loyalist one, to capture the local flavour. In fact, the only flavour he seemed to have captured was that of the local spirits. He could barely stand up, though as usual he was quite articulate.

We had no choice but to go ahead with the programme, which was in any case a tense but difficult one. The youngsters in the audience had seemed friendly and civilized enough during the 'warm-up', but when the programme got under way the old prejudices and partisan slogans began to appear, until at one point we feared actual violence between them. Adrian sat through it all with a slightly dazed look on his face, the proceedings completely out of his control or even comprehension, while the PA – a young English Catholic colleague, who couldn't believe what was going on – and I tried to maintain some sort of order. I have a vivid memory of her kneeling in front of Adrian's desk counting down the last few seconds with huge sweeps of her arms, until we reached the safety of the closing signature music. It was almost, if not certainly, Adrian's last broadcast for us.

He had various attempts later at resurrecting what had been a very promising broadcasting career, until he died prematurely a few years after I left the BBC. Sue and I learnt a great deal about the nature of alcoholism during the months that we worked with him. It shocked both of us to see how intractable the problem was. Adrian tried desperately to fight off his addiction, even spending time in a clinic paid for by the BBC, and aware that not only his job but also a very precious relationship were on the line, but he seemed helpless in the grip of it. It was a deadly warning about the perils of the stuff that sometimes seemed to wash through the corridors of Broadcasting House.

My main claim to respect where Radio 1 was concerned was probably the 'discovery' of Simon Mayo. I had heard him on the 'restricted licence' radio station run during the 'Greenbelt' Christian arts' festival, and made a mental note that this young man – then working for local radio in the Midlands – seemed to have what it took to be a Radio 1 presenter. I asked him to let me have a demo tape of his daily music programme, and then passed it on to Johnny Beerling, the controller of Radio 1. I was very gratified that he agreed with my assessment of Simon's potential, gave him a 'trial' as a holiday replacement presenter, and the rest, in the old cliché, is history.

Simon is a committed Christian – in fact, for some time he was churchwarden of a parish in Holloway – and made no secret of the fact at the BBC, while wisely not parading his beliefs at every opportunity. His wife Hilary worked for a time very successfully as a producer in my department. Simon's arrival on the BBC's most popular network, and his instant popularity with the audience, did no harm either to my own credibility as a talent spotter nor to religious broadcasting's relationship with Radio 1. But I can't claim that either fact led to a flood of religious programmes on its output.

Indeed, apart from Radio 4 our most successful religious output, and by some distance our largest audiences, were on Radio 2. The controller during most of my time as head was Frances Line, and no one could have been more positive or encouraging. I have always believed that carrots are more effective in the long run than sticks, and it proved so with my producers. The team who made programmes for Radio 2 felt affirmed – they knew their work was appreciated, that it was respected and that they were genuinely part of the network, rather than aliens trying to invade it (which was how religion was sometimes made to feel). Consequently, almost everything they did for Radio 2 was successful, from *Good Morning Sunday*, with an audience running into millions every week, to *Sunday Half Hour on Sunday* night and *Pause for Thought* every morning on the *Terry Wogan Show*.

The last of those demanded extraordinary skill on the part of the contributors, because as well as preparing and reading your two minutes of appropriately targeted religious thought you also ran the risk of a live 'viva' at the end by Mr Wogan. It is one thing to write a good little script, neatly avoiding all the tricky bits, but quite another to be asked when you finished, in that innocent Irish accent, how you would explain the one thing you had tried to avoid. Some of our contributors – Bill Westwood springs instantly to mind – actually relished the prospect of crossing swords with Wogan, but for others that moment's pause at the end of the script was charged with nameless terrors.

Good Morning Sunday's first presenter was Roger Royle. I had met him a few years earlier at Ronald Allison's home. At that time he was 'conduct' – which is a fancy name for chaplain – at Eton, and had made a great hit with the boys through his revolutionary approach to school assemblies. With Roger in charge, these were sometimes hilarious, always entertaining and often very thought-provoking. He had an astonishing ability to cajole, inveigle or bribe distinguished men and women to visit the school to take part in them, and he himself presided in the style with which later television and radio listeners were to become familiar. Flamboyant is one word which comes to mind, closely followed by histrionic.

Roger is a born entertainer, with a memorably mobile face, rather large ears, a very distinctive voice and a laugh which was to become the hallmark of his radio performances. It was a cross between a horse scenting a mate and a donkey demanding a carrot. Despite his carefully modulated vowels and public school accent he was born and brought up in Splott, which is an undistinguished suburb of Cardiff. He was a rather shy boy, and perhaps that shyness, or at least an interior anxiety, helped to create the classic introverted clown that he chose as his public persona.

In fact, Roger was far from being just a clown. He is a deeply serious Christian, an intelligent and sensitive man (sometimes too sensitive for his own happiness) and a superb judge of precisely the right thing to say at the right moment. He took his ordination to the priesthood very seriously and both at Eton and later in his career as a broadcaster always ensured that his work gave him the opportunity to exercise that ministry.

It was some time after that meeting at Ron's house that Roger began his radio career, though he was already co-presenting an extremely strange quasi-religious 'comedy' programme on ITV. This seemed to involve placing the 'funny vicar' (as he was cast) into various embarrassing situations. Watching the programme, I got two overwhelming impressions. The first was that this series was doing little to advance Roger's claims on a career in the BBC. The second was that here was a man who would do anything to be famous. In fact, I was wrong about both, though there was just enough truth in these suspicions to cast doubts in my mind about his broadcasting credentials – doubts that were swept aside, I have to say, when he eventually found his true niches.

The first of these was the presenting of *Songs of Praise*, where he brought a welcome breath of enjoyment and fun to a programme which had tended to take itself rather too seriously of late. However, I knew that my colleagues in religious television had more serious doubts about him in this role, or indeed on television at all, and their search for a regular presenter for *Songs of Praise* eventually took them elsewhere.

Television's loss was radio's gain, because Roger was invited to present the 'new' Sunday morning sequence, which we called (not very imaginatively) *Good Morning Sunday*. He was an immediate success, having that great radio advantage, a distinctive voice and style. No one else on Radio 2, or anywhere else for that matter, sounded like Roger. And certainly no one else had a laugh like his, or if they did, took much greater pains to disguise it. I recall the review board, in the early days of his time on the programme, having a very serious discussion about this laugh. The technical people felt that he might damage the ribbon in the microphone. The defenders of BBC standards felt that unedited snorts had no place in the Corporation's output. One or two felt that such levity distracted from the religious nature of the programme. Fortunately, most could see that what it did above anything else was to emphasize that a human being was at work, and one who was not capable of controlling his mirth. Mind you, the producers – myself sometimes among them – did their best to ration him to one outburst per programme.

Good Morning Sunday worked because it fitted. The music was straight-down-the-middle Radio 2. The target audience was older people, who were awake and listening to the network when the nation's youth was still recovering from the excesses of the previous evening. The subject matter was almost entirely people's own personal faith journey. Many of those who were guests on the programme were well known to the audience, which ensured a sympathetic hearing. Roger proved a good interviewer in this setting – firm and probing, but never crudely intrusive, affirming of faith without putting words or beliefs into his guests' mouths, and sensitive when difficult or painful topics were being revealed.

He could sometimes be a little overconfident where ad-libbing was concerned. He was always provided with a pile of listeners' letters, which were reckoned by the researcher to be suitable for what Radio 2 calls 'dedications' – playing a record but 'dedicating' it to the person who had written the letter, or about whom the letter was written. On one occasion Roger picked up such a letter to fill a 40-second gap in proceedings, and after a cursory glance began to quote from it. What he said went roughly like this (with the names changed, of course).

Now, I've got a really lovely letter here from Elsie in Hitchin. Elsie, you tell me, let's see – yes, it's your ruby wedding anniversary today. I hope you have a lovely day. You don't tell me your husband's name – let me see, oh yes, here we are. You say your husband... (noise of page being turned over)... died last Tuesday. That must have been a terrible shock, and so near your anniversary. Still, I hope you'll still celebrate your ruby wedding in thanksgiving for all the lovely and happy years you had together. You can remember them today, Elsie, and we'll remember you in our prayers, as we dedicate our next record to you and to your late husband...

To get oneself into such a hole may be a grievous broadcasting fault, but to get oneself out again with such style and sensitivity is little short of genius.

On two memorable occasions we, and especially I, got into equally deep holes. Strangely enough, both involved my deputy, John Newbury. He had joined the department in the late seventies, once I had persuaded John Lang that birth on a South London suburb and a schooling that ended at 16 didn't necessarily mean that a person had no talent. John Newbury was a Methodist minister, father of a young family, and a man who didn't think it was terribly important to eat your first course with the right knife and fork. In fact, he was of distinctly radical political views, which had been strengthened during a time of ministry on Merseyside. He came to us full of energy and purpose, which was exactly what the department needed, I thought, and began to make some of our most innovative and challenging programmes. He also proved a very able editor of *Sunday*, possibly on the principle of 'set a thief to catch a thief'. John knew all the political tricks and could spot an axe being ground three blocks away.

Anyway, eventually, when I became head of religious programmes John became editor, religious programmes, which made him effectively my deputy. He continued to produce *Sunday* from time to time, and one week had one of those unavoidable disasters that stalk live broadcasting. The programme menu was a bit tight for length, so just as they were going on air John made the decision to drop an item they had prepared about Jewish immigration to Israel. It is customary to give pre-recorded tapes a brief identifying title for studio purposes, and this one was simply known as 'The Jews'. Another convention is that the briefest possible instruction to drop an item is to 'kill' it. As Clive Jacobs, who was the presenter at that time, was about to say 'In this morning's programme' John put down the producer talk-back button, which should convey a message solely and privately into the presenter's headphones. 'Kill the Jews', he said, in rather peremptory tones, as he could see that in a second or two it would have been too late to leave it out of the menu.

Unfortunately, owing to an inexplicable technical error, his words were broadcast, momentarily cutting out Clive's introduction. So what the astonished listeners heard was the barbaric and apparently anti-Semitic instruction to 'Kill the Jews'. It is the sort of moment that makes a producer's blood run cold. John kept his cool, however, and while the programme was still on the air he rang the chairman of the board of deputies, Greville Janner, to explain what had happened. Mr Janner was very understanding, saying that he would get a message at once to the Jewish media and other groups explaining what had happened, and how. The worst political consequences were thus avoided, but not the inevitable jamming of the BBC switchboard with angry and indignant Jewish listeners demanding to know which fascist gang had broken into a studio or intercepted the BBC's Radio 4 wavelength.

That was bad enough, but my own blood still runs cold when I think of the other hole we all but dug for ourselves, again completely unwittingly. It happened on the eve of polling day in the 1987 general election. The Tory government had been angered for several years by what they saw as the BBC's pro-Labour bias. In fact, I think the truth is that every government since the General Strike in 1925 has been convinced that the BBC is 'against' them. After all, it is governments, not oppositions, that actually do things, and most criticism is directed at what is done, rather than what might be done in different circumstances. Certainly the Labour government of the nineteen-seventies under Harold Wilson was quite convinced that the BBC had got it in for them, and those who can remember the new-wave satirical shows on television at that time will feel they had a case.

However, the all-conquering Tories of the Thatcher years were not prepared to wait and find out how the BBC would decide to cover the election campaign. They decided, egged on by their aggressive team coach, Norman Tebbit, to emulate the tactics of the fabled Welsh rugby manager, and 'retaliate first'. So the 1987 campaign was preceded by a blanket barrage of criticism of the BBC's coverage of politics, coupled with dire warnings of the consequences if the alleged bias should surface during the pre-election period. The Corporation's bosses, mindful of the need for an increase in the annual licence fee and of the imminent discussions on the renewal of the BBC's charter, set out to bash their unruly minions into submission. High-level meetings were called and peremptory memos circulated, warning all staff of the BBC's 'incomparable reputation of impartiality'. At one of the meetings I was particularly singled out for a warning. 'That includes religion, David. I don't want some lefty bishop on *Thought for the Day* queering our pitch'.

With those words of the managing director ringing in my ears, I called a departmental meeting and came as near as I temperamentally could to reading the riot act. Every speaker, each sermon, all our stories and features were to be scrupulously overhauled. Fine-tooth combs should scrape through every script. Our broadcasters, even (or perhaps especially) bishops and other turbulent priests, were to be warned as to their future conduct. Everyone nodded. They nodded even more emphatically when I warned that breach of these guidelines would be a dismissable offence. I returned to my desk satisfied that the message had been understood and would be obeyed.

And so it was. Never had we experienced such an uneventful few weeks on the complaints front. Bland 'thoughts for the day' poured from the lips of our safer contributors. *Sunday* kept so scrupulously to genuinely religious topics that someone unkindly remarked that if they kept this up people might think it was a Christian programme.

So when John Newbury and I met for a final review of things on the eve of polling day we felt not only proud of our achievement but safe in our jobs. One task remained: to check through our election-day output. One by one we ticked off the programmes – *Pause for Thought*, *Thought for the Day*, the daily service, even *Choral Evensong*. We could see no possibility of even the most ingenious polemicist infiltrating a political nuance into any of them. We were about to congratulate ourselves and go home when an impulse urged me to ask, 'What about *Prayer for the Day*?'

John laughed. This was the most politically neutered part of all our output – nothing but a reading from the Bible, a short devotional comment and a brief prayer. 'That's OK,' said John, 'The guy's talking about the messages to the seven churches in Revelation.'

'Still, we'd better just check it,' I suggested, responding to heaven knows what providential prompting. 'Let's get the tape out and have a listen'.

John went off to the tape library and we played *Prayer for the Day* back on the machine in my office. Thirty seconds in, we both knew that it was political dynamite. The speaker, dealing with the church at Thyatira and its troublesome *éminence grise* Jezebel, punctuated his talk several times with the insistent divine message: 'The time has come to get rid of this terrible woman.'

Would anyone – would Norman Tebbit, would Margaret Thatcher herself – ever believe that this talk was recorded long before the election date was fixed? Or that the speaker, anxious only to make the scripture come alive, was totally innocent of any political agenda at all? Or that this wasn't religious broadcasting's sneaky way of calling the nation, in God's name, to rid itself of the Prime Minister? John and I looked at each other and knew that in one precious moment our careers had been saved. The talk was scrapped and a completely harmless devotional piece was broadcast in its place. As it happened, of course, the 'terrible woman' was not got rid of, at least for the time being.

It was strange how Mrs Thatcher, more than any other politician in my lifetime, could provoke the ire of the clerics. One of my producers rang me late on a Saturday night to ask my opinion on the text of a sermon for the following morning's Sunday service. 'He can't say this, can he?' he asked, reading me a sentence which spoke of Mrs Thatcher being 'under the judgment of God' because of what she had done to the poor. 'No,' I assured him, 'he can't.'

'But he says it's his church, his pulpit, and he's going to say in it whatever he believes ought to be said'.

'Fine,' I replied, 'So he can. But not on our radio station. If he insists, we'll scrap the broadcast and put on the stand-by tape.'

Even later that evening the producer rang to say that they had agreed an acceptable compromise. The passage in question would now read, 'Those who treat the poor unjustly will be judged by God, whoever they are.' So you can see that the job of a religious producer sometimes requires both the wisdom of Solomon and the patience of Job.

Sometimes it needs other qualities. One of our Scottish producers had a minister die in the pulpit halfway through a live broadcast service. When he left the van and entered the church to see why the programme had suddenly stopped he not only found the preacher slumped on the floor of the pulpit but the entire congregation sitting silently in their pews. No one had left a seat to come to the aid of their stricken pastor. When asked why, one of the elders explained that they had been told very strictly by the producer before going on air that in no circumstances should anyone leave his seat or walk about the church. They were, he said with Highland innocence, simply doing what they had been told.

I suppose, on a slightly larger canvas, I also was 'doing what I was told'. The reward for that came with the surprising invitation to take over as head of religious broadcasting when Colin Morris left that post for an even loftier one in the BBC hierarchy, controller, Northern Ireland. Though how, in 1987, anybody could be described as 'controlling' Northern Ireland stretched credulity to the limits. There was the inevitable 'board', of course, and once again the evening phone call to tell me its decision. As I had been doing the job for several months, since Colin had embarked on a piece of research for the board of management, it meant I simply carried on where I had been the day before, but with a new title.

I had been amused to read a diary piece about the vacancy for a head of religious broadcasting in the *Daily Telegraph*. Various luminaries were mentioned, including Richard Harries, the Bishop of Oxford, and Colin Semper, by then comfortably settled at Westminster Abbey. Eventually I was mentioned, as the 'preferred internal candidate', with 'many years of experience in broadcasting'. It was a strange experience to see one's chances thus assessed.

In fact, the change of role made little day-to-day difference, except that David Hatch took to addressing me as 'God', and I seemed to spend even more time in meetings and conferences, some of them, it must be admitted, in extremely pleasant surroundings.

This was an era when the wind of change began to blow

through the corridors of the BBC. John Birt would soon be appointed director-general, with a reformist agenda which was eventually to change the BBC beyond recognition – and, some would say, very nearly sink it altogether. Already, we all had to learn a new vocabulary. Cost-effectiveness, rationalization, internal market, independent production – this was the new language of broadcasting, apparently. With others, I was not altogether convinced that Mr Birt knew very much about public service broadcasting as such, or anything at all about radio broadcasting. Whether that were true or not, all of this 'new-speak' certainly spelt the end of the Rolls Royce days at the BBC.

As I have said, there was no doubt that there had been wastage and overstaffing in the Corporation. And five years in management had shown me how insidious the 'departmental' system could be. The BBC in those days was organized into many, many small 'departments', each with its own hierarchy. So a head, and probably a deputy head, and perhaps a chief assistant as well, would be chiefs over a quite small tribe of Indians – but a tribe which was quick to defend its territory and assert its rights. Sometimes this led to childish demarcation disputes ('Your department shouldn't have made a programme about that – it's part of our territory'). Sometimes it led to ludicrous duplication of coverage, with two or three sets of producers and reporters turning up from different tribes to mark out their 'rights' to a story. And all the while it created an enormous army of bosses, for all the world like medieval barons raising our own armies to fight – not the enemy, but one another.

The amazing thing is that this tortured and overblown system actually produced very high-quality broadcasting, probably the best and most varied radio broadcasting in the world, and almost certainly, in Milton Shulman's memorable phrase, 'the least worst television'. I was genuinely proud to be part of the empire, even as one lowered the flags and recognized that its days were numbered. The sun might set on the once-mighty BBC, but the hope remained that out of the night might come a new dawn – a hope which may well be fulfilled under the new regime of Greg Dyke, provided there is an honest recognition of the true priorities of public service broadcasting and a determination to correct the grievous misjudgments of the Birtian years.

Personally, I was edging towards retirement by now and also, as I shall later relate, training for ordination in the Church of England. Looking back on my BBC career, I could see what had been good, but also recognized that as a manager I had done little beyond maintain a barely defensible status quo. In my day I had been, I thought, a pretty good radio producer, as attested by one or two prestigious awards that decorate my study wall, but a less than inspirational leader for the department. There were battles I had fought and lost, mostly over the rescheduling of programme slots, but more worryingly there were battles I had not fought at all.

The things I was most proud of were all either programmes or the people who had made them: *Sunday*, *Priestland's Progress*, *The Good Book*, *Good Morning Sunday*, a couple of superb series of Lent talks and a great deal of our worship output. And people: colleagues with whom I had argued, laughed, sweated blood, fought desperate corners, haggled over budgets. I was proud of fighting for, and winning, permission to broadcast an entire Billy Graham mission meeting in 1984, live and complete with the 'appeal' and even a contact phone number. Come the new millennium, the very thought of such a broadcast would give the BBC a collective heart attack.

But I was not proud of various failures of nerve, many the product of a characteristic failure to do things which would make me unpopular. Wanting to be loved can be a deadly flaw. People would sometimes say to me when I visited churches, 'What a wonderful opportunity you have to share the Christian gospel with millions of listeners and viewers.' And then I would think of the 'gospel' we too often presented, a gospel of church politics and controversy, of faith drowned by scepticism, of publicity eagerly given to people whose beliefs and opinions were deeply worrying and even distressing to ordinary Christians. Where, I asked myself, is the 'good news' in all of that?

I just hoped that in the goodness of God the saying would prove true: Great is truth, and it will prevail.

PEOPLE MATTER MORE THAN THINGS

History consists of things that happen, of course, but most profoundly it consists of people. In the beautiful story of the garden of Eden in the Bible, it is made clear that it is not enough, in this place of wonder and innocence, that the man has food, drink, colour and beauty, gold and aromatic spices to meet his needs and give him delight. He also needs human companionship. 'It is not good for the Man to be alone,' says God – and lo and behold, Woman comes on the scene.

Loneliness is a truly deadly thing. All the words we have to describe it are sad, negative ones – alone, solitary, confined, companionless, isolated. The worst punishment we can inflict short of execution is solitary confinement. It is true that all of us at times need to get away, to be with ourselves, but there is something profoundly wrong with a person who cannot stand human company and permanently prefers to be alone. A recluse is not regarded as happy or fulfilled.

So we need people. Indeed, for most of us as we look at our lives, we would have to say that people have shaped us more than events. Telling my own story, I have been reminded of how many people have had a hand in fashioning its course and making me whatever I am. They cannot be blamed for the bad things, but most of the good ones are attributable to a human influence, and often a very powerful one.

Obviously one's parents usually top the list. As I have indicated, my parents certainly did rather more than give me the particular genetic make-up that I have inherited. While not in any sense 'pious' or even especially devout, ours was a Christian and churchgoing home, and those were the standards which my brothers and I were taught from infancy. My grandparents, similarly, reinforced that parental influence, perhaps even more strongly, in some ways, because Sunday evening family hymns and prayers were a feature of life in our Welsh cottage.

However, it was our vicar in London during the early 1950s, Douglas Clark, who did most to shape my own Christian character. Because he was involved in the process by which that childhood religion became a personal and committed Christian faith, I always looked to him as a kind of 'father in God'. Possibly unconsciously, I also learnt by association an approach to Christian ministry which was to be deeply influential in my own life and, later, ministry. Those years of his incumbency at St Cuthbert's, Chitts Hill, were defining times for me and I was glad to have the opportunity, not long before he died, to tell him in a letter how much they had meant and how profound an influence he had been.

I suppose it goes without saying that one's own immediate family is always a major influence on one's life, for good or ill. Parents and grandparents are not chosen, of course, but a wife or husband is, and I can honestly say that I have never regretted the choice that Christine and I made in April 1961. By then I was 30, and for some time had felt that I would really like to be married (in a general sort of way). But it is hard to imagine before it happens what it is like to change from the single to the married state – from 'two into one', as the Bible puts it. No marriage is roses, roses all the way, and as may have been evident already I am more than aware that at times in my working life I took our marriage for granted in a culpable way. But even when I was doing so, Christine's influence was unavoidable. The saving grace was that we enjoyed doing things together, and even at the busiest and most preoccupied periods in my life, I think I can say we enjoyed each other's company.

Among other things, we both came to enjoy tremendously the little cottage we had bought in rural West Wales, a few miles outside Lampeter. It had been an ambition of mine to re-establish a Welsh connection in my life, and Christine had a deep longing for a rural experience, of which her upbringing in inner London had necessarily deprived her. The chance came with a small legacy which was my share of my mother's estate, which was just enough to buy a semi-dilapidated two-up and one-down stone cottage with a corrugated iron roof. Not exactly pretty, I suppose, but in a tiny village tucked away in the Carmarthenshire hills and right opposite an enormous chapel rising out of a sea of grey slate tombstones. Slowly, it was to be transformed into something which one could reasonably call 'cosy', and eventually even 'comfortable'.

That transformation of number one Hendy Cottages would have been impossible without the help of two particular friends, our neighbours and fellow church members Claire and Gerard Disbrey. Their children are almost exactly the same ages as ours, and of exactly the same gender: two boys, one girl. Our children spent almost as much time in the others' house as in their own. Gerard is a solicitor, and a man of great individuality, not given overmuch to anxiety about anything. In tackling Hendy he also revealed a rare skill as a plumber and carpenter. Claire, when we first knew her, was a young wife and mother (the youngest of the quartet, with myself as the senior). Like many others of her generation she later discovered an academic flair through the Open University, eventually getting a PhD in philosophy and working as a tutor for the OU and teaching A-level students as well. Christine was a nurse by training, who as the children reached school age returned to work as a school nurse and later as a health visitor and childcare officer. Her role was often to bring some down-to-earth common sense into the 'team'.

All of this would be of little more than domestic significance, hardly worth mentioning in a book of this kind, were such interfamily relationships not so important a feature of many couples' lives today. True, we don't, for the most part, any longer live in extended 'clans' and 'tribes', but we have created our own smaller ones, not based on blood relationships but on proximity, shared interests and human affection. These new 'mini-clans' are everywhere to be found, as I was later to learn in parochial ministry, and are cemented through such ties as being a god-parent or an 'honorary aunt or uncle' can provide. Nearly 40 years after those far-off Finchley days, it would probably still be true that Gerard and Claire are our closest friends, and our children also remain friends – and in some instances, god-parents to each others' children. Learning from difference and getting to know how other families 'work' seems to be an essential element in adult growth.

In my own journey of faith, no one was more influential than Donald Coggan, who became Archbishop of Canterbury in 1974. Much earlier, in the late sixties, I was his assistant on a mission in Enfield, in Hertfordshire, and learnt from him how it was possible to combine a passionate faith in God and a commitment both to the scriptures and to the gospel, without being tied to a belief in an infallible Bible. It was something I had wrestled with all through my years at *Crusade*, without really coming to a conclusion – except that I was desperately uncomfortable with an approach to the Bible which demanded that the truth of Balaam's talking ass or Jonah's survival in the whale's belly were on a par with the divinity of Jesus or the truth of the resurrection – 'abandon one', I had been warned, 'and before you know it, you've abandoned the lot'.

Donald Coggan was not a fundamentalist, nor even, in the jargon with which I was familiar, a 'conservative' evangelical, but he held passionately to the inspiration of scripture and could preach it persuasively. He was, of course, a biblical scholar of considerable distinction, who had chaired the team that had translated the New English Bible and later was to fulfil a similar role for its successor, the Revised English Bible. I felt that he provided a model I could happily follow, if only I could maintain that inner flame of 'sacred love' which marked his own spiritual life. I could certainly never hope to match his academic distinction.

I did not meet him again for several years after that, indeed until he became Archbishop of Canterbury, when I had the satisfaction of working on a television series, directed by Norman Stone, in which he set out to answer the questions 'ordinary' people raise about Christianity. The Archbishop insisted the series title should be *Simple Faith*, not because he believed faith to be 'simple', much less simplistic, but because he wanted to share his own uncomplicated, focused and personal faith with others.

Many years later, after his retirement and eventual move from Kent, I came to know him well, visiting him in the flat he shared with his wife Jean in Winchester and working on a number of literary projects together for the Bible Reading Fellowship, including his two volumes of commentaries on the Psalms for the *People's Bible Commentary* series. I believe I had by then begun to grasp something, at least, of the heart of his lifelong commitment to teaching and preaching the Bible. At any rate, when a stroke prevented him from applying the finishing touches to the second of the Psalms commentaries, I took over the task, even writing a few paragraphs where there were obvious gaps. Later, in the few months between the stroke and his death at the age of 90, he became a bit more like his old self, though still physically rather frail. He was able to check the book through, and I asked him what he thought of the bits I had written. 'To be honest, David,' he said, 'I couldn't work out which they were. They sounded just like me!' I cherish that as a compliment, just as I value enormously his personal communion set which he gave to me and which I hope to pass on one day to a younger man or woman who tries to follow, however falteringly, in the Coggan tradition.

I have never agreed with those commentators who have been inclined to dismiss his years at Lambeth as a 'caretaker' primacy, or himself as a 'lightweight' archbishop. During my time at the BBC there were three archbishops, Ramsey, Coggan and Runcie. Of Dr Ramsey's personal holiness and depth of spirituality there could never be any doubt. Dr Runcie was a complete contrast, not in the sense that he lacked spirituality, of course, but as a man. Ramsey oozed gravitas, Runcie oozed good humour. What Donald Coggan 'oozed' was a fierce commitment to the Christian faith and an unshakeable faith in the intrinsic value both of his beloved Church of England and of its ministry. All three men contributed notably to the Church's public life, but I think it is undeniable that so far as its membership were concerned it was Donald Coggan who did most to steady a distinctly rocky ship and give Anglicans fresh hope and even optimism. I suppose that was his hallmark, really – Christian optimism, which St Paul would have called 'hope'.

My own struggle to think through a positive yet credible position on the inspiration of scripture brought both heartache and joy. In the early eighties I wrote a paperback book for Hodder and Stoughton, called *But This I Can Believe*. This was aimed, as I said in the foreword, at 'troubled orthodox Christians who want to remain orthodox', but simply could not swallow a view of scripture which required it to be an infallible guide over matters of history or science. It represented my own painful pilgrimage – one trodden by many, many others, of course – from the slightly perverse security of loudly proclaiming my faith in what my reason told me was incredible into a new kind of security, which sees the Bible as a living, dynamic 'word of God', true in a sense that mere facts can never be.

The book was published in 1980 and in its own modest way created something of a storm in the evangelical camp. The reviews in the evangelical periodicals were uniformly critical, of course, while to the others it was all pretty mild, indeed cautiously conservative, stuff. I found myself blackballed in many circles, not invited to preach in a number of well-known evangelical pulpits and regarded with suspicion by many who had previously been friends. I don't know what I had expected to happen. Perhaps I had thought that my lightweight book would win universal acceptance overnight. If so, I was quickly disappointed. What proved to be of more long-term importance was that over a period of 20 years the climate has changed so dramatically that I can think of very few places anywhere, and probably none at all in the Church of England, where I would any longer be considered *persona non grata* (at any rate, on those grounds). And perhaps even more importantly, I still, after all those years, get letters from people saying that 20 or 15 years ago my little book kept them in the Christian fold when everything else seemed to be driving them out of it. Perhaps I could add that a highly critical reviewer in one of the church papers wrote to me a few years ago to say that he had come to regret deeply what he had written and the way in which it had been presented by the editor. I appreciated that enormously, and wondered whether I would have had the grace to do the same.

Alongside Donald Coggan, whose influence on me was mainly, though not by any means entirely, intellectual, I would have to place my late colleague Robert Foxcroft, whose influence was emphatically spiritual, and in a life-changing way. When I first encountered him, Robert was a chaplain to the Green Jackets and – which was why I met him – a successful producer for the British forces broadcasting service in Germany. He was keen to get into broadcasting in Britain, but I wondered if religious broadcasting was yet ready for his slightly mocking, apparently flippant approach.

Several years later, and after marrying Rosemary and fathering a trio of children, he was appointed vicar of St Peter's, Hammersmith, a well-heeled church in a well-heeled district.

Indeed, it stood in a square surrounded by the houses of the rich and famous. Robert fitted this setting perfectly – the quintessential playboy vicar. I remember Christine and I enjoying a typically convivial evening with him and his young wife in their Georgian vicarage.

Although, as I said, I had my doubts about his willingness to curb an impish – indeed, at times waspish – sense of humour, I decided to give him a chance, both at making documentaries for Radio 4 and on the occasional talks slot. At both, he proved remarkably adept. He had a splendid turn of phrase and an original approach to a subject. His idiosyncratic style, about which I had had qualms, proved a distinct broadcasting asset. I recall producing a documentary which he made about churchgoing in modern Britain, which began with a few turgid bars of the hymn 'Holy, holy, holy, Lord God Almighty' before fading to the sounds of pints being drawn and tennis balls whacked. 'Anyone for church?' his voice enquired, as though inviting listeners to choose between these rival claims on their time. He was deceptively easy to work with, entirely unflappable and supremely confident of his own ability to succeed – believe it or not, those are rare qualities in any kind of performer, broadcasters as much as the rest.

Documentaries of quality flowed from him – a brilliant one on the Christian churches and the Sikhs in Southall, a brave and intelligent one on the Freemasons, called *On the Square*, and another on the history of relations between the Church of England and the Vatican, to mark a meeting between the Pope and the Archbishop of Canterbury.

Eventually I gave him a half-time contract as a producer in religious programmes, which he somehow managed to combine with his parochial duties. At least, there were no complaints from the church end, where he was clearly a very popular vicar, with an equally popular wife and a young family. In one sense, Robert, now just 40, looked set fair in his priestly vocation and in his burgeoning career as a broadcaster.

One day, while taking a bath, he noticed what he thought was a lump in his abdomen. Rosemary persuaded him to go to the doctor, who in turn arranged for a scan at the Hammersmith hospital. Robert cycled there, which indicates that he was not feeling very ill at the time. However, the scan revealed a tumour on his liver, tests showed it was malignant, and this time he went to see a consultant oncologist. The doctor studied the pictures of Robert's inside, finally giving his verdict. 'This one shouldn't give us too much trouble.' As the patient remarked in a broadcast a year or so later, it may not have given him a lot of trouble, but it certainly gave Robert plenty.

It was hard for his friends and family to believe that here was a man with a life-threatening cancer. Indeed, as he well knew, the prognosis for any liver cancer is never very good, and the possibility of secondary flare-ups is very real. After a few months, that was exactly what happened to Robert – a hideous ulcer on his shoulder, which needed cleaning and dressing two or three times a day, a task which Rosemary insisted on doing herself, even though the district nurse could have taken it on. 'It was a way of sharing what Robert was going through', was her explanation.

Meanwhile, Robert tackled radio programme after radio programme, as though trying to squeeze a lifetime's output into a few months. What was even more astonishing was the transformation of his ministry. One of his churchwardens remarked to me that it was like a kind of second conversion. Without losing his daft sense of humour or his flair and ingenuity, Robert was suddenly also serious, profound, sensitive in a new way. His congregation began to grow, as people noticed a new depth and insight in his preaching. It was like a kind of divine twilight on his ministry, something quite wonderful and memorable happening before the night would inevitably take over.

His final series of programmes was probably the most effective piece of religious broadcasting I have ever encountered.

I asked him to undertake a series of talks for Holy Week and he chose as his title *All Stations to the Cross*. In a wonderfully adept analogy, he depicted the Christian pilgrimage as a rail journey – but whatever your destination, or the route you thought you had chosen, it would inevitably have to take you 'via the Cross'. He picked up there a feature of travel on London's notorious Northern Line tube, where trains from north to south either go 'via the Bank' or 'via the Cross' (Charing Cross). All through the talks, which were models of radio writing, he wove into the narrative bits of his own story, but completely without self-pity or self-consciousness. I produced him in the studio, where clearly the physical effort involved was telling on him, but he insisted on pressing through to the end. As we recorded the last programme, I knew that here was a classic of religious radio, broadcasts that those who heard them would never forget. And so it proved.

My conversations with Robert during the later stages of his illness were ones that I, too, will never forget. He told me once of a night when he was in hospital, and in the early hours what he called 'the horror of great darkness' came on him. He was terrified, appalled by what was happening to his body, distraught at the thought of leaving behind his wife and three young children. It was, he said, a kind of blind panic, except that it was also, in a sense, completely rational.

Then, he told me, he had a unique experience, which he said could only be described as 'the presence of God'. A voice said to him, 'Robert, you call yourself a Christian and a priest. You've preached to others. Can't you believe enough to trust me now? Whatever happens, I promise that you will never be abandoned.' He said that at once a tremendous sense of peace came over him. He supposed it was, in a religious sense, an act of submission, an acceptance of his own situation and of God's will for him. However it was to be interpreted, Robert said that never again throughout the slow course of his terminal illness did he doubt that he was in God's hands or feel abandoned. That didn't mean, of course, that he was always supernaturally calm or patient, or that he never gave vent to frustration or regrets. But in the heart of things, it felt as though he knew where he was going, or at least in whose company he was travelling. And it was that marvellous assurance that he conveyed in *All Stations to the Cross*.

I had spent a good deal of time with Robert over the last year of his illness and I like to think that we had become very close. I had also got to know and to respect Rosemary, and to see what an appalling strain all of this was on her – a young woman in her thirties – and on the children. But when the end came, I was out of reach, staying for a few days at Hendy. When a neighbour came to say that someone was on the phone from the BBC I guessed what it was.

I was back in London the next day, indeed in time to broadcast a *Thought for the Day* which I made a tribute to Robert, who was admired by many of the programme's huge audience, and by members of the *Today* team, too. And later I had the privilege, at Rosemary's invitation, of preaching at his funeral eucharist at St Peter's, which was probably the most intensely emotional service I have ever attended. The Bishop of Kensington presided, there were clergy from all denominations, and the church was absolutely packed. In fact, I began my sermon by remarking that Robert would have appreciated the turn-out: 'See, standing room only at my funeral!'

For the only time in my life I preached on a rather strange text from St Paul's second letter to Corinth: 'We bear about in our body the dying of the Lord Jesus, so that the life of Jesus may be made visible in our mortal flesh'. Its strangeness lies in the word for 'dying', which is not the usual New Testament word for 'death' – *thanatos* – but one which denotes the process of dying – *necrosis*. And that was what was so remarkable about Robert: not so much his 'death', at an early age and with so much promise unfulfilled, but his 'dying', the manner of it. It was that which had captured the imagination and moved the hearts of people – the people at St Peter's, of course, where there had been a kind of spiritual renewal going on, but far and wide, through his broadcasting. That wider response was signalled in hundreds of letters and cards, including a long and handwritten letter to Rosemary from the Prince of Wales. The words of the apostle Paul had been literally fulfilled in these events: 'So then, death is at work in us, but life is at work in you.'

The whole service was utterly memorable, including the moment at the end when his coffin was carried from the church in a cloud of incense, followed by Rosemary and the children. She had been a figure of great dignity all through the proceedings, though looking, not surprisingly, pale and strained. Over the following months I came to know her very well. I suppose I was the main link between the BBC and the family and between her and his former colleagues, who were devastated by his illness and death. I was glad that both the Corporation and the Church of England were able to be quite generous, so that when the family had to leave the vicarage they were able to move into a house Rosemary had found just a few roads away.

As things turned out, she revealed a personal skill in the broadcasting field, though one rather different from Robert's quirky flair. She worked for us first of all as the organizer of a broadcast charity auction for Children in Need, but did it so brilliantly that she was taken on first as researcher and later as producer of *Good Morning Sunday*, where she proved herself an innovative and also highly competent leader of the team.

Robert's death made a great and lasting impression on me, partly because I was so deeply involved with him and felt that at one level I was sharing the whole experience at second-hand. Another death which impressed me greatly, though I was nowhere near as intimately involved, was that of the great entertainer Roy Castle, whom I had got to know and had worked with off and on over a period of about 20 years.

I first met him when he agreed to be interviewed for *Crusade* in the late sixties. The interview took place in his dressing room at the 'Talk of the Town', at that time one of

London's top night spots, where Roy was the star of the cabaret for a season. You will gather that not all journalistic assignments for *Crusade* took place at churches, missions and religious convocations.

It was fascinating to talk to Roy Castle, who at that time was a sincere and life-long churchgoer rather than the deeply committed Christian that he was soon to become. We found we had a lot in common – we were the same age, had (at that time) the same number of children of the same sexes, and had done our National Service at the same time. We married in the same year, too, though perhaps the nurse I married contrasted somewhat with the showgirl from *The Sound of Music* who was to become Roy's lifelong partner.

Roy was a born entertainer. Indeed, he had more natural flair for it than anyone I had ever encountered. His rapport with an audience was impossible to describe. In a setting like 'Talk of the Town', where by tradition bosses wined and dined their secretaries on the sly, or visiting Scandinavian businessmen were taken for a night's all-star entertainment, many a singer or comedian has died the death, but he revelled in it. Within a few minutes he had the entire audience on his side. He simply oozed energy, good humour and warmth, his repartee with the audience demonstrating how sharp his wit was and his incredible skill at playing just about every instrument in the orchestra stunning the non-English speakers, who inevitably missed most of the verbal humour (some of it – but not unkindly – at their expense).

And humour was what it was all about. I can't remember laughing so much, and yet afterwards I couldn't remember a single 'joke'. You laughed with Roy, at the sheer silliness of things, at the fun of surprise or the ineptitude of the clown. The whole audience reverted to childhood at his hands. He was very, very funny, but from start to finish there was not the vestige of a dirty joke, a sexual innuendo or cruel ridicule. He was a man who truly 'showed his faith by his works'.

The deep – and deepening – reality of that faith was to be revealed 20 years or so later, when Roy Castle, who had never smoked, contracted lung cancer, probably through long exposure to what is called 'passive' smoking – other people's cigarettes. It was a cruel fate for a man who loved life so much and had so much to give, who with his lovely and talented family had begun to forge a distinctive and creative approach to sharing the Christian faith with people through music.

Roy refused to go quietly, which in any case wasn't his style. I remember a marvellous birthday celebration shortly before he died, at which that same bubbly humour constantly burst out, even to ridicule the cancer that was killing him. No one present could possibly forget his trumpet solos, on damaged lungs, or his moving performance of the gospel song 'Here in the grace of God I stand'.

There were other people who influenced me deeply during this period, of course, without making this kind of lasting impact on my life. Our new religious affairs correspondent Rosemary Hartill was one. She succeeded Gerry Priestland, of course, which was quite a daunting prospect in itself. Indeed, there were wide misgivings in the newsroom as to the ability of this young and journalistically unproven woman to rise to the challenge. Yet she managed it: not, wisely, by trying to be another Gerald Priestland, but by becoming the first Rosemary Hartill.

She had several advantages, not least of which was a very pleasing radio voice and an ability to charm church leaders into saying quite indiscreet things in interviews. She also had the ability to write a good script, and to get to the heart of an issue without a great deal of fuss. However, well-organized she was not, and I have many memories (or are they nightmares?) of her rushing into a studio seconds before, or even seconds after, a deadline, to empty from her capacious handbag a small mountain of unedited tapes, with some such comment as 'I've marked the bits I want with chinagraph'. I recall one occasion when a studio manager and I were feverishly trying to identify a particular clip of tape from the bowels of such a pile at the same time as Rosemary's script was bearing her relentlessly towards the point at which we should either have to play it, or let silence reign. I think we found it, or something like it, but as usual the studio session left one feeling that there must be easier ways to earn a living than this.

Perhaps Rosemary felt the same, because at the height of her broadcasting career she left London, bought a little hideaway in Northumbria, and from then on only did such broadcasting as she needed to do to keep the wolf from the door.

Probably the most enjoyable personality I encountered during my years at the BBC was John Betjeman, who was poet laureate and probably the first man in modern times to make a small fortune out of writing poetry. I had approached him with the idea of presenting a series on the radio about the words of well-known hymns and slightly to my surprise he not only agreed, but with enthusiasm. What I came to learn was that he did everything with enthusiasm, mainly because if it didn't enthuse him he simply didn't do it at all.

Two instances will exemplify this. On one visit to Broadcasting House he asked if I would show him the council chamber, which he had heard was 'rather special'. In fact, to those of us who had to sit in it for hours on end at meetings it was a pretty ordinary example of 1920s' municipal architecture, with wood panels and a rather pretentiously gubernatorial feel to it. However, John Betjeman stood rapt in the doorway for several minutes, before murmuring under his breath, 'Magnificent. Reformed Metropolitan.'

Some time later he came in to record some programmes just after completing a lecture visit to Canada – 'Some minor university somewhere', was his most precise description, I think. They had paid for him to ride on a train through the Rockies, and I said I imagined that that was very memorable.

'Not really,' he replied, head slightly to one side and with a typically half-mocking expression. 'After about an hour one rocky looks much like another rocky'.

However, mocking or not, I quickly discovered that he knew a great deal about hymns and their writers, especially those of the Victorian era. He was a particular admirer of Fanny Alexander – or 'C.F. Alexander' as the older hymn books preferred to call her. I can still remember sitting in a studio while he rhapsodized over the sheer verbal felicity of verses such as 'There is a green hill far away' and 'All things bright and beautiful'. 'Could you imagine better words than "bright and beautiful" or "wise and wonderful" to capture a child's delight in birds and animals?'

One week he produced a first edition of a book of Fanny Alexander's verses – not her hymns, which are universally known, but verses on such topics as father coming home from work or the need to be kind to the village idiot. They were utterly charming, echoes of a different era and a culture totally unlike our own. Eventually he inscribed the book and gave it to my daughter, Becky, which she has to this day.

The programmes – in the end there were 39 of them, spread over three series – were entitled *Sweet Songs of Zion*, and I would consider them some of the most satisfying I ever produced. Betjeman had a completely distinctive broadcasting style. His voice was technically unexciting, lacking in dynamic range and trapped in a slightly camp Oxbridge accent, yet it was undeniably arresting to the ear. The listener was invited to share his boyish enthusiasms and fascinations. And there was, of course, that quite wicked sense of humour, made all the more mischievous by the artless way in which the barbs were delivered.

I received a quite hurt letter from a descendant of the hymn-writer Sabine Baring-Gould (author, among other gems, of 'Onward Christian Soldiers'), refuting Betjeman's droll account of her ancestor, as a bachelor curate, lining up a selection of likely wenches from the village mill and choosing one to be his wife – and the mother of a large brood of little Baring-Goulds.

Not surprisingly, my correspondent felt that this was a slur on the family's reputation. When I put it to the poet laureate that his story was being denounced as a malicious invention, he thought for a moment, sucked his teeth and then muttered something like, 'Well, I'm sure I heard the story somewhere. And anyway, it was not malicious. Surely it was rather charming?'

Sweet Songs of Zion was a great success in terms both of audience size and appreciation. The researcher for it was my own father-in-law, Bernard Martin, who had an encyclopedic knowledge of hymns and their backgrounds, but it has to be admitted that many of the most memorable moments in the programmes were provided by Betjeman himself, who would chuckle quietly and then incorporate yet another jolly anecdote into the narrative. But there was also a serious note to his scripts. He was a genuine and sincere Christian, reared in the Anglo-Catholic tradition, and imbued with a love of liturgy and hymnology – though one would have to add, the more outlandish the ritual or the hymn, the greater its appeal.

I can remember, however, a very moving and haunting passage where he soliloquized on the work of the fathers of the Church who wrote its very earliest hymns in Greek. He evoked a picture of mists and mountains, of an era of faith constantly under threat from barbarian and Goth, and of little groups of believers gathering in the evening twilight to sing 'Hail, gladdening light, of his pure glory poured'. John Betjeman felt things deeply, even when he was joking about them, and I think that was why he was so much the 'people's poet' of his day.

I already knew his poetry quite well – indeed, I sometimes felt that I knew it better than he did, though one could never be sure that he was professing an ignorance that wasn't entirely genuine when he disclaimed all recollection of this or that line or stanza.

One of his abiding terrors, as anyone who has read his poetry will know, was of death and dying. He could make a hospital ward or the bed of a dying patient an object of sheer horror. For him, the dark abyss always seemed to lie across even the most golden of paths. He knew that this was inconsistent with his own Christian faith, but for a long while regarded it as simply part of his own psychological make-up. So I was very surprised, in between series of programmes, to get a letter from him to say that he had come across my little book *Hereafter*, which was about the Christian case for life beyond death, and had found it more helpful than anything he had encountered before on the subject. 'As you know,' he added, 'this has always been a particular problem of mine.'

I could not believe that my book had done what hours of conversations with his many priestly counsellors had failed to do. What I think had in fact happened was that his reading of it coincided with a period in his own life when a combination of advancing years and the slow onset of Parkinson's disease had made his morbid obsession into much more than a poetic affectation. He saw it now as a weakness in his own character and a denial of many of the things which he most profoundly believed. Perhaps *Hereafter* helped him along the process, but I am convinced he was already moving into a period of something like serenity.

Certainly our last occasion together was marked more by serenity than obsessive fear. It was the recording of the very last edition of *Sweet Songs of Zion*. We did it at his home in Cheyne Walk, Chelsea, with the aid of a BBC engineer and my PA, who at that time was a young woman called Maria (a Roman Catholic, needless to say) who was of decidedly pre-Raphaelite appearance. At any rate, John was entranced by her, even at one point breaking off in the middle of recording to enthuse that she 'looked like an angel, sitting there on the sofa'. At about 4 o'clock he enquired whether we would all agree that the sun was now below the yard-arm. We weren't quite sure of the significance of this question, but all agreed that it probably was. At this point Maria was sent downstairs to bring up a couple of bottles of bubbly from the fridge in the kitchen, which we then consumed with much conviviality. He later revealed that these had been flown in from France that morning.

The rest of the recording session was rather difficult, because although the alcohol seemed to help John's Parkinson's, it didn't help either the engineer in his manual dexterity nor Maria and the producer in keeping tabs on the script. Eventually it was all done, though the consequences of our indulgence required several hours in an editing suite to correct. We bade John Betjeman farewell, and I did not see him again. I was glad to hear, however, that he died in the garden of his beloved Cornish hideaway at St Enodoc's, apparently slipping into eternity while dozing peacefully in the sun. No sign there, one noticed, of the feverish terror of death as some of his poems had depicted it.

Having mentioned Maria – Maria Comerford, to be more precise – I should mention some of my other PAs. Originally they were simply called production secretaries, but as more and more was asked of them they were given the title of 'Producer's Assistant' – though not, in true BBC fashion, any extra money. In the radio set-up of those days producers and their PAs worked very closely together. Indeed, in the tensions and joys of the studio, especially on live programmes, an enormous sense of mutual trust developed, so that the personal chemistry needed to be right for the dual role to work effectively. I was fortunate to have a quite outstanding series of PAs working with me, and two of them, Sue Doggett and Sarah-Jane Elbourne, remain close friends to this day – indeed, Christine and I are godparents to Sarah's youngest, and Sue and I still work together on projects for the Bible Reading Fellowship, where she is a commissioning editor. I think those who have never experienced this kind of 'working partnership' cannot quite understand the degree of bonding which is necessary to make it work. Its downside, I suppose, could be seen in the way in which these rather intense work relationships could sometimes damage people's marriages – not an uncommon scenario in the broadcasting world, it has to be said.

Another of my PAs, Marina Avraamides, was of Greek Cypriot parentage. Her courtship by a young Englishman, a lighting engineer, was an hilarious saga, though possibly not always for Marina and certainly not for her parents. They couldn't at first see why she was so reluctant to go through the normal Cypriot process of arranged marriages, but kept on turning down a succession of highly suitable second-hand car salesmen, rag trade entrepreneurs and café owners. Finally she confided in her mother, who contrived to work the English lad, Michael, into the 'system', so that both honour and Marina's preferences were respected. All of this romantic drama – and indeed more, especially when she was wooed at long distance by a handsome but over-emotional soldier in the Greek Cypriot army – was acted out within the routine of a fairly frantic production office. It was all pretty nerve-wracking, but entertaining.

Marina was a brilliant PA, who went on to a responsible job in BBC television production until her career was overtaken by marriage (to Michael, of course) and then by motherhood. I must add that her wedding, in a Greek Orthodox church in Haringey, followed by a marvellous party in a West End hotel, was quite the most memorable I have ever attended. And all paid for by her parents, who lived in a council house in Tottenham, but had saved all their married lives in order to give their daughters just such an occasion and also what amounted to substantial dowries.

Sometimes even the briefest of encounters is capable of conveying the quality of a person's character. I remember negotiating with some difficulty an interview with George Thomas, then Speaker of the House of Commons, for the *Sunday* programme. It was finally agreed that our reporter, Ted Harrison, and I could utilize the Speaker's precious tea break to record the piece.

We duly turned up and were escorted to the very prestigious quarters of the Speaker. Tea was brought in on silver trays and served from bone china cups, of course. 'I sometimes think,' George Thomas said wistfully, 'If only my old Mam could see me now!' And it was indeed light-years away from his childhood in the South Wales valleys.

The interview went well, as they always did with the splendidly articulate member for the Rhondda, but when we got the precious tape back to the *Sunday* studio we found that there was nothing on it. It was bafflingly blank. Somewhere down the line one of us had failed to push a switch or open a volume control dial.

In desperation I rang the Speaker's office again. No, there was no question of a repeat interview. It had been difficult enough fitting that one in, and Mr Speaker Thomas would be presiding in the chamber for the rest of the afternoon before leaving for a speaking engagement in the North. Still, could our request be somehow conveyed to him? The interview had been trailed on air, and listeners would wonder why it was not being broadcast. Reluctantly, his secretary agreed to get a message to him, but held out no hope at all of a favourable response. Indeed, the implication of her tone was that we were pushing things quite unreasonably, which (in the arrogant manner of the media) we probably were.

Half an hour later the studio phone rang. It was the same secretary. Mr Speaker had agreed to do the interview again. He would arrange for the Deputy Speaker to take over for 20 minutes at exactly 6 o'clock. If we presented ourselves at the Palace of Westminster at that time, we would get our interview.

We did, feeling like a pair of naughty schoolboys outside the head's office, guilty of flagrant neglect of duty and wilful incompetence. Our embarrassment increased as we heard the shouts of the flunkeys clearing the way for the Speaker's procession. George Thomas eventually burst into the room. We grovelled. He grinned. 'Come on,' he said, 'We all make mistakes. That's what grace is all about.'

We did the interview again. It was as good as the first time. We sped back to Broadcasting House clutching the precious tape. Ted said to me in the taxi, 'Now that's what I call a real Christian.'

In any consideration of people who had a profound influence on me Bill Westwood would have to rate very near the top, but this was partly because he was part of my non-working life as well as my broadcasting one. As I have already mentioned, he came to London to be Bishop of Edmonton, and very soon picked up on a national stage a broadcasting career he had begun in East Anglia. I admired his broadcasting skills, of course, but I also came to appreciate a warmth and depth of both humanity and spirituality that some of those who worked with him, and some of his clergy, seemed to fail to detect. Beneath a sometimes brusque, and occasionally downright rude manner, there was a man who cared deeply. That was what made him such a good broadcaster, but it also made him a most unusually effective bishop, especially in the strange culture of north London, where his writ ran.

Bishop Bill's approach to the episcopal task was a distinctly proactive one. Much of his area consisted of vast estates of terraced and semi-detached houses, their occupants varying from the traditional English working class (Tottenham and much of Edmonton) to the upwardly mobile tribes of Hampstead, East Finchley and Totteridge and everything in between. It also embraced an astonishing racial mix, including the Greek and Turkish Cypriot community in Haringey, the Afro-Caribbean population of Brent, Wood Green and Camden, the relatively new Hindu and Muslim centres in Finchley and Barnet and the long-standing Jewish communities in Golders Green, Southgate and Edgware.

It was not an area that was 'natural' territory for the Church of England – in fact, there were probably as many Roman Catholics as practising Anglicans, and almost as many Greek Orthodox. There were a number of flourishing evangelical centres (Cockfosters, Muswell Hill, Barnet), but also many parishes where churchgoing, as a weekly habit, had all but died out.

Bill's approach was to be almost ferociously upbeat. Few who had been to one of his confirmation services would have forgotten the experience. He insisted that churches group together for these events, in order to ensure that there were plenty of candidates and a full church. The service would be carefully planned and then exuberantly, almost theatrically, led by the bishop. His sermons on these occasions were models of communication – funny, moving, personal, but also challenging. He believed that young people responded to a challenge rather than to a placebo.

He was equally upfront with the local media, always willing to co-operate with a photo-call or a brief comment for publication. He accepted invitations to address gatherings of almost any kind, but especially non-religious ones. His broadcasting reputation ensured a steady flow of such invitations, and he was a witty and effective after-dinner speaker, especially to groups such as Rotary, Round Table, Chambers of Commerce and professional associations. Increasingly, people in the area would refer to him as 'our' Bishop Bill.

His style and approach provoked a stream of anecdotes, most of them doubtless apocryphal. However, I was actually present on the occasion when Bill confirmed one young candidate by the wrong name, a mistake which might cause little confusion in heaven but evoked an angry protest from the boy's parents. Bill apologized profusely, but they were not going to leave it at that. Relatives had come from all over the country. Godparents who hadn't set eyes on him for a decade had dragged themselves to the service. Why should their big occasion be ruined by a bishop who couldn't even get the lad's name right? In vain did the bishop protest that all he had done was misread the writing on the little card which the candidate's vicar was holding surreptitiously behind his back, or that it all made little difference in the sight of God. It wasn't the sight of God they were worried about, but the family's reputation. In the end, somewhat reluctantly, Bill agreed to confirm the boy for a second time, on this occasion by his right name. Theology may have been flouted, but honour was apparently satisfied.

The other story concerning a confirmation was told me by Bill himself. He was taking a confirmation at a very smooth Hampstead church, the last place at which one would have feared an eruption of red-hot religion. As he laid his hands on a middle-aged woman, she began to speak aloud in tongues. Bill said he withdrew his hands in shock, and stood back as the manifestation continued, and after a minute or two ended. As he remarked to me, bishops go around laying their hands on people's heads praying for them to receive the gift of the Holy Spirit, but when something actually happens it comes as a bit of a surprise. As it happened, I met the woman later, when I interviewed her as part of the selection procedure for readers, and she related much the same story, though from a rather different perspective, of course. Though she assured me that the phenomenon took her every bit as much by surprise as it had Bishop Bill.

So far as the rank-and-file churchpeople were concerned, this was all very positive and helpful – something of his charisma rubbed off on the rest of us. Certainly during his five years at Edmonton Church statistics in the area began to pick up, but the main difference was in morale. Congregations stopped feeling irrelevant and anachronistic.

Mind you, while the laity on the whole thought that Bill was distinctly a 'good thing', I am not sure that all of the clergy would have agreed. No one could have accused him of wasting time on lengthy consultation, and undoubtedly his highly directive style of leadership deeply irritated and upset some of them. He could be particularly fierce with PCCs (Parochial Church Councils) whom he felt were dragging their feet over schemes to encourage parishes to collaborate and even close redundant buildings and churches. It was all rather heady stuff, by Church of England standards, but as an active lay member of a struggling parish I was inclined to suspend criticism and back anyone who was prepared to tackle the problems of a dying institution so positively.

In fact, I was rather more than just an 'active layman',

because from as long ago as 1958 I had been a lay reader (as they used to be called) – a licensed lay minister in the Church, with authority to preach and conduct services, except holy communion. Over the intervening years I had probably preached about a thousand sermons, the earliest in St Cuthbert's, Wood Green, then during our short time living in Holloway at Christ Church, Highbury, and latterly at St Paul's and St Luke's, Finchley, one of the 'united' pairs of parishes that Bishop Bill had helped to bring into existence. Among them were some stinkers, I am sure (I can remember, but decline to describe, one or two of them), many that were adequate and a few, by the grace of God, which actually seemed to make a difference for people.

I have always believed in preaching, even in the dark days of the seventies, when the received wisdom was that the days of the sermon were over for ever. Partly this belief sprang from personal experience. Preaching had been a means that the Holy Spirit had used to speak to me and I had seen the impact of honest, biblical, relevant and persuasive preaching on the lives of many others. In 1982 the vicar of St Paul's and St Luke's, Frank Sears, had left, and there followed an uncomfortably long interregnum. Frank had done a pioneer job in keeping things going at St Luke's, which, with an ethnically and credally diverse population, was in a very difficult area for any Christian church, but it now seemed that the future lay with an amalgamation of the two parishes. As the only reader at the time, it fell to me to organize the services and generally try to hold things together until a vicar was appointed. That was probably a full-time task on its own, but I also had the little matter of a more than full-time job at the BBC. Bishop Bill was very supportive, and after a while provided us with the help of a retired priest, Bob Parsonage, who presided at the eucharist, took baptisms and was there with advice and help whenever it was needed. Nevertheless, I found myself preaching at least once most Sundays, and also getting involved in various pastoral matters that I would rather have avoided, to be honest.

I had always felt, from the early days of my adult commitment as a Christian, that God might be calling me into the ordained ministry. It was a possibility that I put to Christine before we got engaged. I even on one occasion went to a conference for potential ordinands. But two things consistently opposed this sense of call. One was the sheer busyness of life. Without my initiative, and sometimes even without my say-so, I seemed to get drawn from one job to another. I know that sounds rather helpless, but I can only describe how it felt. Teaching, journalism, broadcasting: it would be hard to say that I had 'pursued' a career. More often, it felt as if various careers had pursued me. Weakly, perhaps, I had followed along, but at each stage I could genuinely say that it seemed the 'right' thing to do.

The second opposition force was rather more subtle. I was quite drawn to the public elements of the Christian ministry – preaching, leading worship, planning and conducting services and so on. It is not at all to my credit, but it is true that I enjoyed the performance element in it all. What held me back, and in my darker moments appalled me, was the other and even more important side of ministry, the care of people at the moment of their greatest need. To be honest, I simply could not see myself at the bedside of a dying person, or praying with a newly bereaved family, or wrestling anonymously with the problems of a collapsing marriage or a moral casualty. Yet I knew that this, more than the public face, was what true ministerial priesthood was all about.

During that two-year interregnum at Finchley I began to discover that my terror was misplaced. Indeed, my very reticence and hesitancy over it was a vital part of doing it well. Nothing is of less help in situations of that kind than the glib, articulate priest who has all the answers. In the life-changing experience of the prophet Ezekiel, I learnt to 'sit where they sat'. And I found that even if I didn't like it, I could do it, and do it in ways that people found helpful.

So one of the opposing elements was removed. The other was much more in my hands. I had a good and satisfying career at the BBC, and had no desire to move either out of it or upwards into greater responsibility. So perhaps now was the moment for the restless Spirit of God to have another go at me.

When he did, it was through Bishop Bill. I was driving him back to his home in Gower Street, in Holborn, one night after a service in Finchley. We sat in the car outside his house talking, and he asked me how I felt about work and career at the moment. I told him that I was happy professionally, but – perhaps – unfulfilled, and that I had found the past 18 months at St Paul's more satisfying that I had expected. 'Have you ever thought of ordination?' he asked. I gave him an honest answer and then said that I was entirely open to the possibility that though I had resisted for many years, if God were really calling me then this time the answer would be 'yes'.

'I think he is,' Bill said. 'I'm willing to start the process, but you'll have to submit yourself to the Church's selection procedures. That way, your sense of call will be tested, and so will my own guess that this is the right time.' I agreed, and I suppose from that moment the next, and in many ways most important, phase of my life began.

CALL ME EARLY,
CALL ME LATE

Once Bishop Bill had pointed me in the right direction, things began to happen with an apparently unstoppable momentum. In the spring of 1985 I attended an ABM conference – I think the mystic letters stood for 'Advisory Board for Ministry' – at which I and 15 other aspirants to the Church of England's ministry were put through our paces for three days. Bill Westwood had been 'translated' (what a gorgeous thought) to Peterborough a few months earlier, so the result of the conference was relayed to me by our new Bishop of Edmonton, Brian Masters, in his bachelor flat in Mayfair. I had been 'recommended for training', with the suggestion that I should do a shortened two years' study, part-time, on the non-stipendiary course at Oak Hill College, not far from our home in north London.

So far, so good. Though actually to be starting training brought home the fact that I had set myself on a course that would inevitably change the whole of life. Christine was entirely supportive. She was by now herself a licensed reader – lay minister – and was actually working on a church-planting project in what was the old 'St Luke's' area of our parish. Our hope, which we dared not push too hard, was that prompt, if not early, retirement from the BBC might coincide with the possibility of a move outside London, preferably to a rural location, and the opportunity to share in parish life together. This probably sounds, and may indeed have been, a slightly selfish ambition. Our justification would have been that a working lifetime in London surely exempts one from the duty of living out one's days in the increasingly squalid, noisy, crime-ridden and godless metropolis. We knew, of course, that it was not 'godless', in the sense that God had no more abandoned London than the Cotswolds, but that was how it was beginning to feel, and we wanted to move before many very happy memories, especially of the thriving and warm-hearted congregation at Finchley, were completely extinguished.

By now St Paul's and St Luke's had a new vicar, Peter Templeman, a man in his thirties with a wife and young family. He had come to us from St John's College, Cambridge, where he had been chaplain, and with warm endorsement from Bishop Lord Coggan. After a two-year interregnum there was a great deal of rebuilding work to do, but there was also a solid base of lay support and commitment.

Peter brought a freshness and enthusiasm that was infectious. After the gospel and his wife Anne, his great passion in life was sport, and few services passed without several references, jokes or illustrations from what was going on around the world's playing fields. He was a very good cricketer, who eventually captained the successful London diocesan clergy cricket team.

At the human level we got on very well and he supported me strongly during the time that I was in training for ministry. He was more conservative in his biblical theology than I was, and I knew that he was keen to abandon the wearing of robes for church services. However, he not only simply agreed to differ from me over such matters but delayed the abandonment of robes until Christine and I had left the parish, which was both generous and, I suppose, wise.

The issue of wearing robes or not was quite a big one at

that time among the younger evangelical clergy, especially those influenced, as Peter was, by the then Rector of St Helen's, Bishopsgate, Dick Lucas. The rationale was that robes separate 'clergy' from 'laity' in an unbiblical manner, implying that there was some intrinsic 'difference' between the presbyter (as they would have called him) and the people. That was the theory. The practical concern was that robes – 'dressing up in skirts and poncing about' was how one of them described it to me – created yet another barrier between the outsider and the worshipping life of the Church. People, they claimed, and especially men, were put off by all this 'dressing up'.

It was not a view I shared, though life in the increasingly Anglo-Catholic and, it must be said, camp clerical life of the Edmonton area under its then leadership could easily have persuaded me otherwise. However, theologically I would argue that ordination does create a 'difference', and always has, right from the time that Paul and Barnabas were 'separated' for God's work (Acts 13:2). The problem is not the 'difference' but the notion that one state of life is 'better' or superior to the other. Those who minister in holy things have donned special robes for the purpose all through the history of God's people, and apparently this persists beyond time as well – the presbyters around the throne in heaven will be wearing 'white robes'. I hope my Protestant friends won't refuse to put them on. As for people, men especially, being put off by 'dressing up', what on earth are young men doing when they don the 'robes' of their chosen football team, or when older men are delighted to wear the robes and regalia of various organizations, clubs and orders to which they belong? I am afraid the evidence is that men, especially, love 'dressing up', possibly to a fault.

In fact, ministering in recent years in churches of all kinds, I have been forced to modify my views. I still believe that the wearing of modest, simple and appropriate robes by those ministering in church is absolutely right and proper, not to glorify themselves or their office but to render themselves, as it were, anonymous in the service of Christ. But I have come to be deeply suspicious of ornate, costly and flamboyant robes, which (whatever the wearer's intention) serve to focus attention on the glory of the minister rather than on the glory of God.

At any rate, I am glad to say that this never became an issue during our remaining and very happy years at Finchley. I appreciated Peter Templeman's enormous 'people' skills and indeed modelled a great deal of my subsequent parochial ministry on his approach. For his part, he seemed to appreciate my own style of preaching, and we would often compare notes and discuss themes, outlines and approaches to preaching together. The five years that we were together at Finchley were good ones and made the eventual transition to ordained ministry much easier than it might otherwise have been.

The course at Oak Hill posed a quite different set of problems. It required a considerable commitment of time and energy – every Tuesday night, for a meal and some three hours of lectures, every fourth weekend and a summer 'residence'. Then there were the essays, projects and placements, all of them necessarily time-consuming.

And time was my biggest problem. I was now head of religious broadcasting, and responsible for the day-to-day running of radio's religious programmes, with a staff of 40 or more scattered over the country and a budget running into seven figures. It was simply not possible to abandon that responsibility, day and night, because in the end I was very often the last point of reference for a programme or budget decision, and many of them emphatically brooked no delay. My colleagues on the course, and the staff at the college, got used to the fact that phone calls tended to pursue me wherever I was, though at least the dreadful mobile phone was not in widespread use in the BBC at that stage.

My fellow students were an interesting group of men and women, mostly younger than I was – though I was not by any means the oldest – and from a variety of backgrounds and professions. There were a couple of teachers, a couple of doctors, a compositor from *The Times*, a university tutor, a farmer's wife, several younger business people and two or three who would happily have described themselves as 'housewives'. We were from a variety of church backgrounds, by no means all sharing the strictly evangelical ethos of the college, but the staff looked benignly on such eccentricities as people crossing themselves during the creed or when receiving communion, while presumably praying that the regular students would not be infected by such ritualistic practices.

Tuesday evenings were particularly demanding. I would leave Broadcasting House after work and drive straight across the northern suburbs to Southgate. My mind was usually still buzzing with the day's people, events, problems and disputes. Sometimes, to be honest, there was a major crisis looming over some issue or other – a serious complaint about one of our programmes, perhaps, or a disciplinary matter with a member of staff. It was hard to prepare oneself for an evening on the prophet Isaiah and Contemporary Spirituality in the circumstances. My only antidote was a tape which I kept in the car and which eventually wore out with use, Rutter's 'Gloria'. I found his settings of 'All things bright and beautiful' and 'For the beauty of the earth' had a kind of cleansing effect: they radiated normality, simplicity and gratitude, not qualities which sat easily with the broadcasting environment, especially at management level. At any rate, by the time I pulled into the college car park to face the truly awful student food – certainly not designed with middle-aged digestion in mind – I was in a more peaceful frame of mind. Halfway through the first lecture the issues of the day had usually slipped into the background.

The course was intellectually stimulating, to an extent which surprised me, and slowly began to shape a new mindset in all of us. Many of the students on the NSM (Non-Stipendiary Minister) course were people with a good deal of experience of preaching and leading services, often as readers. The added factor was what I would call now (in very non-Oak Hill language) 'priestly formation'. Though the college might not have used the phrase, that was exactly what the course gave us. It began to convert us from active laypeople, in other words, into ministerial priests.

The weekends were for the most part fairly relaxing, except when some of the more intense of my fellow students cajoled us into sessions of 'sharing' or what they liked to call 'ministry'. This usually involved some open expression of need and the eager proffering of laying-on of hands and prayer. Sometimes one could think of a good excuse and walk the grounds in a meditative frame of mind instead, but at times, for the sake of mutual respect, one would submit.

I remember one long Saturday afternoon in summer, when we had enjoyed two lengthy morning lectures and the air in the room where we met was hot and stale. One of our members called us to open prayer, as we sat in a wide circle. There was silence. I suspected that several others, like myself, were either fighting off a splitting headache or longing just to fall asleep. We waited for someone to lead our prayers, and eventually one of our more intense colleagues spoke up. In a tone which was heavy with prophetic insight, she said that the Lord was telling her that there was someone in the room who had a headache. I saw the shoulders of the person next to me convulse slightly and thought desperately of serious things to stave off the terrible discourtesy of laughter. I felt like saying that the Lord had told me that there was someone there who hadn't got a headache, and could they explain where they had been all day?

The course made considerable demands on the students, naturally, but it also made demands on their families, particularly on those with young children, when weekends were a vital part of parenting. For my family it was less stressful, I think, because our children were now beginning to pursue their own lives, and Christine had a demanding and responsible job of her own, as a health visitor. Philip had tried the life of a gardener, which suited his nature but not his financial needs, and had finally ended up – rather to my surprise – working in the BBC music library, where he was very happy surrounded by people who shared his passion for music-making, even if not always his particular taste in the music he fashioned.

Becky was at university, reading political science at Reading, and Adrian was at college doing business studies. Although we weren't to know it at the time, each of these decisions crucially determined the shape of their subsequent lives – Philip staying at the BBC in a variety of capacities (but always connected to music) right into the new millennium, while engaging in music-making at a professional level; Becky meeting her future husband, Phillip, at Reading, an architecture student of excellent Welsh stock, to my great delight; and Adrian getting a taste for the retail business, which was to become both his employment and his ambition.

Halfway through the course, Christine's mother died very suddenly of a heart attack, the news reaching me at Oak Hill during a residential weekend. Peggy Martin was of good Brethren provenance, in every sense of the word a strong woman, and although she had not been in robust health her death came as a shock. This was also, of course, the first death in Christine's immediate family.

Eventually the course came to an end and ordination to the diaconate loomed. I was unsure what precise difference this would make to me. I was clear that I could not possibly do more, in terms of church work, than I was already, but I sensed that turning the collar round might also involve turning around a few other things, too.

The ordination retreat offered a few days to think and pray, though it was rather odd to be separated from those closest to me at such a moment of profound change in our lives. In fact, we met at St Paul's Cathedral after the service, but along with a crowd of well-wishers from our church, of course. It was some time – to be honest, perhaps some years – before the strange dynamics of this change of life were properly absorbed into home and marriage. I have since found that this is quite a common experience, but I don't recall anybody talking about it on the course or at the retreat.

For a year I continued in a life split between the BBC, home and church – not divisively, exactly, but certainly not comfortably. I knew that my priority from now on would be Christian ministry, but couldn't yet tell in what way that would work out in practice.

However, by the time of my ordination as priest in 1988 things had become clearer. I had let the managing director know that I wished to begin my scheduled retirement earlier rather than later – he had offered me the option of an extended contract – and I had written, in consultation with Christine, to a few episcopal friends to ask whether they had anything in their dioceses which would fit the shape of this rather odd ordinand.

My ordination as priest was an occasion of personal commitment on a level I had seldom if ever known before, but the service itself was bizarre, though sadly typical of the Edmonton area in the late eighties. There were perhaps a dozen of us to be ordained, including three or four male deacons, and the service was to take place in a barn of a church of extreme Anglo-Catholic style at Chalk Farm. The Bishop of Edmonton would preside and celebrate at the eucharist.

So far, there was nothing particularly disturbing about that. Although all of the largest churches in the area were evangelical, and between them they contributed an enormous proportion of the archdeaconry income, it was quite normal for their wishes to be ignored completely on episcopal occasions. The four of us of evangelical sympathies – none of us by any means of an extreme persuasion – accepted that our ordination would take place in a positive fog of incense, ringing bells and to the strains of 'Soul of my Saviour'. We were all happy to be vested in a white stole, something which many of our evangelical forebears would have regarded as a total sell-out to Rome.

It was not, to be honest, the service, but the indefinably exotic atmosphere which pervaded the proceedings which made it oddly disturbing. In the vestry the Anglo-Catholic deacons decked themselves in their gold and lace dalmatics. These gorgeous garments would become redundant, of course, when they were priested in a year's time, but they had been purchased at heaven knows what expense for a purpose that eludes rational thought. The four evangelicals were offered – I think I could say strongly offered – the opportunity to receive the eucharistic vessels as well as the Bible at our ordinations – the *porrectio instrumentorum* of Roman usage. We declined, accepting that at this particular feast we were half-hearted participants. We similarly declined to take part in the concelebration of the elements not, in this case, I think, through any deep feeling that it was out of order, but because we couldn't see how the bread and wine would be any more validly or fruitfully consecrated if 12 people said the prayer rather than one. Not only that, but we weren't by then in a particularly co-operative frame of mind. Although people were perfectly nice to us, and Bishop Brian could not be faulted in his pastoral concern for our ministries, it was hard to avoid the feeling – perhaps unjustly – that we were taking part either in an elaborate show or, worse, a defiant protest against all that was currently changing in the Church of England, which some of us, after all, wholeheartedly endorsed.

My first celebration of communion the following Sunday at our home church was a great occasion for me, only slightly marred by the fact that at the 'Lift up your hearts' I managed to say the people's response instead of the priest's, and that my rather new and shiny stole, weighted by a radio microphone, slid slowly and unnoticed by me to a ludicrous angle during the eucharistic prayer.

An important family event followed – Becky's wedding. This took place at St Paul's in Finchley. My only role in the service was to 'give her away', but I was more nervous than if I'd been giving the address. All went well, including the reception, which took place at Oak Hill College, with the students' dining room transformed for the occasion and a jazz band led by a long-time colleague from the BBC providing the music. The only hitch to the day's proceedings was the rather late arrival of the coach bringing the groom's relatives from South Wales. When they realized that it was all going to be touch and go to make it to the church on time, the entire party changed into their wedding gear on the coach, which must have provided some eye-opening entertainment for a few drivers on the M4. In fact, we delayed the start a few minutes so that they could compose themselves and subsequently they played a great part in keeping the occasion down-to-earth, genuine and human.

We all took to Phillip. As I said in my wedding speech, he endeared himself to me by two unalterable characteristics. He is Welsh, and he is, like me – how shall I put it? Not tall. Becky fully justified the usual bridal adjective, 'radiant'. By now she had embarked on a career in publishing which was to see her become within a couple of years one of the youngest directors of a publishing company in Britain – an event duly noted in *The Bookseller*.

During the following autumn and winter the feelers I had put out began to bear fruit. George Carey, then the Bishop of Bath and Wells, suggested an interesting post at Bath Abbey. Bill Westwood, now 'Bishop William of Peterborough', also came up with some helpful suggestions, though on inspection Christine and I felt they were all either too much like the life we were about to leave in London, or so radically different that it would be hard to cope. It was Richard Harries, the Bishop of Oxford, whom I had worked with over many years on *Thought for the Day* and *Prayer for the Day*, who came up with the two ideas that seemed to fit most neatly into what I felt I had to offer and we could together cope with satisfactorily at this stage of life.

The first was a rural parish in Buckinghamshire, where the previous incumbent had been in post for nearly 50 years, maintaining a rigid Prayer Book ministry and running matters in the style of a Trollopian country parson. Although the village was lovely and, as I later discovered, there were people in the church longing for a fresh start, it didn't seem right for a novice in the parochial stakes.

The second was Ducklington, a rural village near Witney in Oxfordshire. Both of these posts would be half-time as priest in charge of the parish, and the other half as diocesan adviser on evangelism – the Decade of Evangelism was about to start. We drove down to Ducklington on a cold and grey February day, not one to show the true glories of its Cotswold stone or rushy village pond to best effect. Despite that, and despite not being able even to find the rectory, we felt very positive about the place, the church and the job, which would enable me to do something I did know something about, communicating a message, while I learned the life of a parish priest, which was completely new to me. I told Bishop Richard how I felt and he arranged for me to meet the area bishop, Anthony Russell, then the Bishop of Dorchester.

I met him (at the Public Schools Club, in Mayfair) and apparently passed muster, because there followed an invitation to meet the churchwardens at Ducklington. They, wise men both, decided that we should actually meet the whole PCC, which we did, in the farmhouse in the middle of the village where one of the wardens and his family lived – and kept, at that time, several hundred pigs. It was not quite Finchley and definitely the other side of the moon from the BBC.

A formal invitation followed and was accepted. I would be priest in charge of Ducklington and half-time bishop's officer for evangelism in the Oxford diocese. Christine and I had a lot of family matters to put in hand, of course, and for me there was the little business of completing my career as head of religious broadcasting. I discussed developments with the managing director, and it was agreed that I should retire, a few months before the 'proper' date, in time to be licensed at Ducklington before the summer holidays.

Farewells at the BBC were warm, genuine and protracted. There would be friends and colleagues whom I would miss, of course. But I cannot say that then, or at any time since, I have found myself longing to be back. For several years people in church circles would say to me, 'You must miss the excitement and buzz of life in the media', to which I always replied that I had never for one moment regretted leaving or consciously missed whatever mystique broadcasting is assumed to have. I had enjoyed being a producer. I had enjoyed the camaraderie of a creative team. I had achieved a few things, made a few programmes, that I was very glad to have tucked away in my file of good memories. I would miss the daily contact with a number of my colleagues – mostly those who had other things to talk about and other interests in life than broadcasting.

But the BBC, which it had been a privilege to serve through the seventies and eighties, and whose standards and values I could happily defend, was beginning to change in directions that I found unappealing and in some cases indefensible. I certainly suspected that the great era of religious broadcasting was over, probably for ever, sunk to the bottom of the sea of multi-cultural slogans and secular pressure.

I was delighted when Ernie Rea, who had been a friend and colleague for many years, was appointed as my successor, but I did not envy him the task of managing religious programmes through the changes that lay ahead. In short, it was probably a good time to leave, at any rate for a moral coward like me.

In my working life, as I have recounted, I have had broadly three careers: a short one in teaching, in my twenties; a slightly longer one in print journalism, in my thirties, and a third one in broadcasting, starting in the year when I became forty. Now, in the year that I reached 60, I was going to embark on a fourth 'career', if one can call it that, as a parish priest.

Whatever else my life has taught me, it has underlined the value of fresh challenges at different points in one's life. This one, as we packed up home in London and set off for rural Oxfordshire, was in many ways the most challenging, because this was completely uncharted territory for me.

In June 1989 we moved from Finchley, actually leaving our 18-year-old son Adrian alone in a five-bedroom semi to fend for himself. There is a lot of argument about when children should leave home, but less advice about how parents should do it. We were reassured by the presence a few doors away of our friends the Disbreys, and had in any case set in motion plans to sell the house and then to buy a flat for our two boys to share in London. Of course, that took time – in fact, until November – but Adrian survived and even, we suspected, rather enjoyed the experience. Most of the furniture had come with us to the rectory, so he was really rattling around a largely empty house.

Many of our friends from London, including some from the BBC, came to my induction and licensing service. Largely because of them the Norman church, with its newly restored peal of bells, was full for the occasion. I had been to many such services, of course, but never as 'the rector', and I have to record that it is a strange experience. Although no one knows you at all, they do know precisely who you are, so that unlike any other newcomer to the village you are immediately 'located', as it were.

The service, and the inevitable bun-fight afterwards in the village school, went without any hitches. My only gaffe was to ask a young girl standing among the youth group which school she went to, only to be told – very courteously – that she was well past schooldays. Judith was in fact the youth leader, by then a trained youth worker, and was later to become one of our readers – probably the youngest in the diocese.

It didn't take long to get to know the pillars of the church, partly because, like all pillars, they were always there, and partly because they all knew the way into the rectory, preferably by the back door into the kitchen. Our predecessors, Chris and Gwynneth Drummond, had only been in the parish just over three years, but in that time Chris had completely transformed the church's style, approach and worship, and as a couple they had pioneered a sort of 'open house' policy which had removed a great deal of the traditional and unhelpful deference to 'the Rector'. At any rate, it was good to feel immediately among friends, even though slowly over the next couple of years we did manage to steer most of our visitors to the front door, so that the house's nether regions became just a little more private.

Life in a village was very, very different from life in London, of course. Ducklington is only a mile or two from the market town of Witney, but cherishes its independence. Indeed, Chris Drummond had been able to use the threat that failure to implement necessary changes – have a Sunday school and a family service, for instance, and introduce modern language services – would inevitably lead to the then tiny congregation being absorbed in the Witney Team Ministry. Even the hint was enough.

Ducklington is on the river Windrush, a gentle tributary of the Thames, a village originally grouped around its ancient and beautiful church, which itself stood above a small green with a pond. The area around the church is a listed conservation area, and so it should be, with its Cotswold stone cottages and the former village school, with its little bell tower and church-style arched doors.

Of course the village had grown in recent years. During our time there the population had reached 1600. But it had never lost the 'feel' of a village community. People around would say, 'Things go well in Ducklington', and they did: the football team, the two pubs, the 'Good Companions' for the over-sixties, the village shop and post office. And, one must add, the church, which since the Drummond revolution had become a focal point of village life, with 60 or 70 weekly communicants, a thriving toddlers' service on Fridays and even (almost a miracle in a village parish) an active youth group. It was a good place to arrive and a good place to learn the 'trade' of country parson.

One elderly lady, who was then into her nineties, told me

of one of my fabled predecessors, the Reverend Mr Tristram. He was rector before, during and for a long while after the first world war. She was a girl in the village school when he arrived, and she told me how the teacher lined up the boys and girls to instruct them in the correct protocol should 'the Rector' approach them in the street. The boys, he said, should salute – and they practised doing it. The girls, he added, should curtsey. They also practised this tricky art. 'Don't forget', he said. 'There's the cane for anyone I see not treating the Rector with proper respect.'

A few days later, the rector approached her home, where she was playing outside. Dutifully, as he drew near, she offered her very best curtsey. When she went indoors, her mother confronted her. 'Did I see you a-bobbing to that parson?' The small girl admitted that she had, adding that the teacher had said she would get the cane if she didn't.

'Don't ever let me catch you bobbin' to no parson again,' her mother warned, 'or I'll give you a far worse hiding than he would.'

I asked what she did subsequently. She smiled, and said, 'When the teacher was around I bobbed, and when my mother was around, I didn't.' I wondered if Mr Tristram spotted the difference.

I took communion regularly to this lady, who had lost two brothers killed in action within a few days of each other in the last fortnight of the first world war. Seventy-two years later she could recall the details with moving clarity – the telegraph boy on his motor bike with the telegram, coming to their house near the mill in the village, and then riding up again a few days later with an identical message. I always thought of them, and of her, when we read out the names – a terrifyingly long list – from the war memorial on Remembrance Sunday.

Another elderly lady to whom I took communion regularly was Alice, one of the few remaining residents to speak in the genuine local patois. In this version of English nominative and accusative pronouns became indistinguishable, thus: ''Er 'as no idea what 'er's doin' to 'er, 'er 'asn't'. She knew the Prayer Book communion service off by heart, and threw me occasionally by getting a few words ahead, even in the prayer of consecration. Alice knew absolutely everything that was going on in the village, spending the entire day seated at a table in front of her large front window, which offered a panoramic view of anyone waiting for the bus or going to the post office. This led to another disconcerting habit, which was to break off at sundry points during a prayer to draw attention to something which had captured her eagle-eyed attention. Thus, 'We do not presume to come to this thy table, O merciful Lord (What's 'e doin' now?), Trusting in our own righteousness, ('e don't come till Tuesday) but in thy manifold and great mercies. (Now what's 'er up to, nosy baggage?) But thou art the same Lord...'

Alice was at heart a generous soul, desperately proud of her family in America, who twice during my time came over to spend time with her. What on earth they made of her disorganized cottage after their splendid Texan ranch-house I can't imagine. Sadly, she was robbed of £200 by two con men who lured her out into the garden to inspect a fictitious defect in her roof while an accomplice nipped indoors and stole whatever he could find. I'm glad to say the village charity, of which the rector was, of course, a trustee, was able to make good the loss.

Christine and I began our ministry in the parish by printing and delivering to every house a brochure, headed by a photo of the two of us, inviting people to contact us if they would like a visit, and also letting them know about the church's services and other activities. We had no idea what the response would be, though people in the church seemed to think it was a good idea. In fact, only one person responded by requesting a visit, but that had such remarkable consequences that it probably made the whole effort worthwhile.

The one respondent was a woman called Sue. She was in her fifties, handicapped by partial paralysis of her lower limbs and an ileostomy, the consequences, she told us, of an operation in an RAF hospital which went sadly wrong. She lived alone in a bungalow in a road in the village provided for her by SSAFA – the Soldiers', Sailors' and Air Force Association, a service charity. Her husband had been an RAF firefighter, who took his own life while on service in Northern Ireland.

My first visit to Sue was on my own. I was confronted by a chain-smoking and somewhat aggressive woman, who waved our leaflet at me and said, 'Can you give me one good reason why I shouldn't take my own life?' It was not a question I had ever been asked before. To the best of my recollection, I replied that such an action would be murder, but murder of herself. She seemed to think that was an interesting reply, and we then embarked on a long and convoluted discussion, which certainly included my conviction that God was the one Person who could really change her life, if she would let him. Again, she found that idea interesting. Would I say a prayer for her? Of course, I did. She explained that she had never been to church since she was a child – and that was rather an odd experience, taken to some religious group that her foster parents, who appeared to have been a middle-aged lesbian couple, belonged to. As I was taking my leave, she said that she would come to church the next Sunday.

She did, negotiating the awkward stone steps into church with the aid of two sticks. After the service, she told me that it had been 'lovely', though totally unfamiliar (it was parish communion), and that the people had been very friendly and welcoming. And yes, she would come again.

She did, regularly, and after a few weeks she called me aside to say that she had 'taken my advice'. She had asked God to change her life. I went to see her the next day and prayed with her. I was astonished at the almost instant change in her outlook. She acquired a Bible, hobbled along to our mid-week Bible study and our Friday prayer meeting, and joined the adult confirmation preparation group. In due course she was confirmed, along with half a dozen other adults, the first fruits, I liked to think, of what God was going to do in Ducklington.

However, that Easter – indeed, on Easter Day itself – Sue fell making her way to her car after church. When she finally got home, it was discovered that she had suddenly, completely and irreversibly lost the use of her legs. Those of us who had been praying for healing for her were shattered by this set-back. As St Theresa is reputed to have said, 'No wonder God has so few friends if this is how he treats them!' yet, far from undermining Sue's newfound faith, it seemed to strengthen it. She started her own mid-week Bible group, complementing several others that were now being held in different homes in the parish. She felt supported and cared for in a way she had lacked before – largely, in those early days, by Christine, it must be said – and she became a woman of prayer. It really was a most remarkable conversion, which deepened and strengthened in the face of adversity, until her death a few years after we left the parish.

Sue would sit in church in her wheelchair at the front, near the organ. One of her little tasks was to keep Norman, our octogenarian organist, alert to the arrival of the last verse of a hymn. Next to Sue, in another wheelchair, would sit Bernard, an equally remarkable person in his own way.

Bernard was a scientist of some repute, who had held down some mysterious but vital post throughout the war, eventually marrying a young woman from the WRNS who was many years his junior. They had one child, a girl, before the wife died prematurely, leaving Bernard to bring her up on his own. He clearly did this very well, because the 'girl' in question was now our reader-in-training and youth leader, Judith – herself now a mother.

When Bernard retired he had a period of serious ill-health which resulted in the amputation of both his legs. It was following this that Philip and Judith invited him to live in the cottage adjoining theirs in Ducklington, where he became amazingly self-sufficient.

Bernard was a very devout Christian of the Anglo-Catholic tradition, taught the faith by the Cowley fathers and meticulous in matters of ritual and vesture – not exactly my strong points. He was generous to my failings, however, just occasionally drawing attention to a stole or frontal of inappropriate colour or a minor saint's day overlooked.

Eventually – and now well advanced in his eighties – he collapsed and was taken into Oxford's John Radcliffe hospital. Judith phoned to say that he was very ill and not expected to survive the night. I grabbed my home communion set and a phial of oil and set off, arriving to find a patient who was, even to the untutored eye, clearly unconscious and at death's door. Knowing what Bernard would have expected, I went through what used to be known as the 'last rites' – prayer and anointing for those about to die. I then commended this Christian soul on his journey to the new Jerusalem, attended by saints and angels. That duty completed, I packed my box and went home, convinced that I had seen Bernard for the last time on earth and leaving the family to attend his bedside until the expected end.

In the morning I phoned the ward to find out what had happened, and Judith was put on the phone. To everyone's surprise, Bernard had not only lasted the night but seemed, if anything, rather better. I said that I would come in to see them, and him.

When I arrived at his bedside, I was astonished to see Bernard sitting up drinking a bowl of soup and apparently very much his old self. 'Your prayers really did the trick, Father,' said his Irish nurse admiringly. Bernard leant forward conspiratorially to ask me whether he was right in thinking that I had given him the 'last rites'. I admitted that I had, which seemed to give him an almost wicked delight. 'Apparently a bit premature,' he commented, 'but very nice all the same.' He assured me that he had been fully aware of what I was doing, and heard the prayers and felt the oil being applied. It was a further reminder of the danger of assuming that a patient who is apparently completely unconscious is entirely unreceptive to sound and touch.

Bernard was 'of riper years', as the old Prayer Book so delicately puts it. Two of the most vivid memories of pastoral ministry in Ducklington were of sad events touching much younger members of the congregation. One such quite early in our time was a rude awakening to the realities of parish ministry.

One of the young husbands in the church was a police officer. He and a colleague were called out one night to what seemed to be a minor disturbance in Wantage, a rural town about 17 miles or so away. When they got to the town square, they found it full of young people, most of them well soaked in the amber liquid, creating a lot of noise but with really not much very serious going on. As they stopped their car, a section of the crowd noticed them, and a shout went up that the 'Filth' had arrived – and suddenly they became the completely innocent victims of a vicious and unprovoked assault. Before they could summon help they were kicked, hit with missiles, knocked to the ground and generally subjected to a quite brutal mass attack. Eventually reinforcements arrived and they were rescued, and my friend, much the more seriously injured of the two, was taken by ambulance to hospital in Oxford.

At some unearthly hour of the morning the phone by the bed rang. It was his wife. She told me what had happened – could we look after their children so that she could go to see him in hospital? Of course, we could – while I was still talking to her Christine was pulling on some clothes, and within a few minutes the young woman was on her way to hospital. As quickly as I could, I followed – and was appalled to see the extent of her husband's injuries. He had broken ribs, massive bruising to his face and body and various cuts. But far worse, as we only gradually discovered, was the long-term psychological damage which this incident had done to him. He never really recovered, eventually being invalided out of the police force, which lost exactly the sort of officer most needed, a man of compassion, integrity and intelligence. As it happened, he later took up a successful career as a writer and librarian. The incident was a forceful reminder to me of the strange volatility of people (especially young people) in crowds, but also of the danger of demonizing people like police officers, as though all the normal rules of civilized behaviour can be suspended where they are concerned.

The other case was totally different – the death from a long-standing congenital heart condition of a lovely little 10-year-old girl, a pupil in the village school, and a member of a local farming family who had a long and committed relationship to the church. Her death, though both a shock and a tragedy for her family, was not unexpected, but it was the occasion of a beautiful and spontaneous response from the schoolchildren. They wrote verses and letters, they drew pictures, they put into words what Mary had meant to them. And the funeral, with the church packed out with family, friends and her immediate classmates, was lovely, gentle and inspiring. What was good was the free expression of emotion, not controlled by protocol or social acceptability but by that glorious juvenile confidence about right and wrong, which usually enables them to get things absolutely right on such occasions.

It took me back to the very first funeral I ever attended, which was of a little girl from our village school in Wales. Her classmates, including me, stood around the grave and sang a beautiful Welsh hymn to Jesus the Good Shepherd, asking him to look after her. In that setting, and through the innocent eyes of a child, there seemed to be no terror, no ugliness about death. While in later life I often approached funerals with some apprehension, from that moment I think I always knew in my heart of hearts that they were occasions of healing and good memories.

Our five years at Ducklington were astonishingly productive and hugely enjoyable, apart from the inevitable overload of two jobs, both of which could well have been full-time. I felt I needed to 'succeed' in the parish, because who was going to listen to a diocesan 'adviser' who was a failure at his church? To be frank, I knew very little about parochial ministry outside the metropolitan setting when I arrived in Oxfordshire and the learning curve needed to be steep. Villages, I learnt, were not like towns, and country towns were not like cities, and cities – most of them, it seemed – were not very much like London.

In London, it was perfectly reasonable to ask someone 'Do you belong to a church?' and they would understand what you meant. I think that simple question would have bewildered many a village resident. 'That's our church,' they would say, not meaning that they went to it, or particularly shared its beliefs, but that it was *theirs*. The notion of 'joining' or 'deciding' that you 'belonged' was largely foreign to their thinking. Almost every baby was baptized. Indeed, in my time at Ducklington the only babies I heard of who were not baptized were those of Baptist or Community Church members, and one family in our congregation – very committed Christians – who genuinely felt that baptism should be delayed to await an adult response. All the others claimed their right to baptism, and with it, however subconsciously, the right to regard the church as 'theirs'. Mission was more a matter, in a phrase of Cardinal Hume, of 'evangelizing the baptized'.

Part of that work was fulfilled in our church by the Tiny Tots' service, which we had inherited as a thriving weekly event. It happened on Friday afternoons at 2 o'clock, was led by an enthusiastic group of Christian women, mostly themselves young mothers, and aimed very clearly at the pre-school age group. It consisted of a little service, following an absolutely unchanging ritual (which the children loved and knew by heart) with a simple Bible story or talk. It lasted no more than 20 minutes and was followed by 'drinks and biscuits' for the children and the adults who had brought them – mostly their mothers, but sometimes grandparents or 'minders'. It was our staple follow-up to baptism and a wonderful way of introducing the mothers to the life and worship of the church, without the need to involve dad, who often resented any intrusion on his Sunday morning routine.

Tiny Tots was brilliant, and got even better after we started a Mothers' Union branch – something I would never in my wildest dreams have seen ourselves doing. However, it met an obvious need for something specifically Christian for women. We tried to avoid the danger of its becoming an exclusively Grandmothers' Union, which many branches seemed to be, by having a regular evening meeting for working women and young mothers, and again it seemed to meet a genuine need. Not only that, but the members were only too willing to help in practical ways in all sorts of church events, including coming along to Tiny Tots, making the drinks, serving the biscuits and chatting with the parents.

The Mothers' Union was almost entirely Christine's idea, as was the even more strategic one of a 'pastoral team'. As the congregation grew, there were more and more calls on our time. People asked us to visit them, there were church members or other parishioners in hospital, there were elderly people who couldn't get out, and dozens of other opportunities for friendly and caring contacts – but never enough time.

The pastoral team was to be the answer: a voluntary group who would work under one of three categories: 'friendly visitors', who would be expected to do little more than call on people regularly and check that they were all right; practical helpers, who could offer lifts to hospital or help with simple jobs in the home, and – fewer in number, because this required some training and supervision – those who would offer prayer, a listening ear and advice about further counselling. We were able to appoint as our 'Lay Pastoral Assistant' a young woman who was a psychology graduate and had taken a course at the Oxford Christian Institute for Counselling, and she supervised this part of the team.

It was never quite as simple or as 'organized' as this may sound, but the team, which met together regularly, in fact made an enormous difference and brought the caring ministry of the church into many of the homes in the parish. In addition, of course, the members of the team themselves felt affirmed and strengthened by the experience.

Ducklington church was, in fact, a joy. I often said to people that these years were by some distance the best of my working life. At 60, I had started a new life and I suppose something of the freshness and thrill of that communicated to the congregation. For a year or two Christine and I ran the services more or less on our own, but slowly a ministry team came into being, and by the time we left that team was strong enough to carry the church through what might otherwise have been a difficult interregnum. By then we had three readers – Christine, Judith and Dave – and an NSM curate, Bob, who had been ordained the previous year, having started his training soon after we arrived. Our Sunday evening ministry team meetings were thoroughly rewarding occasions – a meal together, a review of services and sermons, sharing of pastoral information and then prayer.

Having since seen something of the other side of rural experience, where the 'parson' is more or less left to get on with it while the laypeople turn up on Sundays (or don't, as the mood strikes them), I have come to believe that one is the future of the Church and the other is doomed to be part of its history.

Arriving early in one village where I was to lead a PCC study day, I had a few minutes to spare so I popped into the village shop for a bar of chocolate (oh, carefree days). I asked the talkative shopkeeper what the church was like in her village. Her reply came without a second's hesitation: 'Him? He's dreadful.' I felt a bit smug about that, reckoning that the same question in Ducklington would have evoked a kinder response, but then reflected that the same problem might well underscore both replies – if 'he' was 'dreadful' and I was 'nice', then in both cases the parson was the church and in terms of the future each was just as unhelpful an attitude.

The one real drawback in Ducklington was the dual ministry in which I was involved, though both the parochial and the diocesan tasks could be mutually nourishing. I certainly felt that my experience as a rural incumbent gave me some degree of credibility in the country chapters and synods, and I learnt things about church life from the diocesan job that were quite foreign to the work in our village.

The Oxford diocese is vast, both in terms of its geography – Ducklington was over 60 miles from Slough on the map and about a million miles apart culturally – but also in numbers of clergy and parishes. In the course of five years I visited over 200 churches, but that left 400 or so unvisited, though many of those would be very tiny village congregations. There was, to be honest, very little in common between the stockbroker belt around Amersham and Gerrards Cross and the multi-racial and cosmopolitan world of Reading, Slough and Bracknell, not to mention the vast new towns of Milton Keynes and Bletchley.

The diocese was – and still is – blessed with a splendid and varied team of area bishops, acting as regional deputies for the scholarly and poetic diocesan bishop. In that sense, it is a well-managed diocese with clear spiritual priorities. But in the sense of a location of church life, 'Oxford' is an awkward historical misfit, too big to feel one thing, too varied to feel a common pulse, too diffuse to have a sense of Christian community. It was a splendid diocese to work in, because it was home to so many gifted Christian people, but it was a strange base to work from, which was what I had to do.

Still, I did my best. My arrival in the diocese coincided with the start of the Decade of Evangelism, an ecumenical initiative to encourage the churches to share the Christian message with as many people as possible in the last 10 years of the second millennium. The whole idea was ridiculed in some circles from the very start – 'doomed to failure' was the verdict of Clifford Longley in *The Times* – but there are worse initiatives than to tell Christians to do precisely what Jesus had told them to do: 'make disciples', 'be my witnesses', 'preach the gospel to the whole creation'.

The problem at ground level was not 'what?' but 'how?' It was frequently alleged that the churches couldn't even agree about their basic message, but in my experience that simply wasn't true. I conducted an experiment with nearly 2,000 churchpeople in those 200 churches, but also including several groups of clergy and one of bishops, inviting them to summarize, in not more than 26 words, what they felt was the core of the Christian message. Put together and analysed, they did not vary greatly, mostly emerging somewhere along these lines: 'In his love for the world, God sent his Son Jesus to forgive sins, offer a new life and bring us into the kingdom of heaven.' Some stressed one aspect more than another, some were eager to include a reference to the Holy Spirit, some wanted more emphasis on issues of justice, some felt that the creation was too important to be omitted. But in the end the consensus was very much along those lines, and it made little difference whether the group was evangelical, catholic, free church or liberal.

It was not, in other words, the 'what' of the message that held people back, but the 'how'. How, in the modern world, where every opinion is tolerated so long as it is not proposed as the 'truth', can we proclaim a message that is fundamentally validated not by human reason but by divine revelation? And beyond that, how do we go about sharing it with a people who don't seem all that eager to hear it? Different churches had different answers to those questions, of course, and, it must be said, different expectations and different levels of success when they tried doing it.

What the critics could not seem to understand was that it was never going to be possible to evaluate the results of the Decade in terms of crude numbers. No matter how successful the churches were to be in sharing their message, and even winning people to the cause, decades of decline would continue to be reflected in church statistics well into the next millennium. The average age of congregations was so high – I often visited churches where no one in the service appeared to be below retirement age – that the ordinary processes of mortality were going to be knocking people off one end faster than any campaign for growth could add them at the other.

In fact, I am convinced that that is what has been happening, with the result that churches keep on reporting the recruitment of new members and yet the overall membership figures stubbornly refuse to rise. As a result, journalists simply don't believe us when we say that a large number of people, especially in the 25–40 age group, are coming into the churches. Why, they say, don't the figures go up? The answer, sadly, is in the churchyard and the crematorium. But, by the same natural processes, if current trends continue one would be entitled to see church growth as a positive factor of life after, say, 2010.

However, statistics were not my concern, I am glad to say. I spent my diocesan time on things such as PCC conferences, parish days, mission weeks, training courses and clergy consultations. They were all, in different ways, stimulating and some were positively eye-opening.

I recall one meeting of a PCC in Buckinghamshire where I was asked by a gentleman sitting at the back (who addressed me as 'padre', which I always find highly revealing) whether I would agree that one's religion was entirely a private matter between oneself and God? I could see both the provenance of the question and the probable consequence of my expected response.

'Yes,' I agreed, 'it is true that my faith is always at heart a private matter between God and my own conscience, partly because only God knows whether my faith is truly genuine.' He looked relieved, but I went on. 'However, it's just as well the first disciples didn't hold too rigidly to this view, or I suppose the Christian church would have died out some time in the late first century when the last apostle fell off his perch wondering whether he shouldn't have told somebody that Jesus had risen from the dead.'

In fact, most parishes and synods were prepared to accept that it was their responsibility to share the Christian message with others. The problem was not in the intention, but the execution. I have never been a great believer in special 'missions' and campaigns, especially in a parish setting – not since one such effort in Finchley, when we worked our socks off with a team from a church in Essex, including visiting every single house in a parish of 15,000 people, and ended up with fewer people in church than we had at the beginning.

What seems to 'work', in terms of growing churches, is the day-by-day shared involvement of the congregation in the life of the community, backed up by effective and well-run little 'islands' of contact – toddlers' activities, lunch clubs, men's discussion groups, healing services, bereavement support. Then, of course, the worship offered on Sundays must be such that people who venture to turn up feel welcome and involved, rather than odd and isolated. It also helps, needless to say, if that worship has a genuine air of the divine about it: not simply well-presented entertainment or polished liturgy, but the genuine touch of God.

Three times, in my short parochial experience, people have simply 'turned up' in church and sat through what must have been a totally unfamiliar service, yet felt the reality of the presence of God in such a way that they embarked on a life-changing journey of faith. We can work towards that, but only the Spirit of God, I believe, can actually bring it about.

What I did learn, on my 200 and more visits to different churches, was how to 'smell out' the quality of an empty church – or even a locked one. In the first place, one can tell a great deal from the church noticeboard – especially if there isn't one at all. A church that is interested in those who are not yet inside will want them to know what is happening, and when. Yet it is astonishing how many church notices fail to provide even this most basic information. My classic example was a church in a holiday area which proudly announced on its front gate, 'Details

213

of services in the church porch', but then kept the porch locked all day.

Equally frustrating are the churches where the monthly programme of services is so complicated that to interpret it you need a calendar, a diary and a table of sunrises and sunsets. 'Third Sunday, Evensong 6pm (Winter months, 3pm)' is an example. In any case, the whole business of 'first, second, third, fourth and fifth Sundays' is so foreign to the way ordinary people conduct their lives that it is asking to be ignored. So is the constant variation of times of services – 'Sung Eucharist 9.30am (first and third Sundays), 11am (third Sunday), Family Service 10 am (fourth Sunday)' is an invitation to confusion. In practice, it is far better to say that each church in a team will always have its Sunday morning service at a specific time, whatever the form of the service may be. At least then people who are occasional attenders know that there will be a service of some kind at the advertised time. We managed to work this system quite successfully in the rural team where I finished my parochial ministry, despite having seven churches to cover.

Once one has got past the noticeboard and into the church there are many more clues, of course, to the kind of church one is visiting. Personally I look for a clean, bright and unfussy interior, with well-kept service and hymn books – preferably not dog-eared copies of the Book of Common Prayer and Hymns Ancient and Modern – and some sign that children are welcome and involved. A few artistic efforts by the Sunday school may not please the heritage lobby, but they lift the heart of the visitor who cares about the church's future as well as its past. A well-presented bookstall is a bonus, I suppose, but a simple takeaway sheet welcoming the visitor and explaining what the church is and does, with an invitation to its various activities, is an inexpensive necessity.

With the mobility of modern society, village as well as town churches need to be on the look-out for migrants seeking a new church home. For such people first impressions are very important, and it is in these simple things that the answer usually lies.

A survey run on the back of some BBC research in 1981 showed that 60 per cent of non-churchgoers had attended church at some time in the past, and that 70 per cent of 'occasional churchgoers' were more regular attenders in the past. Indeed, even 30 per cent of those who described themselves as 'frequent churchgoers' were 'more regular in the past'.

The reasons people gave for this lapse in church attendance were fascinating. Less than 10 per cent stopped attending 'because they did not believe in Christianity any more'. In contrast, three times as many stopped attending 'because they had too much to do' and 28 per cent simply because they had 'lost the habit'. Many of those in the last-named category admitted that the change of habits coincided with moving house.

Simply in terms of church growth (and I accept that that is not the same as evangelization), if the churches could somehow stem this haemorrhage of members, reversing habits, altering people's priorities of time, church attendance would be transformed. It was a principle I tried to introduce at Ducklington, and I think we enjoyed some success. At any rate, during my six years in the parish weekly communicants rose from 70 to 120 and the church electoral roll (which we ensured was a 'live' one) from 86 to 240. Contributing to those figures were 32 adult confirmations candidates and 28 teenagers, it is true, and there was also some 'transfer growth' from other local churches and from people moving into the village. Yet it seemed that the key to it all was to make church worship and fellowship a relevant, live and important part of people's lives. That is the 'change of habit' which is really a conversion of life, and nothing less will produce lasting change in our churches.

In the end it is this 'conversion', which may be sudden but is more often a point in a journey of faith, which is the goal of evangelization. People matter more than statistics, and the Great

Commission was to share good news, not worry about how many signed up to join the club. It is always reassuring to remind ourselves that if something is true, it is true whether anyone believes it or not. The truth or otherwise of the Christian gospel, in other words, can never be decided by popular vote. There will be times when people 'crowd into the kingdom', and times when the way seems narrow with few travelling companions – oddly enough, both pictures offered by Jesus himself. It is wonderful when we can see people responding to God's good news, but the good news remains true, valid and unalterable whether or not they do.

Put like that, the Christian faith sounds an uncompromising kind of thing, and doubtless that is how some Christians feel it should be presented. However, in my experience it is that very 'totality' of faith that tends to frighten off the casual, agnostic, would-be believer. They are very wary of being drawn into something odd or fanatical. They do not want the ordinary pattern of their everyday lives turned upside down by a conquering deity. They don't want to abandon friends, hobbies, pastimes, or very probably, what they would call their 'little sins'. They are aware that there are benefits in faith. They know their need of a sense of security, direction and meaning in life, and probably long for inner peace of mind. But they gibe at the demands of the gospel. Consequently they come just so far – to the family service, to harvest festival, to the midnight eucharist at Christmas, perhaps – but hold back at the point of real commitment.

Church people can view such half-hearted adherents in one of two ways. Either they can be seen as parasites on the church body, wanting all its goodies but not paying the price for them, or as an enormous potential 'harvest field' of faith. After all, the object of Christian ministry is to draw everyone into the very heart of the Church – nothing less. The fact that some hold back, that some move only slowly towards the centre and that some also drift away from it does not alter that objective. Good ministry cherishes the grain of faith 'like a mustard seed' and the 'smoking flax' of spiritual longing. But always with the intention that the former will spring into growth and the latter will burst into flame.

But that ministry has to be carried out sensitively, and is completely invalidated if words such as 'parasites' or 'hangers-on' are employed. We are not calling people to become religious fanatics, to abandon their friends, hobbies or pastimes, provided they are, by the grace of God, prepared to turn from their sins, whether 'little' or large. We are inviting them to believe in a Saviour who can transform, not demolish, the ordinary bits and pieces of everyday life. The church of Jesus Christ does not exist to limit life, but to offer it 'in all its fullness'. That, in summary, was the position I took in my work in the diocese, and to a great extent it was the approach I employed during my five and a half years in Ducklington.

When we left in 1995, at the end of my 'contract' with the diocese, it was with both regret and relief. The regrets were obvious. This was a place and a people we had come to love. There were memories here which would remain, and many shared joys and sorrows. If I have given the impression of a kind of fantasy village, where everything was sweetness and light and the church simply grew and grew, like Topsy, then I must correct that impression. I made plenty of mistakes and had plenty of failures as well as successes. I think we tried too hard, too soon, to model a village church on a big urban one – Cotswolds folk don't take too kindly to study groups, action teams and the like. My predecessor told me that I would find it impossible to start house groups, for instance, and indeed it was a long and at times discouraging process. Yet by the time we left there were five groups, involving up to 50 people, including many of the long-term village residents. But they had to come to it in their own time and in their own way.

The other great struggle was with the church building – a beautiful Norman church with a double nave and a long, narrow chancel which (in true pre-Reformation style) kept the celebrant at the altar safely out of view of lay eyes. It was light and airy, with several lovely plain glass windows on the north side. But it could be wickedly cold in winter. The rather pathetic little overhead heaters took the chill off your top but left legs and feet to freeze in the mini-gale that howled between the huge north and south doors, distressingly sited exactly opposite each other. There were no toilets in the church, no proper vestry and nowhere even to make a cup of coffee. In other words, it was the sort of English country church that guide books and conservationists drool over, but actual, living congregations find a sore trial for most of the year.

We tried to tackle these problems one by one, driven forward by our unlikely new churchwarden, Denis, a true product of London's East End and a highly successful senior manager at Unipart in Oxford until he took early retirement. Denis hit the church like a minor whirlwind, with a 'can-do' approach which at first shocked but gradually came to impress people. It could be done, and slowly much of it was. By the time I left, the heating was improving (and is now very good), the lighting had been upgraded, the old and splintering seating had been replaced (with pews Denis had picked up cheap from a local Methodist church reordering scheme) and the walls had all been restored, cleaned and lime-washed. Then the outside drainage was tackled, to remove the constant threat of damp in the church. In five years we raised and spent over £100,000 on the church building alone, quite apart from meeting our diocesan share and maintaining the weekly ministry. I am glad to report that since we left the work has proceeded and I have even heard that toilets are now in the offing, given the approval of the dreaded Diocesan Advisory Committee.

Yet, what one remembers about a church is seldom the building, however beautiful, or the finances, however sound, but the people. A parish pilgrimage to the Holy Land, with 36 members of the congregation jetting off to Israel to 'walk where

Jesus walked' and two parish holidays in Devon, with 60 of our people the first time and almost 100 the second, were marvellous opportunities to build a genuinely Christian fellowship. Certainly on the first of the Devon holidays many barriers between old and young, traditionalists and reformers, village folk and 'incomers' were broken down. These occasions were hard work for everybody, but in terms of ministry and personal spiritual growth they were utterly invaluable.

So it was quite a wrench to leave, and yet the truth was that the job, at least in the way I had gone about it, was rapidly becoming too demanding for a man of my age working half-time. I was amused to discover, when the diocese planned a day conference for clergy in charge of 'large churches', that Ducklington was well up the list – but I was certainly the only part-time priest-in-charge on it!

However, I fully accepted the diocesan policy, which was that clergy are allocated not by congregational size but by population and pastoral need. On that basis, a part-time priest-in-charge was probably right, and one could expect a congregation of this size to produce a ministry team from within its own ranks – which, indeed, they had begun to do. Now, six years later, my NSM, Bob Edy, is the NSM priest-in-charge of the parish, supported by three readers and a lay pastoral assistant, and the church is a healthy and growing one. In many ways, this must be seen as the long-term future of the Church of England in rural areas. The tragedy would be if we simply abandoned the villages, as the Free Churches and Roman Catholics have increasingly tended to do.

When we knew we would be leaving Ducklington, I again put out 'feelers', this time about a 'house for duty'. This is an arrangement by which a priest is given rent and rate-free occupancy of a vicarage in return for an agreed number of 'duty days' a week. Usually it involves Sunday services and two days' pastoral work. Christine and I felt we had a few more years of energy for parish work, and we were not yet ready to sell our

London flat and eject the boys on to the streets, so a 'house for duty' seemed an honourable compromise. We also wanted to be within babysitting distance of Becky and Phillip, who were hoping to start a family. Would-be grandparents are allowed to hope, too, I suppose.

Mike Hill, the archdeacon of Berkshire, came up with one or two suggestions, and much the most attractive, in almost every way, was St Mark's, Cold Ash, one of five parishes (at that time) in the Hermitage Team Ministry. Cold Ash was a rather larger village than Ducklington, a mile or two from Thatcham and perhaps four miles from Becky and Phil at Shaw. We moved in during February 1995 and I was licensed to the Team in March.

So for five more years we put our roots down in a village church, but the big difference this time was being part of a team. Not long after our arrival the vicar of a neighbouring pair of parishes decided that the ordination of women was too much for him and he left to become a Roman Catholic. The response of the diocese was to add those two parishes to the Hermitage team, which now sounded like a country branch line in pre-Beeching days: Hermitage, Cold Ash, Frilsham, Hampstead Norreys, Yattendon, Compton and East Ilsley.

Our first team rector was Philip Allin, who was an extraordinarily gifted man and probably the most adept liturgical improviser I have ever encountered. He needed to be, because a serious sight defect meant that reading from a text was painfully difficult, both for him and for the congregation. But Philip overcame this handicap by sheer inventiveness. I would guess that few people realized the extent of this, because if he couldn't read the set Collect he would instantly compose one that was usually superior to the one in the book. He was also masterly with children at family services, and a preacher of rare originality and insight.

However, his many gifts did not, excusably, extend to organization skills, and his own problems with mobility made the duty rota for the team, especially in its extended form, a complicated exercise. After a couple of years he left, for a post which seemed made for him, to be pastor to the much-abused and spiritually shellshocked congregation of the 'Nine O'Clock Service' in Sheffield.

He was succeeded by a man who was in almost every way his precise opposite. John Coombs brought order out of near chaos and a high degree of liturgical propriety. While he was not, on his own admission, a man of great flair or eloquence, he knew how to release gifts in others, which is probably a more important grace in the ministry of a large team. He certainly had the vision to back a proposal to take on a team youth worker, whose contribution absolutely transformed the work with children and young people in several of the parishes and in the local comprehensive school. And he gave his enthusiastic backing to a scheme which had been discussed, but lay dormant, to build an extension, or annexe, on to the side of St Mark's Church at Cold Ash, to provide facilities for meetings, children's and youth work, meals and offices – and including, praise be to God, toilets.

It was very exciting to be involved in this process from its beginning, and to see how what seemed at first a daunting challenge helped to energize, unify and then inspire the congregation. When we began, the average Sunday attendance was probably about 50 people, and the parish just – but only just – managed to pay its contribution to the team budget. The projected cost of the extension was £130,000, towards which the PCC already had a legacy of £30,000, left by a former organist, Vicky Fisher, who had specified that it should be used to enhance the work among children. Even then, raising £100,000 within the space of two years, which was what we needed to do to avoid burdening the congregation with a long-term debt, seemed an extremely tall order.

The astonishing thing is that it was done, and without too many tears or much bullying or public pleading for help. We did invite the village community to support the project, but to be honest giving from beyond the church membership was not significant – the community was already trying to raise money to improve the village hall. But the congregation responded in exactly the way one had hoped, seeing this as a wonderful opportunity to take the church's ministry forward and to meet needs that everyone had recognized for decades but had felt powerless to tackle. Not only that, but congregations in general grew and parish giving increased all round. In May 1999 the 'Fisher Room' was opened and dedicated by the Bishop of Reading. Today, I think the people of St Mark's would question how they had ever managed without it all those years.

The five years at Cold Ash provided a transition to retirement. I was not the 'incumbent', I wasn't even on the PCC, and all those infuriating and sometimes distracting administrative questions could be shunted elsewhere. On the other hand, I took many services (probably more than I had at Ducklington, simply because there were more) and found pastoral ministry as demanding and as rewarding as ever.

Again, we saw growth in the 25–40 age group, with almost all of our confirmation candidates at Cold Ash coming from adults who were now ready to take on a commitment to the Christian faith. Again, Tiny Tots, which Christine started, was a crucial element in reaching the younger mothers. Again, I enjoyed spending time in the village school and taking assemblies.

But the things I shall remember most about Cold Ash are family ones, especially the birth of our two grandchildren, Lydia and Harry, and people – people, very often, in moments of pain, anxiety and at the threshold of death. It would be insensitive to say that I 'enjoyed' such ministry, and yet the sober truth is that nothing in my working life has given me a greater sense of worth. One of my favourite poets, Gerard Manley Hopkins, a Catholic priest, captured the feeling exactly in 'Felix Randal':

> *This seeing the sick endears them to us,*
> *us too it endears...*

Of those people, one or two stick most vividly in the memory. Elizabeth was a rather daunting lady of frail health but robust opinions, to whom I took communion each month – Prayer Book, of course, as nothing else was 'quite the same', as she put it. Eventually her chronic weakness became a critical, indeed terminal, illness, and I visited her in the Battle hospital at Reading. I sat by her bed, chatting, when she suddenly said, 'What do you think about life after death?' I began to frame a suitable reply, but she cut across my words. 'You see, year after year I've said the creed, and I always supposed that I believed it... I mean, you do, don't you? But now, well, it's not theory any longer, is it?'

That led into a wonderful, deep and honest exploration of what it meant to each of us to believe, most of all in the sense of trust, in God and Jesus Christ. She was in fact a woman of great faith, far stronger, in some ways, than I had thought, yet this conversation was a kind of working-through of things that had never been expressed – not exactly doubts, but hesitancies, holding-backs, reticences. When she finally sank back on her pillow exhausted, I could say with complete honesty that I didn't know how much that had helped her, but it had helped me a lot. She smiled, and said very softly, 'Oh, it has helped me, David, too.' Taking her funeral a week or two later was, of course, made special by the moment of shared exploration.

It reminded me of John, an irascible but loyal member of the congregation at Ducklington, who had been ill for years with a chest problem which eventually seemed to develop into cancer. He, too, was one of these 'silent majority' of Anglicans, very like Elizabeth, not given to talking much about faith, God or prayer, but devout in a dogged, disciplined kind of way. He spent his last days in the John Radcliffe hospital in Oxford, where I visited him just before he died. It was immediately obvious that something had happened, because he was – it seems a ridiculous word to use of John, but it is true – radiant.

He told me that the previous night he had been unable to

sleep, worried about his health, about his wife and children, and about his own faltering faith in the face of the final enemy. He tossed and turned in bed. Eventually, he said, a nurse came over and asked him if he was all right. She seemed to be inviting something more than the customary, 'OK, thanks', so he said that he couldn't sleep because of so many things on his mind. She sat on his bed and they began to talk, and slowly it emerged that she was a committed Christian herself, who was able and willing in the middle of the night to sit and listen, and then to share her own faith, tested, as she said, time and again on a ward where many patients were terminally ill. At last she offered to pray with him.

'David,' he said to me. 'Will you tell Marian I'm all right, really all right. At last, I actually know where I'm going.' It was a wonderful tribute to the value of simple, honest testimony, simply given. It made me pray that the day would never come when nurses no longer had time to sit down in the night and talk with a patient.

There were others at Cold Ash, in one sense, too many of them – three deaths in the village of leukaemia during our five years, one a five-year-old boy, one a 40-year-old woman and one a man in his late fifties, all of them connected with St Mark's. There was a young student, a schizophrenic, with whom I spent many hours and who died suddenly of a heart attack while in a mental hospital. There was the woman in her fifties who had never bothered about church since her teens, until she found she had an inoperable brain tumour. She asked if I would call, and that began a wonderful, moving and necessarily swift journey of faith, which culminated in a private confirmation in the bishop's chapel a few weeks before she died.

And there were the 'quiet' deaths, too, in the fullness of years and the serenity of faith. In an odd way, and perhaps because during my last year or two in the village I discovered that I had a chronic, though stable, heart condition, I felt better able to 'sit where they sat' than I would have done in the confident days of youth.

Leaving Cold Ash for retirement was quite different from my two previous 'retirements', both of which, I knew, would lead on to other things. This was genuinely the end of my 'working' life as a parson. Called late, I was glad I hadn't entirely missed the bus.

POSTSCRIPT

The end of my life as a parish priest marks the end, as a narrative, of the story, but not, I hope, of the whole play. Retirement offers to many people today space to be themselves, to do some of the things they have always wanted to do but never had the time. I have never been one to agonize about missed opportunities, and I have a very short wish-list of things I still want to do, but the space to write more, and under less pressure, to do a bit (but not too much!) broadcasting and to spend much more time with family and at home are probably the main ambitions of the evening years for me. I still enjoy preaching, I must admit, and leading worship, and in the countryside there is little likelihood of being deprived of opportunities for either.

My own personal story has been wrapped around two public activities, the media and the Church. Now, in the evening of life, and with that crystal clarity of vision given to those who are the pensioned-off veterans of the golden years which are always and permanently 20 years ago, I can sit back and reflect on my own experience of both.

That reflection leads me to the inescapable conviction that the media, and especially television, take themselves too seriously, and that the rest of us, including church leaders, collude in that. The television director Norman Stone – the man who created the award-winning play *Shadowlands* – has described television as a 'tickle medium'. It is there for fun, more than anything else, not to be regarded as the Fifth Estate or the Source of Ethical Judgment, which is how some of its practitioners like to present it.

Malcolm Muggeridge described television as a 'harlot medium', one which always and inevitably corrupts everything it touches. In the manner of prophets, he somewhat overstated the case, as he was wont to do. Yet there is more than a grain of truth there. Once the picture replaces the substance, reality becomes fleeting. Time and again, watching what purports to be a serious documentary investigation, I have had the irresistible sensation of being manipulated. I feel that what I am being fed may be true (in the sense that a lawyer could defend it in a court of law) but yet far from 'the truth' and nowhere near to being 'all the truth'. And even when it is 'true', it may not be 'right', which is often another matter altogether.

The trouble with a tickle medium that takes itself seriously is that it may in turn persuade others to take it seriously, too. I think that has happened with politics, and increasingly with the churches. Instead of holding on to what we know is true, good and honourable, we have been tempted to play the media's own game and dress it up in a guise more acceptable to them. The harsh truth is that where the Church, and especially the Church of England, is concerned, the media have two coshes ready for use. One is labelled 'too soft' and the other 'too hard'. If the Church appears to be condoning 'sin', or what the media imagine the Church has traditionally believed to be sin, then the 'too soft' cosh is brought out: 'Archwimp of Canterbury!' as a tabloid newspaper once cruelly dubbed the late Robert Runcie (and this of a man who won the Military Cross for bravery in battle). But if the Church stands firm on something which it sees as a matter of principle, but which runs contrary to transitory popular taste, then the 'too hard' cosh can be brought into action. Hence 'Church maintains tough line on gays' as a Sunday headline.

There is really only one answer, and that is to ignore what radio, television and the papers say about us, and simply get on with whatever we believe God has called us to do. Christians will make mistakes, even bishops and archbishops, but at least it is always safer to follow one's conscience than the fruitless hope of pleasing so capricious a mistress. If Jesus, Paul or Peter had taken notice of the popular opinion of their day the Christian Church would never have turned the world upside down. Indeed, it would never have survived years of abuse, persecution and ridicule. The Church in modern Britain is spared the first two of those fates, but not the third, yet that is probably the most potent weapon of destruction in our media-saturated society.

There are some phrases, for instance, which broadcasters seem incapable of pronouncing without that heavy emphasis which distances the speaker from the topic and also implies a faint whiff of the ridiculous: 'born-again' is one; 'committed Christian' is another; 'evangelical enthusiasm' is another. Any worship which departs from the decorum of public school matins three decades ago is by definition 'happy-clappy'. In these ways the impression is conveyed that any kind of committed or enthusiastic Christian faith belongs to someone quite alien to the common culture, another sort of people altogether. In the long run this is probably more damaging to the Christian cause than a full frontal assault on its beliefs. It simply marginalizes ordinary Christians, turning them into social oddities.

Possibly they are, and possibly they should be. To be seen as marginalized from a loutish, lager-soaked, materialistic and hedonistic society is hardly to be disadvantaged, and that is how much of contemporary Britain might appear. Of course, that is as unfair a portrait of our society as the one the media generally offers of the Church, but life from both the media and the Christian ghettoes can encourage such caricatures.

Certainly the days when it was assumed that any decent, respectable British person was a Christian, and when Sunday school and church were part of most people's lives, are long past, if indeed they ever truly existed. Today Christians, and probably any other people of deep commitment to a set of beliefs or code of behaviour, are oddities, and perhaps should not be ashamed of the epithet.

John Reith saw the BBC as a partner of the churches in creating a Christian civilization in Britain. Modern broadcasters would not only, and understandably, reject that view but instead see the BBC as existing to challenge or test traditional values rather than to foster them. At the same time, they would feel that it is not the role of a public service broadcaster to shape society's attitudes, but to reflect them.

Slightly reluctantly, I have come to agree with that. There is enough of the evangelist left in me to long to use every possible means to persuade people of the benefits of Christian faith, but enough of the liberal to know that to try to use public service radio and television in that way is to open a Pandora's box of horrors. The history of religion, in institutional terms, should be enough to warn us that the distinguishing line between persuasion and brainwashing is easily ignored by those who have no doubt that they know what is good for everybody else.

So I accept that the BBC, in the religious as well as the political realm, should be as neutral as is humanly possible. That does not mean, of course, that it cannot provide at times a platform for persuaders, but that it cannot align itself with their views nor silence the contrary arguments. Equally it does not mean that it should provide a platform for those who dissent from our society's fundamental moral principles. Few would wish to see the BBC providing time for anti-Semitic, racist or anarchist views. Those who wish to use a platform must not at the same time try to dismantle it.

However, while recognizing all of that, and recognizing the necessary restraints under which the BBC has to operate, I have come to alter my views about the value of specifically Christian radio and television channels (or, for that matter I suppose, Muslim, Hindu or humanist ones). Since 1998 I have been a trustee of the Trust which supports Britain's only licensed Christian radio station, Premier Radio, broadcasting to the vast potential audience of Greater London. It has taken the station several years to bed down and especially to understand what it really means to claim that it broadcasts from 'the whole of the Church to the whole of London'. But it has begun to get there and to build a viable audience, reaching nearly a quarter of a million people a week, the majority of them already church members of one kind or another. Remarkably, calls to its 'Lifeline' telephone help service run to more than a thousand a week.

I feel Premier in a small way meets a need which the BBC and the commercial broadcasters can no longer do. There are about 7 million active members of Britain's churches, spread across the Christian traditions, but their interests and priorities can only be addressed by the BBC in a fragmentary way, and barely at all by most commercial radio and television stations. As a large minority – possibly the largest single 'minority' in our society – it seems to me that they are entitled to something more than the increasingly marginalized fare offered to them by the Corporation.

I realize that the BBC still does much to reflect a Christian presence in our society (far more than any other public service broadcaster in the Western world), but I am also aware that in the modern world of multi-media choice there is no convincing reason why Christians should not also be served by one or two dedicated broadcasting channels. They will never be able to match the size of audience which *Songs of Praise* can reach – one of the largest audiences for a Christian programme anywhere in the world – but they will be able to offer a rather more challenging style of worship than the daily service and a rather less querulous and confrontatory style of religious news coverage than *Sunday* on Radio 4.

There are people, including some at the BBC, who would argue that there is no longer any justification for specifically 'religious' broadcasting on publicly funded radio and television.

Indeed, some would say it should be left to the exclusively religious channels, as happens in the United States, where virtually no religious broadcasting at all is originated by the major networks. But while so many people in this allegedly secular society continue to practise their religious beliefs, it would seem to be the duty of responsible public service broadcasters to reflect that. Religious ideas and issues are still of great and wide interest to people, including many who are not conventionally 'religious', and vast numbers of people continue to pray, even if they choose to do it at home or in the caravan rather than in church. It would seem that current BBC thinking is also along these lines, and so were the policies argued by Ernie Rea, my successor as head of religious broadcasting, a post which is to be identified by the mysterious title of 'Head of Religion and Ethics' and without either a 'department' to lead or a budget with which to make programmes. In the developing marketing climate at the BBC, and with the present stress on the multi-cultural nature of our society, Ernie's was always going to be a difficult role – one I was glad to be spared, to be honest. Settling for a policy of keeping religion, God – and, I suppose, ethics – somewhere in the output seemed a reasonable enough policy, but early in 2001 he resigned, leaving the case to be argued by someone else. In the current BBC climate, no one could blame him.

I have always regarded the *Today* programme's *Thought for the Day*, to which I have contributed off and on for over 30 years, as a valuable means of 'keeping the rumour of God alive', in Robert Foxcroft's phrase. I take courage from the fact that it has survived some withering criticism down the years, mainly because the audience, by and large, actually wants it to be there.

Over the years *Thought for the Day* has changed radically, of course, from the reassuring religious certainties of *Lift Up Your Hearts* to the slightly strained news-based topicality of today. In many ways that change epitomizes the general change in approach to religious broadcasting during my adult lifetime. It is no longer there as a public duty or out of a sense of mission, but must justify itself in purely broadcasting terms. Few, I imagine, would seriously expect to see it otherwise.

I remember researching the 1930 Sunday radio schedules for an article I was writing marking the BBC's fiftieth anniversary. The 'National Service', which was the core provision for all the regional radio services at that time, offered nothing on Sundays but classical music, religious services and 'serious talks', until a blessed respite at 8.30pm, when *Palm Court* tempted the sabbath audience with dance music from Max Jaffa and his orchestra.

The late Lord Soper once related to me how he was engaged in the thirties to present a half-hour programme of hymn-singing with children at 5.30pm on Sundays. This should have given him plenty of time to jump in a cab and nip across to Kingsway to take the evening service at his West London Mission. In fact, in the nature of classical concerts and 'serious talks', they regularly overran, so that he would be sitting at the studio piano surrounded by anxious children waiting desperately for the red light that always came late. Apparently the church officers got quite used to the fact that he would arrive hot and breathless at the Mission and about 15 minutes behind schedule.

The stipulated radio diet for Sundays faithfully reflected John Reith's view of the BBC as an instrument of social improvement. Whether people liked it or not, they were going to be educated and civilized. Just occasionally, and usually incidentally, they might be entertained as well, but one never felt that was very high on the director general's priorities. It was a brave experiment in social engineering (or cultural brainwashing, according to one's point of view), but like all such it was doomed to failure in the end.

The story was told of the time when the BBC Symphony Orchestra was playing its way through the entire works of Mozart on Sunday afternoons. One of the violinists arrived at Charing Cross station and hailed a taxi to take him to St George's Hall, next to Broadcasting House, the venue for the concerts. As he got in the cab the driver asked in an apparently appreciative tone whether he were a member of the BBC orchestra. The musician smiled modestly and admitted that he was. That's the orchestra, the cabbie enquired further, that is currently working its way through the music of Mozart? Yes indeed, he was assured. The driver switched off his engine, got out of the cab and opened the passenger door. 'In that case,' he said, 'you can bloody well walk.'

It was not surprising that very early in the war it was decided that this Reithian diet was too sombre to sustain the morale of our fighting men, and so the 'Forces Programme', forerunner of the Light Programme and then Radio 2, came into being. Suddenly the Christian sabbath was lit up by sundry brilliant comedy series, enjoyed not just by the men and women of the Forces but by just about everybody else as well. There was *Happidrome*, *Much Binding in the Marsh* and, most popular of all, *ITMA – It's That Man Again*. The last-named still probably retains the record for the largest radio audience in the BBC's history, over 33 million people tuning in to its half-hour of corny slapstick and endless catch-phrases, presided over by Tommy Handley. That is the sort of audience a modern television channel controller would kill for, and only a royal wedding, coronation or the funeral of Princess Diana has ever been able to equal it. The entire works of Mozart, no matter how exquisitely performed, had no chance in competition with that.

The contrast between the broadcasting ethos of the thirties and that of the last couple of decades could not be more marked, yet this transformation has all happened within the lifetime I have been relating in this book. Go back a dozen years earlier still, to the generation now in their eighties, and you have many, many people who were born before the first radio broadcast was even made, in 1922. It has not felt like a revolution, mainly because human beings are communicating animals and this was at one level simply another advance in the skills of communication. Yet a revolution is what it has been, and it has turned our lives and our society inside out.

In fact the whole communications world is currently in turmoil. It is as though everything which has long been familiar has been thrown up into the air and the bits haven't come down yet. I think it is true to say that while there are many who will confidently tell you what is going to happen, the wise ones among them don't put money on it.

The fragmentation – ghettoization, even – of broadcasting is likely to produce a complex mix of 'narrow-casting', with every conceivable interest, fetish, preference and whim catered for, always provided customers can find it in the jungle of sites and options.

On the other hand (and just as likely) people may revolt against this Anoraks' Charter, demanding instead a return to high-quality television and radio on recognizable and accessible channels, offering programmes you can discuss at work the next day: 'Back to the Future', one might say.

When the BBC began its radio broadcasts the *Methodist Recorder*, in a doom-laden editorial, saw this as the end of Christian civilization as we knew it. Eventually no one would go to church, but simply stay at home to listen to the 'wireless'. Manners would be eroded and behaviour undermined.

Oddly enough, in many ways the paper was absolutely right. As broadcasting audiences have risen, church attendance has fallen – the graphs match almost perfectly. 'Manners' have been eroded and behaviour undermined. We have moved from an era when BBC producer guidelines specifically ruled out jokes about women's underwear to one when no comedy programme is complete without jokes about their private parts. Until relatively recently 'bloody' and 'my God' were banned on air. Now blasphemous language is two-a-penny and the once-excluded 'f' word occurs scores of times a day.

However, the change is much more significant than a mere matter of vocabulary. We live in an age of open debate, of 'rights', of extreme sensitivity over gender and no reticence at all over sex. Compared with the thirties, or even the immediate post-war period, personal privacy counts for little. No one, rich or poor, famous or obscure, is immune from the searchlight of media scrutiny.

In many ways this is a less hypocritical and repressive society, but it can also be a good deal less gentle. Crudity of language on the media seems to have been matched by crudity of behaviour on the streets. Only by the most simplistic logic could the latter be seen as a direct product of the former, but it is hard to resist the conclusion that both have their roots in a cavalier indifference to the feelings and sensitivities of others.

From this it might be deduced that I am not all that enamoured of some of the cultural changes that have so profoundly altered society during my lifetime – indeed, that I share the views of the editor of the *Methodist Recorder* 80 years ago. On the contrary, I would not wish to put the clock back even to the 1950s, let alone the days of my childhood. What is sad is that it seems to be impossible to have the more open, tolerant and honest approach of today without the violence of language, crudity of behaviour and constant rubbishing of serious religious belief which marks so much of contemporary society and especially the media. I suspect that most of the population don't actually want it, any more than they want football thuggery or drunken fighting on the streets, but this is the age of the overwhelming minority and most of us feel powerless to alter things.

The enormous transformation of the media in my lifetime reflects not only the technological advances which have added television, satellite, cable, digital and the internet to the basic medium of radio, but also the struggle to adapt our communication processes to a rapidly changing society.

The broadcasting world, for instance, has been transformed from one dominated by establishment values and paternalistic attitudes to one which is audience driven. The determining factor in programme decisions today is what listeners and viewers want, not what is 'good for them'. To an extent that the first governors of the BBC could never have imagined, broadcasting is now almost entirely a commercial enterprise, even for those who are working in the publicly funded sector. After all, they too are aware of the fate that awaits them if they fail to deliver whatever is deemed to be a 'viable' audience – what is known in some circles as the 'ABC' effect, after the disastrous experience of the Australian Broadcasting Corporation in the eighties, when the Australian government came close to shutting it down because its audiences had shrunk to unacceptably low levels.

Behind this lie the changing patterns and pressures of the modern world. It is no longer possible in Britain to speak of a 'national culture' or even a universally shared set of values. We are a multi-credal, multi-ethnic and multi-racial society, with not a great deal in common, to be frank, between the values and lifestyle of the large Islamic minority and the equally large minority of sexually promiscuous, heavy-drinking, pleasure-bent twenty-somethings. Somehow or other, and rather to our credit, we manage to live together. There is probably still a large minority, possibly even a numerical majority, of people who would subscribe to what might loosely be termed 'Christian values', which could be taken to include a degree of tolerance of others, respect for law and other people's property and honesty in interpersonal dealings. It is that core of what some religious broadcasters like to call 'people of goodwill' which makes Britain still a tolerable place to live in, and to which the Christian churches are increasingly looking for their natural support.

In fact, the churches too have gone through a revolution of their own in my lifetime. To compare the church in which I was a choirboy just before the war, or the church in Darowen in mid-Wales in the forties, with the church in which I minister today is to see the extent of that revolution. True, as in any revolution, there are pockets of resistance, areas where there is still 'mopping up' to be done, but for the most part Christians have accepted that if the faith is to have any relevance to today's society, or the Church's message any genuine appeal, then a quantum shift of thinking is required.

We no longer live in a society where it is enough to add 'the Bible says' to what we say to give it mandatory authority. This is not an age without religion, but an age that likes to make its own spirituality, and inevitably that affects both religious broadcasters and churches. The problem for the churches, however, is that they are bound to a set of propositions, whether they like it or not. I mean, Christ died for our sins or he didn't, Christ is risen from the dead or he isn't. We are not free to rewrite the faith simply to make it more acceptable to an agnostic generation, mainly because if we do there will soon be no faith left to rewrite.

In fact, most of the changes which have transformed church life in the last two decades have not concerned the faith itself but the way the Church presents itself. There have been many important developments, including probably the most dramatic change in English Christianity since the Reformation, the ordination of women as priests in the Church of England. But I think the biggest change has simply been in the way church 'feels'.

In the sixties, Britain began to change radically. These were the so-called 'swinging sixties', when many younger people felt freed from emotional inhibitions. It became not just acceptable but even praiseworthy to get excited about soccer, sex and showbiz. The restrained English handshake – the only way my parents would have dreamt of greeting a friend – was rapidly giving way to the continental kiss. Football players could be seen on television week after week hugging and kissing each other after a goal had been scored. In less exotic circles – offices, schools, factories – the same process was under way. At the BBC it was becoming normal to address colleagues, even senior ones, by their Christian names instead of by the ludicrous acronyms which had prevailed since the thirties – 'Could I speak to HCAMP, please? Yes, this is HRP(R).'

The Church of England was rather slower to get there, but eventually that cool Anglican reserve and ecclesiastical formality began to melt away. The liturgical renewal movement made common cause with the fast-growing charismatic renewal to change the face of Anglican – and Roman Catholic – worship. While both of these movements would claim to have their roots in theology, they were also reflecting profound social changes in Britain. There was a widespread desire for less formality and restraint, for more warmth, emotion – and even passion. People began to clap in church on suitable occasions – welcoming a new bishop or vicar, for instance, or visiting guests. And then came the Peace.

When the first experimental revised services came into the Church of England in 1966 they introduced, or rather reintroduced, the liturgical 'kiss of peace'. No less than five times in the New Testament Christians are commanded to 'greet one another with a holy kiss' or 'with the kiss of love'. This seems to have been part of the normal ritual of 'gathering', if one can describe it in those terms. It was now to be restored, both in the Roman and the Anglican liturgies, to an honoured place in the eucharist, but there is no doubt some Anglican congregations found all this a step too far in the direction of warmth and friendliness.

The service books simply set out the formula: 'The peace of the Lord be with you', 'And also with you', adding that 'all may exchange a sign of peace'. This was generally interpreted, with true Anglican reserve, as a straightforward handshake. But in the prevailing climate, this was not enough for some members of congregations, who set out on a minor orgy of hugging and kissing in a most un-English way. At the same time, others declined to get involved at all, standing rigidly with their hands folded beneath their arms or even, as one man in our last church did, resorting to kneeling in prayer to avoid the hands outstretched in greeting.

However, for most churchgoers it has been a very welcome innovation – indeed, no longer an innovation for younger people, for whom it has been a normal part of Christian worship all their lives. It helps to emphasize that worship is an expression of unity and fellowship as well as beauty and dignity, and that this is as true when it takes place in a national shrine like Westminster Abbey as when it happens in a charismatic house group.

When I conducted a survey with the youth fellowship at Ducklington on their feelings about Sunday services they marked the Peace as their favourite item and the notices as the second. This may not be quite as quirky a response as it sounds. What the Peace and the notices have in common is that they are the ordinary stuff of life – greeting friends and catching up with the news are uniquely human activities. We are perhaps most Godlike when we are being most truly human, being 'made in his image'.

I have greatly appreciated the changes in patterns and style of worship and now feel distinctly deprived if I find myself in a church which has ignored them and stuck to the 'old' ways. Brought up on the Book of Common Prayer – indeed, its communion service is still the only one I can conduct without reference to a book – I now find its repetitive language, elaborate Tudor sentence structure and sin-soaked theology quite oppressive. I am more than willing to take Prayer Book services for the shrinking minority of older churchgoers who were raised on them, and to do them as well as I can, but I can't bring myself actually to enjoy them.

Although conservative – I should prefer to say 'orthodox' – in my theology, I have never found serious difficulty in accepting changes of this kind. Christine and I sat emotionally drained as we watched the closing stages of the vote on the ordination of women on television. It was a cause I had come to believe in passionately, not on the for me spurious grounds of 'feminine rights', but on the fundamental nature of the Church. If the whole Church, male and female, is the Body of Christ, as the

Bible teaches, and if (in St Paul's memorable words) 'there is neither male nor female, but all are one in Christ Jesus', then such distinctions of gender in Christian ministry are contradictions of a profound truth of the gospel. All human beings, male and female, are 'made in the image of God', as Genesis tells us, and all Christian believers, male and female, are part of the Body of Christ, what the New Testament calls the 'royal priesthood'. Consequently, it seems to me, a woman may 'represent' God or Christ to the people, and the people to Christ and God, as fully and effectively as a man. That, for me, is both the heart of ministerial priesthood and the core argument for admitting women to its ranks.

This would provoke some of my evangelical friends to take a different line of objection. In the divine order of things, they would argue, a man was to be the 'head' of the woman, and never vice versa. It is a case painfully worked out in the first epistle to Timothy, using an argument based on the stories in Genesis of the creation of woman and the role of Eve in the downfall of Adam in the garden of Eden. I do not profess to follow the writer's argument, which may well have related to domestic relationships in the first century, or to a specific situation in the church at that time. What I do know is that it is simply not possible to draw a general and for-all-time conclusion from it about female leadership of men.

'I do not permit a woman… to have authority over a man', says the epistle. But God himself not only permitted a woman to have authority over men, he actually called and commanded her to do it. I refer to Deborah, judge over Israel by divine authority, as one can read in Judges 4. A few words banning women teachers (in a letter which also refers to women deacons, incidentally) seem a poor basis for the permanent exclusion of women from the leadership and ministry of the Church.

As will be clear, I am happier about the changes that have served to transform the modern Church than about those which have transformed the modern media, though in the latter case, too, there have been many positive gains. Change doesn't suddenly stop, of course, and learning to live with change is no more than a part of being alive. Living things adapt; dead things wither. In a diocesan study 12 years ago it was established that 'good management of change' was one of 10 factors marking genuinely growing churches. Conversely, bad management of change, where the issue is either funked or driven through with a ruthless disregard for people's feelings, has helped to empty churches up and down the land.

Managing change in one's own life is also a challenge. I recall one senior bishop confessing to me that he had made a 'bad retirement', and it was a phrase that stuck with me. For myself, despite two previous opportunities to practise this kind of transition – leaving the BBC, and leaving stipendiary ministry – I approached what might be called the 'real thing' with some apprehension.

For 40 years I had been 'somebody' – the editor, the producer, the head of department, the vicar. It seemed a bit of a come-down suddenly to become 'nobody' – just another retired pensioner. I couldn't help thinking of all those anonymous headlines: 'Pensioner mugged'; 'OAP robbed in her home'. I found it quite a challenge to put myself into that category. A working lifetime of being recognized and respected had ill-prepared me for the loss of status that accompanies the loss of role.

All of this revealed a side of my character which surprised and slightly depressed me, because I would have said that I had never cared about titles and status. But clearly they had meant much more to me than I had been prepared to admit. Just facing that fact was in the end a positive experience. After all, I was not any longer the editor, the producer, the boss or the vicar, but just another man of 70, a husband, father, grandfather, friend and, in God's sight, to put it in starkly biblical terms, a 'sinner saved by grace' – nothing else, and nothing more.

I had been on retirement courses (actually, two of them)

and at one level was looking forward to being free of the more irksome responsibilities of parish work, tied to the phone, to service rotas, to funerals and baptisms and weddings – and to the ever-changing needs, anxieties and fears of my parishioners. Such demands could at times be tiresome, and I cannot say that I never muttered imprecations under my breath when these demands conflicted with some anticipated leisure pursuit. But it was the feeling of being useful that gave the ministry its particular appeal to me. However ineptly or even reluctantly, I was doing something, and that something was appreciated. The by-product of this for me was, quite simply, value – being valued, and valuing myself.

Now that was to come to an end and I must admit I couldn't quite see what was to replace it. There are rewards from the world of work that have nothing whatever to do with monetary payment, things that I don't recall retirement courses talking about: meaning, respect, goals, status. I knew that it would be good to have time to do other things, but I am not a great hobby person. What would those 'things' be?

In the event, my fears were largely dispelled. It was deeply satisfying to own our own house again and plan its decoration and improvements. It was good to have time to be together and to do things Christine and I had always promised ourselves we would do 'one day'. This was the day. And, as it happened, other things I had been involved with over the previous few years expanded to fill the available 'spare' time that had now become available.

Probably the biggest of these new involvements was with the Bible Reading Fellowship, which had moved to Oxford from London about 10 years earlier. I had been a contributor to its *New Daylight* daily Bible notes for some years, but suddenly a tragic event catapulted me into a more central role.

The editor of *New Daylight* was Shelagh Brown, a woman priest whom I had known for a few years and who had enlisted me as one of her writers. Although she was well into her sixties,

Shelagh was a person of enormous energy, so that one thought of her as permanently no more than youngish middle-aged. She hustled and bustled her way through an enormous workload, with an almost total disregard for organization, records or delivery dates, but also the kind of charisma that earns forgiveness, or at least amused tolerance, of such idiosyncracies.

In the August of 1997 Christine and I had just arrived at a *gîte* in Brittany which we were to share with Becky and her family, although they wouldn't be arriving until our second week. The phone rang, which was a surprise, as I didn't think we had given anyone the number. It was Becky, with the shocking news that Shelagh Brown was dead – killed falling down the stairs of her cottage in Wolvercote while hurrying to open the door to some guests.

It was a devastating shock at the personal level – Shelagh had been to tea at our vicarage a few days earlier in that week – and I knew it would also be a terrible blow to BRF. She would have had several books on the go, both as author and commissioning editor, and the relentless process of publishing daily Bible reading notes left no room for gaps in the production schedules.

By the time I had got home from holiday things had moved on, and I found myself taking over Shelagh's role as editor of *New Daylight*, as temporary relief at first, but then more permanently. To no one's surprise, things were in a fairly catastrophic state in her office – letters were coming to light six months later – but I did my best to read her mind and to second-guess what she had probably asked people to do. A few dozen phone calls got things more or less back on track and it was then possible to bring a rather less frantic style of editorship into being.

I knew that I could never match her own particular flair, nor sweet-talk contributors into writing 'just a few days' notes – by tomorrow afternoon?' as she frequently did. But I tried to continue to work on the same editorial principles, which I had always enthusiastically endorsed, and which had rescued BRF notes from the verge of extinction to an enormous and growing popularity. Those principles involved a respect for the scriptures, but not a slavish neo-fundamentalism of interpretation, and a readiness to come to them with what Shelagh liked to call 'heart and mind', taking context and background seriously, but also trying to apply the word of God in a dynamic way to the issues of everyday life. At the time I took over *New Daylight* it had over 85,000 readers each day, and with the other series of BRF notes the total readership was well over 100,000.

As I soon came to realize, that is a lot of people to satisfy! It is some kind of tribute to our very varied band of writers – right across the denominational spectrum and embracing a wide variety of approaches to scripture within our published principles – that most *New Daylight* readers are both loyal and enthusiastic. Shelagh was missed, at a personal as well as professional level, but I felt she would have been pleased to see the work go ahead very much as she had envisaged it.

Her funeral was a marvellous occasion. Her will had omitted, in typical fashion, many of the details which would have made life easier for her executors, but it did specify that there was to be champagne at her funeral, and that it should be Lanson 'Black Label'. It was a lovely touch, perfectly complementing the stories about her with which the occasion was replete.

I think my favourite was told by Bishop Gavin Reid in his address. Apparently not long after her ordination to the priesthood Shelagh was invited to celebrate the eucharist at some grand occasion in Southwark Cathedral. When she made her way to the high altar, she was confronted, in true cathedral style, with rows and rows of gleaming silverware, some apparently to convey wine and some to convey the wafers – though it was not immediately apparent which was which. A server appeared at her elbow, handing her a silver box containing a large number of wafers. She opened what looked like a capacious ciborium on the altar, and with something of a flourish emptied them into it – and then watched in horror as they floated soggily to the surface of a chalice full of wine.

This would have been enough to finish off a lesser spirit, but Shelagh, quite undaunted, seized the chalice, carried it as though in measured procession to the side of the sanctuary and handed it, with a gracious little bow, to a surprised verger. She then returned to the altar and resumed operations, simply requesting the server for 'more wafers, please'.

Editing *New Daylight* was a very satisfying responsibility, but I thought it wise to establish a time limit to my involvement – 'Until the end of 2000,' I told chief executive Richard Fisher. I wanted to ease myself into retirement, but as so many people find, promises came home to roost – especially books I had promised to write or weekends and retreats I had promised to lead. For a little while it almost felt as though the daily routine of parish life would be less demanding. However, as it was my fault that the problem arose, so it was within my competence to solve it, even if that meant postponing some activities and abandoning others.

Ever since my first little effort back in the early sixties, I suppose I have always had a book on the go. There is something peculiarly satisfying about writing, at least at the ideas level, but like most authors I am not enamoured of the actual physical business of transferring the ideas to the computer screen, disk and then paper. I find that I can manage about a thousand words at a time quite comfortably, but more than that begins to feel like a chore. In any case, advancing years and fading eyesight mean that screens send my eyes dancing in all directions after an hour or two.

But nothing – nothing in the work context, at least – can quite equal seeing the finished product in your hands. Whatever may lie in the future of written or recorded communication, for me nothing could ever surpass the sheer intellectual beauty and satisfaction of a book, especially, I must admit, one I have written.

Of course, the more ephemeral pursuit of journalism also has its joys, especially in its immediacy. It also has a common touch, which appeals to my innate vulgarity. Books can be a touch precious at times and certainly authors tend to take themselves very seriously – just listen to any group of writers getting their heads together at a literary weekend!

As in many other spheres, my real weakness as a writer has been the 'jack of all trades' syndrome. I have never been able to resist the temptation to dabble. So my literary output has included one novel, one biography, one anthology of poetry, three paraphrased translations of Christian classics, the lyrics of two musicals (one stage, one a television series) plus scripts for countless radio and TV programmes – for schools programmes, for documentaries, music strands and even an ITV comedy series called *Beyond Belief*. In the event, it *was* beyond belief, by far the biggest disaster of my professional life. All of that is on top of my staple diet of devotional and apologetic books, of which there is by now an embarrassingly long list, and articles for magazines and newspapers on everything from cricket to obituaries and from church affairs to broadcasting. If variety were the guarantor of quality I would rank above Shakespeare. Sadly it isn't, and I don't. Indeed, I long ago reconciled myself to the role of literary butterfly: come autumn, all is forgotten.

But not pointless. Time and again I have been reminded that books, more than anything else, shape our thinking. That is why nothing tells you more about a person than an inspection of their bookshelves. For writers, it is genuinely rewarding to be told that something one wrote 20 or 30 years ago in a book long out of print has been a turning point in someone's thinking. That is why it is so important that Christians don't abdicate from the wider fields of the arts. Indeed, I see it as a chief justification for the existence of the Arts Centre Group or the Association of Christian Writers. You can't be heard if you don't speak and you can't be part of the argument if you refuse to enter the forum.

One of the greatest encouragements of the last couple of

decades has been the emergence of writers – novelists, dramatists, biographers – who see the world through the eyes of Christian faith. I hesitate to call them 'Christian writers', because that might seem to imply that their writing is simply a tool of their faith, rather than their faith being the inner illumination of their writing. That is not to say that their work sets out to convey a Christian 'message', nor that it is suffused with some kind of beatific vision, but that it offers a view of reality, sometimes harsh, sometimes beautiful, that is seen through the eyes of faith. I am thinking of writers such as Susan Howatch, Libby Purves, Murray Watts and, in recent years, Melvyn Bragg.

Long before their day, my own approach to writing was greatly indebted to G.W. Target, a novelist of some stature back in the sixties, who seemed to pioneer this particular approach. I can still remember with joy the Christian member of staff in his novel *The Teachers* (which was dramatized on BBC television), one of the few examples I can think of where sheer 'goodness' was presented as powerfully attractive.

Writing, then, is a thoroughly rewarding occupation, though demanding both of time and commitment. This is especially true, of course, of writing books. Many authors – though not this one, as my wife will confirm – go into a kind of purdah while the thoughts and ideas are being transferred laboriously from brain to paper. Journalism is less all-consuming, though everyone engaged in it knows the frustration of those moments when a deadline is pressing and the wretched ideas simply will not come. Even then, the printed words, often dashed off with insufficient thought under pressure of time, have a kind of authority simply by being published. That is quite frightening. As Jesus said, we shall answer for every idle word one day.

Broadcasting has much in common with print journalism, of course, but it is even more immediate (indeed, in its live form, instant) and hence ephemeral. I have never wanted to put my broadcast scripts into storage files, feeling that what I have said, I have said, for good or ill. On the other hand, there is the feeling that what is written, especially in books, has some kind of 'eternal' quality about it. At any rate, it becomes part of the archives of the human race and of our civilization, for better or worse. I think of poor Pilate. 'What I have written, I have written', sounds so bold, so masterly – and yet what he had written has remained part of that archive to haunt him to the end of time: 'Jesus of Nazareth, King of the Jews'. By his sole authority – bold and masterful as it might have been – probably the best and noblest man who ever lived was put to death on a trumped-up charge of treason. I wonder what Pilate would give now to be able to erase that damning superscription?

My journalism, post-retirement, has involved three fairly regular columns: a diary for the *Church Times*, an 'Across the Irish Sea' perspective for *The Church of Ireland Gazette* and a monthly column in our free diocesan paper *The Door*. As well as those, I have written occasionally for three of the national broadsheets, one of our cricket monthlies and various religious journals here and abroad. It has been enough, I hope, to keep my hand in.

It has been *Thought for the Day* that has done most, however, to keep literary skills sharp. The need to write three minutes on a topical issue – which by its very nature can't be chosen until the last moment – keeps even the dullest brain alert. I once rewrote an entire script in the car park of Radio Oxford, sitting in the darkness of the early hours of a winter morning, because the Californian earthquake had just struck, and one simply knew that the whole *Today* programme was at the moment being revised, and the piece I had written would have stood out like a yawn in the middle of a party. I remember a similarly swift piece of rewriting on the morning of the Manchester holiday plane crash, when I was taking the daily service on Radio 4 as the news of the disaster was breaking.

Live broadcasting certainly stimulates the adrenaline, but it can also lead to mental paralysis. Most broadcasters know the awful looming void which sometimes swims into one's brain at crucial moments. You know words are needed, yet no suitable ones seem to form themselves in your consciousness. It is at moments like those that the professional slips on to automatic pilot and the amateur – sometimes, and sadly – into embarrassed silence. Of course, it is probably true that silence is preferable to some of the inane banalities which can emerge from the mouth on such occasions.

If I try to find one embracing theme or motivation in my working life I should like to think that it is to share something of my own enthusiasm for the Bible with people, and that is why working for the Bible Reading Fellowship in recent years has given me so much satisfaction. In fact, I suspect that those who know me best would say that my embracing theme and motivation is to be liked or admired, and I would find it hard to argue with that.

Still, the Bible has always figured largely in my adult life, and I have come to appreciate more and more how 'special' it is. Part of that appreciation has been the product of liberation from a rather tired fundamentalism, which meant that one had to go around fighting every little corner of 'Bible truth' as though God's own honour somehow depended on it. I have always appreciated the profound fact that 'the Truth', in the absolute sense, is literally beyond us. We do not have it within us to fathom the answers to the ultimate questions of existence, relating to meaning, purpose, consciousness and origins. If there is a God at all, then the saying is surely true, 'God alone knows'. In which case, if we cannot work our own way to these most profound truths, God must reveal them to us. I have always felt that revelation is a better key to understanding than reason or, rather, that reason is best employed in the pursuit of revelation. Hence, I suppose, my fascination with the Bible, which in what one of its writers calls a 'fragmentary' way offers us many different 'glimpses of truth'. Those phrases are from J.B. Phillips' astonishing paraphrase of the New Testament letters, which had a considerable influence on my early shapings of faith.

In the 'Translator's Preface' to that book he wrote something which has in a way come to mean more and more to me as the scriptures have shaped my beliefs and ministry. Phillips wrote: 'Without holding fundamentalist views on "inspiration", [the present translator] is continually struck by the living quality of the material on which he is working. Some will, no doubt, consider it merely superstitious reverence for "Holy Writ", yet again and again the writer felt rather like an electrician re-wiring an ancient house without being able to "turn the mains off".'

I know the feeling exactly, and have felt it time and again when working on the actual text of scripture. This living quality – a dynamic element in the words and ideas – convinces me that a heavy-handed literalism, or an arrogant minimalism, are the wrong ways to handle the 'living and abiding word of God'. In some way, perhaps principally in our reception of them, these are inspired writings through which God speaks to the human heart with unique power. There is a mystery here, I have to confess, but it is one that is tested not by the question 'Is it a fact?' but by the rather more contemporary one, 'Does it work?' The answer of experience to that, time and again, is 'Yes, it does.'

Instances abound from my time working with BRF, but none is more dramatic, nor makes the point more powerfully, than a letter we received at BRF in the summer of 1999, at the end of the Kosovo conflict that caused such suffering in the Balkan region. It was from Neville Lee, who in May of that year was a driver on a convoy of 30 lorries taking humanitarian aid to refugees from the fighting. It had been, he wrote, a 'fairly arduous' journey. On the morning of Saturday, 22 May he slipped away from his colleagues to the front seat of his vehicle for a 'quick, quiet read' of that day's text from *New Daylight*, before they continued their drive across northern Greece. That day's target was the Macedonian border. The reading for that day was Acts 16:6–9. Its final verse reads, 'And a man of Macedonia was standing beseeching him and saying, "Come over here to Macedonia and help us".' As our correspondent remarked, 'You can imagine how that extraordinary verse hit me, read in those circumstances, and within that day it affected many members of our convoy.' That night they reached the Macedonian border under a sky filled with the reflected light of missiles attacking Belgrade.

Of course, one can reject that story as just coincidence, but the impressive thing about it to me is that the verse wasn't discovered by sticking a pin in the pages of the Bible, or plucking a 'promise slip' from a box. It was read by a man following a plan of daily readings worked out long before such a conflict in the Balkans was even under discussion, and it was the reading for that very day which spoke so directly to the immediate need of that group of people.

I would reject with some vehemence any tendency to think of the Bible in a superstitious way, as a kind of 'magic'. It doesn't yield its richest treasures to pin-stickers and searchers for secret codes. Yet it is a demonstrable fact of experience – brought home to me forcefully over the years I have written for BRF – that the Bible does have this uncanny way of speaking to people at the very moment that they need its message, and with immediate relevance. Time and again it has happened, and we have scores of letters to prove the point. In any case, it shouldn't surprise Christians who believe that the scriptures contain the living and dynamic word of God.

So I have enjoyed talking and writing about the Bible, not as a theologian or biblical scholar, which I am not, but as a Christian communicator who recognizes something of the dynamic nature of the written and spoken word. The Judeo-Christian God is a God who speaks, who reveals himself and his purposes to people, who longs that human hearts should be open and responsive to that purpose. I have never believed that the pulpit is the place for human speculation, but for exploring and applying the Christian revelation to the situation of the hearers. The Bible is not an 'easy' book, and sometimes it only yields its deepest treasures to those who are prepared to dig for them, yet there is also truth here which will light up an infant heart with simple joy.

So there may be time left to pursue the 'ministry of the Word' in different ways. Or, of course, there may not. That is the essential truth of mortality, which for the most part we can ignore in younger life, but which begins to invade one's consciousness as contemporaries die, and as the inevitable frailties of advancing years make themselves felt. The sudden death of my brother Geoff in the summer of 2000 brought this home to me. After running the coconut shy at the church fête on Saturday, he was stricken with a heart attack the following morning. It was desperately sad to be at his funeral. He had been a part of my life from my first conscious moments. But it is not a cause for regret, surely. There is a 'completeness' about a human life, whether it has been short or long, and that completeness is a work of God.

For me, that life has involved so many good things. Best of all has been marriage, family and friends, but I have also been able to enjoy three different and each in its own way satisfying 'careers'. Briefly as a teacher, for rather longer as a journalist and broadcaster, and finally as a priest, I have experienced three rather different ways of doing the same thing: relating to people, relating to truth and communicating ideas.

Teaching was good. Writing and broadcasting was better (for me, at least). But best of all, in 'career' terms, was ordination. Perhaps I should have responded earlier. Perhaps I was not so much a 'late call' as a 'late response'. But a generous God has given me a marvellous late afternoon of a working life, in the most satisfying calling that a human being can have.

The introit to the thanksgiving service for the life of my great hero Donald Coggan said it all, in the words of C.H. Sorley:

Call thou early, call thou late,
To thy great service dedicate.

FOOTNOTE

After the book was finished, Christine became ill
with ovarian cancer and died two weeks after our
ruby wedding anniversary, on 1 May 2001. As is
evident from these pages, she was both a stabilizing
and an inspirational element in the whole story.
Her moment of passing, like so much of her life,
was gentle, holy and a precious gift to the three
of us who were there.

INDEX OF NAMES